D1570290

June Jordan

WOMEN WRITERS OF COLOR

June Jordan

Her Life and Letters

Valerie Kinloch

Joanne M. Braxton, Series Editor

Westport, Connecticut
London

Library of Congress Cataloging-in-Publication Data

Kinloch, Valerie, 1974–
  June Jordan : her life and letters / Valerie Kinloch.
    p. cm.—(Women writers of color, ISSN 1559–7172)
  Includes bibliographical references and index.
  ISBN 0–275–98241–6 (alk. paper)
  1. Jordan, June, 1936– 2. Poets, American—20th century—Biography. 3. Women and literature—
United States—History—20th century. I. Title. II. Series.
  PS3560.O73Z55 2004
  811'.54—dc22   200600844

British Library Cataloguing in Publication Data is available.

Library of Congress Catalog Card Number: 200600844
ISBN: 0–275–98241–6
ISSN: 1559–7172

First published in 2006

Praeger Publishers, 88 Post Road West, Westport, CT 06881
An imprint of Greenwood Publishing Group, Inc.
www.praeger.com

Printed in the United States of America

The paper used in this book complies with the
Permanent Paper Standard issued by the National
Information Standards Organization (Z39.48–1984).

10 9 8 7 6 5 4 3 2 1

Copyright Acknowledgments

The author and the publisher gratefully acknowledge permission for use of the following material:

Excerpts from the book *Naming Our Destiny: New and Selected Poems* by June Jordan. Copyright
© 1989 by June Jordan. Appears by permission of the publisher, Thunder's Mouth Press, a division of Avalon Publishing Group.

A Eulogy for Theodore R. Rutledge, delivered at St. Mark's Church in Brooklyn, NY, August 25,
1984 and April 3, 1991, by June Jordan. Courtesy of Valerie Orridge.

"What Would I Do White?" and "On the Spirit of Mildred Jordan" reproduced from *Lyrical
Campaigns* by June Jordan by kind permission of Virago Press, an imprint of Little, Brown Book
Group.

Let this work live in the memory of June Millicent Jordan (1936–2002), poet of passion, lover of justice, and warrior for freedom.

Contents

Acknowledgments

There is not enough time, space, or memory for me to thank everyone who has contributed to bringing this book to life. For such shortcomings and oversights, I take complete responsibility and offer my apologies. In this, I extend my sincere appreciation for the thoughtfulness of the many people I have not recognized here.

First, I want to thank the subject of this biography: June Millicent Jordan. Without her writings, speeches, recordings, and commitment to universal justice, I would not have been able to begin this project. The legacy she left behind is nothing short of extraordinary, and I am honored to contribute to it, even in a small way. I can only hope that this biography adds to both the preexisting and future scholarship on this marvelous poet. I thank her cousin, Valerie Orridge, for inviting me into her home, sharing stories and pictures with me, and entertaining my many questions about June Jordan and the history of their family, a history that began in Jamaica and traveled to New Jersey and New York. To Orridge's son and friends, I offer my gratitude.

Jordan had many close friends. I would like to thank Adrienne Torf for agreeing to engage in an extensive telephone interview and for providing me with invaluable information on her work and collaborations with Jordan. I do agree with you, Adrienne, that June Jordan was an exceptionally talented poet whose life and writings should be remembered. I am indebted to you. To E. Ethelbert Miller, your generosity is heartfelt. Our conversations and e-mail exchanges added another dimension to my work, one that would not have surfaced in the absence of your kindness. Thank you for your support and direction. To Julius Lester, a man of remarkable words and writings, I am honored to have received quick, detailed, and honest responses on Jordan from you. Your graciousness is forever admired.

I am indebted to many individuals and institutions for providing me with assistance as I completed this book: Karla Y. Davis, Curator of the Givens Collection of African American Literature at the University of Minnesota, for engaging in e-mail exchanges with me and for mailing me resources from the Collection; Donald Glassman, Archivist at the Wollman Library at Barnard College, for his kindness and speed in giving me reference articles on Jordan; and Robert Vejnar, Archivist at the Library at Emory and Henry College, for his willingness to send me information should I ever need it. I must also recognize the many archivists and reference librarians at the following research institutions: the Donnell Branch of the New York Public Library, the Schomburg Center for Research on Black Culture, the Library at Stanford University, the Houston Public Library, the Library at the University of California at Berkeley, and the Library at the University of Houston.

This project began when I was an Assistant Professor of English at the downtown campus of the University of Houston. While there, I received encouragement from many people: friend and colleague, Professor Jia-Yi Cheng-Levine and the students in her Ethnic Heritage courses; Professor Margret Grebowicz, my coeditor on our very first book project, *Still Seeking an Attitude: Critical Reflections on the Work of June Jordan* (2004); and Professors Jane Creighton, Merrilee Cunningham, Sara Farris, William Gilbert, Michelle Moosally, Lisa Read, and Lorenzo Thomas. I must also acknowledge Dagmar Corrigan and the faculty and staff members on the Women's Month Planning Committee (2005) at the University of Houston-Downtown for sponsoring my visit to the campus so that I could deliver a talk on my research on June Jordan. To my former student and dear friend, Ursula Dorsey, what can I say besides, "Thank you, thank you!" I still have that packet of reference articles on Jordan that you gave me four years ago because you thought it would come in handy. It did! And to Latoya Hardman: our journey began at the University of Houston, Downtown and has extended to New York City and the students at Bread & Roses Integrated Arts High School. I am looking forward to the next chapter.

It is important to recognize the faculty, staff, and students at Teachers College, Columbia University. To my colleagues in the English Education Program and in the Department of Arts & Humanities, I thank you for listening to my many talks on June Jordan. I am also indebted to Janice Robinson and the Office for Diversity and Community for sponsoring my fall 2005 talk, "Fighting Boundaries: Locating June Jordan in the Academy." As well, I thank the Teachers College Office of Student Activities and Programs for inviting me to speak during the Casual Conversations Series in the spring of 2005. Gratitude is given to Dean Darlyne Bailey, her office, and the Subcommittee on Race, Culture, and Diversity for supporting my work and acknowledging my research with a Faculty Diversity Fellowship for the 2005–2006 academic year. To the many supportive students, Rebekkah Hogan, Lena Tuck, Catherine DeLazerro, Leonda Whitaker, Chanika Perry, and many, many others, I owe you more than I can say. And to the countless other students, teachers, and activists whom I have encountered, I am happy to know that we are the ones doing this work. Thank you!

To my writing partner, Maisha Fisher, your research on literacy and spoken-word poetry is more important now than ever before. Sorry for not responding to your e-mails in a more timely fashion.

I thank my editor, Joanne M. Braxton, over and over again, for believing in June Jordan, in me, and in the importance of this book. I am so fortunate, Joanne, for your expert editorial advice, detailed responses to my manuscript and my inquiries, and for your patience, kindness, and friendship. You have been an important force in bringing this book to print. Thank you for being there for me. Senior Editor Suzanne Staszak-Silva has also been an important force in shaping *June Jordan: Her Life and Letters*. I thank you for your sensitivity and patience.

To my parents, Virginia and Louis, my brothers Wendell and Louis, and two of my closest cousins, Kesha and Cheryl, I say thank you for the surprise phone calls, unexpected interruptions, and the many laughs, especially when I did not realize I needed them. (I did!) I am lucky to know you and to be of you.

That special someone who always listens to my disjointed ramblings with eager ears and a big heart deserves a huge thank you for dealing with me while I dealt with June Jordan. Your understanding and care are more than appreciated.

And to the readers of *June Jordan: Her Life and Letters*, may my work inspire you as others have inspired and continue to inspire me.

Series Foreword

Intended to include biographies of women writers of Hispanic, Asian, and Native American descent, the "Women Writers of Color Series" begins with a focus on African American women writers. Overlooked for too long, these women, like other women writers of color, deserve a place in our libraries and on our bookshelves.

Among women writers of color in the United States, women of African descent have been preeminent, setting high standards, and opening doors for women writers from other ethnic groups. Beginning in the eighteenth century, the tradition of black women writers in the United States has been one of long struggle, or perhaps a series of interrelated struggles. For the earliest writers, there was the struggle to achieve freedom from enslavement and physical abuse. Literacy, self-definition, autonomy, and self-respect are some of the goals that eighteenth- and nineteenth-century poets, orators, novelists, and essayists promoted among the general black population. But first and foremost, they were concerned with physical survival—the survival of their families, loved ones, and themselves; survival is something that no black woman writer has ever taken for granted.

Graced with few weapons other than what they could carry with them, Africans new to the Americas brought with them a rich cultural heritage that included a vibrant oral tradition. Having endured the dreaded middle passage to the New World, the first Africans in America had still to survive its harsh climate and the cruel conditions they would suffer as enslaved men and women without legal rights with which to resist rape, disfigurement, starvation or the separation of their families. Not only would they endure, but—to borrow Faulkner's phrase—they would prevail.

Contemporary women writers of color, including those women of color who are not of African descent, have looked to these foremothers as heroes and miracle makers. It is because of such women that this series exists. It exists for every woman writer of color whose work we will never know. It exists for everyone of any race who can read these words and appreciate them, and for every little girl of any race who ever wrote a poem and hid it. This general audience series is intended to be enjoyable reading for an enlightened multiethnic audience that knows both the cost and the necessity of creativity, for poets, writers, schoolboys, and librarians who will read with their eyes wide open. Naturally there will be something new and refreshing for the scholar and the critic, but this series is also for the daughters of those mothers whose creativity and intelligence were suppressed, hidden, targeted and denied—women like June Jordan, whose mother, Mildred Maude Fisher Jordan, might have been an artist, but instead succumbed to madness and suicide; and Lucille Clifton, whose mother, Thelma Moore Sayles, burned her poems because her husband didn't approve. Audre Lorde's mother also wrote and hid the poems that she wrote in secret.

Therefore, this series exists. It exists so that girls and women of all races everywhere and in all layers of society will know that there were those who went before them who survived beatings, sexual violation, and all manner of psychological and emotional abuse, as well as various other attempts to degrade and silence them. Instead of becoming silent victims, these women of the word went on to become poets, novelists, and essayists. Inspired by the models offered by the brave literary women who are the subjects of these biographies, the coming generations will refuse to write their poems and novels in secret; and those who have written in secret, and without the affirmation of friends, family and loved ones, will come out of the literary closet, bravely bringing their once hidden works into the light of day. Each volume is published with a user-friendly bibliography so that the readers of the Life and Letters Series can pursue original readings by these writers and find literary criticism more easily.

June Jordan: Her Life and Letters is one of the first in the "Women Writers of Color Biography Series." This volume is the work of Professor Valerie Kinloch of Teachers College, Columbia University. June Jordan was one of the most prolific black women writers of the twentieth century. She worked successfully in multiple genres, making profound contributions not only to African American life and letters, but also to the global discourse on race, color, class, gender, and to an improved understanding of the politics of language and experience.

As a student at Sarah Lawrence College in the late 1960s, I took Jordan's "Literature of Social Change" class, reading widely from Percy Shelley's sonnets, Amiri Baraka's *Dutchman* and *Slave*, Berthold Brecht's *Good Woman of Setzuan*, and Buckminster Fuller's *Spaceship Earth*. Even then, Jordan's students knew that studying with her was an extraordinary opportunity. She challenged us to think and write clearly and cleanly; she could use a piece of sculpture like Alberto Giacometti's "The Palace at Four a.m." to shake up our ideas about poetic structure and to inspire us to think in new ways about what a poem could be.

I will never forget the first time I saw June Jordan, as she ascended the staircase on the way to her office: as always, she was a study in beauty, grace and elegance, but above all, *energy*. Like many others, I was much affected by her essay "Black Studies: Bringing Back the Person," which appeared in *Esquire*, and I would follow the publication of her early works, including *Who Look at Me*, *Some Changes*, *Soulscript*, *His Own Where*, and *New Days: Poems of Exile and Return*. In my adult life, we became friends, and I last saw June in the summer of 1993, when she met me and my daughter for sushi in Berkeley, but I have always found her an elusive personage.

Working with author Valerie Kinloch on this project, I have discovered the June Jordan that I never knew. Kinloch not only examines Jordan's work and takes us through the chronology that comprises the visible aspects of Jordan's life, she lifts the veil from these experiences to shed light on the ways in which Jordan actualized her belief that the personal is political. Having coedited an earlier volume of critical essays on June Jordan's work, Kinloch is a seasoned Jordan scholar, and she will no doubt produce other volumes on this distinguished author and activist, especially as the June Jordan literary papers at the Schlesinger Library, Harvard University, become more accessible. For now, though, she has given us an exceptional first look at June Jordan's extraordinary life.

Joanne M. Braxton
College of William and Mary
Series Editor

Introduction

June Millicent Jordan was born on July 9, 1936 in Harlem, New York, to Mildred Maude Fisher and Granville Ivanhoe Jordan, natives of Jamaica and Panama. Before her death on June 14, 2002, after a long struggle against breast cancer, Jordan had published more than twenty-seven books, including *Some of Us Did Not Die: New and Selected Essays of June Jordan* (2002), *Soldier: A Poet's Childhood* (2001), *Haruko/Love Poems* (1994), *Naming Our Destiny: New and Selected Poems* (1989), *Civil Wars: Observations from the Front Lines of America* (1981), *His Own Where* (1971), and *Who Look at Me* (1969). Her political writings have appeared on the pages of *The Progressive*, the *New York Times*, *Chrysalis*, the *Herald Tribune*, and the *Harvard Educational Review*. She was, and continues to be, one of the most versatile and widely published black American writers who employed democratic and uncensored language in order to convey, with passion, truths about race, gender, sexuality, violence, war, and human rights.

Even though her writing spans poetry, nonfiction, children's and young-adult literature, and drama, it is important to recognize that fixed labels will never contain this poet, a woman of charm and laughter who fell in love with people just as easily as she fell in love with words: eagerly, willingly, and with great excitement. Her writings, teachings, activist efforts, and her calls for universal love transcend all the limiting boundaries that oftentimes place people, especially black women, into static roles. As much as Jordan was a poet, she was also a professor, a lover, and a mother who fully embraced efforts toward universal justice. And yet, she was more than these things combined. Her writing serves as proof of the magnificence of a woman who could not abandon the journey toward human freedom. The problematic nature of naming Jordan's experiences suggests the difficulty of writing her biography. To accomplish this type of work, one needs to begin with Jordan's personal, autobiographical writings, for they hold the key to her familial interactions, her interracial marriage, her early teaching positions, and the ending of her political involvement, freedom struggle, soft yet strong voice, and fascinating life.

June Jordan's work reveals the splendors of her public personas as storyteller, poet, essayist, librettist, dramatist, journalist, and educator. It also demonstrates her more private personas: she was an only child, a single mother, a classically trained pianist, a passionate lover, and a candid friend. A writer of precision, power, and detail who would craft political manifestos against violence with the same fire that ignited her many love poems, Jordan has often been referred to as a "dissident poet," a "people's poet," and a "universal poet." These monikers find their roots in the literary tradition of Walt Whitman, the exceptional letter-writing style of Langston Hughes, the magnificence of Pablo Neruda, and the musicality of Beethoven. Jordan admired these prominent figures from whom she learned both the seriousness and truthfulness of honest, startling, lyrical, and painful writings. Her writing is, in fact, a brilliant compendium of stories that offers political commentaries on the difficulties of living, loving, and surviving in America as a raced and gendered person, the daughter of West Indian parents who immigrated to the United States during the "roaring" 1920s, a black mother, and one of the most published black American writers of the twentieth century.

Jordan's writing, illuminative of her life experiences as a child in New York City, a protégé of Fannie Lou Hamer, a participant in the Civil Rights Movement in the United States, and an activist who called herself a Palestinian, jumps off the page with an urgency that beckons its readers to gather, plan, mobilize, write, and act. The black woman who emerges from this writing is a skilled poet who refuses to be hindered by labels and acts of racism, but who insists on using words to search for freedom and justice for all people. This person, this June Jordan, this headstrong and outspoken poet, was a woman whose writing is politically savvy and unconventional in its brutal honesty. Her writing points to her bravery in asserting a public voice against injustices, from the violent acts perpetuated on black and Puerto Rican youth in New York City to the dangers of marginalizing black women in political movements. Jordan was, by any stretch of the imagination, an extraordinary writer.

This unauthorized biography, then, is a glimpse into the life and literary contributions of June Jordan. While this work does not pose as a "critical biography," it does provide a detailed treatment of Jordan's various writings, her family encounters, teachings, and reachings beyond the confines of restrictive identity stereotypes to become a public, revolutionary artist. This work, supported by in depth studies of all of Jordan's published writings and many in print and archived critical commentaries of her works, is the result of collected data from a number of significant sources: the Donnell Branch of the New York Public Library, the Schomburg Center for Research on Black Culture, the Library at Stanford University, the Houston Public Library, the Library at the University of Houston, and the archives at the Barnard College Library.

Interviews and personal exchanges with Jordan's first cousin, Valerie Orridge, and with author Julius Lester, poet E. Ethelbert Miller, musician Adrienne Torf, and countless activists, teachers, and students provide invaluable information on aspects of Jordan's life and the value of her literature as they were influenced by her commitment to language and human life.

As a "people's poet," June Jordan fought for justice with words and actions. Where did her strength come from? In what ways was her strength a result of her childhood experiences with an allegedly abusive father and a silent mother? What motivated the poet to marry a white man during the onset of the Civil Rights Movement in the United States? How are Jordan's literary and political commitments to social change connected to her lifelong search for personal love, physical safety, sexual freedom, and quality education for others, especially women and children? In what ways did Jordan make use of Black English Vernacular, and how did her commitment to its form enrich the ways language is currently used and understood? Can Jordan's life—from her childhood, involvement in New York City literary communities, participation in the Civil Rights Movement, and creation of Poetry for the People at the University of California, Berkeley—be brought into the spaces of public school classrooms? How did she come to define power and, at the same time, interrogate the power possessed by some and not others? In what ways does Jordan connect power, activism, leadership, and love?

To answer these questions is to examine the changing circumstances of Jordan's life—her father's abuse, mother's death, academic appointment as professor at several colleges and universities, international campaigns for justice, and prolific writing career. Revered by many social activists, political figures, writers and poets, professional associates, and personal friends, Jordan's life and poetic works are marked by a unique brand of honesty. It is this honesty that *June Jordan: Her Life and Letters* attempts to capture and convey in its discussion of how Jordan used democratic language so as not to become a victim of language misuse and abuse. She knew of the consequences of linguistic and physical abuse, for her life was a daily battle with these realities. She was raped twice, yet this victimization did not stop her from declaring her love for women, men, and children. Her struggles, as articulated in this biography, fueled her life and work, making her an important American writer.

In Chapter 1, "Soldier: A Poet's Childhood," I investigate Jordan's early years as the only daughter of West Indian parents. I pay particular attention to the poet's following lines:

I wasn't too happy about maybe having to choose
between having brains and being pretty.
I wasn't too happy that maybe somebody else
had already made that choice for me.[1]

Jordan was always unhappy with the status quo, and what is known of her childhood in Harlem and Brooklyn—particularly surrounding her documented love–fight–punish relationship with her parents—testifies to this fact. However, there were many moments when she was happy, including the time she spent with her father at the Harlem River Bridge; when she was in the company of her grandmother, Marie "Nanny" Taylor, who lived in East Orange, New Jersey; or when she would listen to stories told by her step-uncle, Theodore "Teddy" Roosevelt. Such significant relationships connect with one another and reiterate significant points from Jordan's memoir, *Soldier: A Poet's Childhood* (2000). They also provide invaluable insight into what is known of Jordan's intimate relationships with, and growing fondness for, the poetic writings of Paul Laurence Dunbar and Shakespeare—literary geniuses whom Jordan studied while under her father's supervision. The chapter concludes by highlighting how Jordan, as a young adult, happily embraced her freedom to choose by boldly making her own decisions. In 1953, she matriculated to Barnard College in New York City, where, two years later, she married Michael Meyer, a white student at Columbia College. After a short stay with Meyer in Chicago, Illinois, Jordan returned to New York City, reenrolled in Barnard, and became active in the college's student literary publication, *Focus,* before ending her studies there. The significant events of her youth parallel her later life of activism, writing, and love.

An analysis of not being "too happy about having to choose" and the events that defined Jordan's childhood leads into Chapter 2, "Who Look at Me," with a discussion of the birth of Jordan's son, Christopher David Meyer, and her separation, and eventual divorce, from Michael Meyer. These encounters encouraged the poet to evaluate the personal and political implications of her role as mother, writer, freedom fighter, and activist at the brink of the U.S. Civil Rights Movement. Such reconsiderations occurred in the face of her divorce and her pursuit to establish a life of passion and fulfillment marked by the publication of her first poetic text, *Who Look at Me* (1969), and her first novel, *His Own Where* (1971). Her growing literary and political involvements reiterate the influence of her childhood, marriage, and divorce on her professional choices and literary accomplishments.

Chapter 3, "New Days: Poems of Exile and Return," delves into descriptions of the poet's early jobs and teaching appointments by focusing on her burgeoning devotion to human life, civil liberties, and political rights. It is this devotion that shows itself in her art, freedom rides, and participation in civil rights movements. Starting in 1966, Jordan worked as a researcher and writer for the Technical Housing Department of Mobilization for Youth and as a poet-in-residence with Teachers & Writers Collaboration, both organizations located in New York City. Soon thereafter, she received teaching positions in English and composition at several universities, including the City University of New York, Sarah Lawrence College, and Yale University. This discussion leads into an investigation of Jordan as a serious literary and political public figure who was awarded a prestigious National Endowment for the Arts Fellowship in Creative Writing (1982), and who went on to pen, among other works, *Soulscript: Afro-American Poetry, Some Changes, New Days: Poems of Exile and Return, Things That I Do in the Dark: Selected Poetry, Passion: New Poems,* and *Living Room: New Poems 1980–1984.*

In Chapter 4, "Moving Towards Home: Political Essays," I discuss how the work of the civil rights and black arts movements, and the philosophical teachings of Malcolm X and Martin Luther King, Jr. influenced the direction Jordan would follow with her politics and art. She often questioned the black leadership of rights movements, exhibiting concern for the implied roles and responsibilities of women in movements. In addition to her interrogations of black leadership were her increasing public campaigns, rallies, and freedom rides for the rights of black people in politics and education. Jordan's writings on such topics found a home on the pages of various New York-based magazines and periodicals. This chapter analyzes some of the sociopolitical tensions that surround race, gender, sexuality, and freedom, which led Jordan to confront the dynamics of being a poet and essayist, and an activist and educator concerned about global injustices and the coalitions needed to combat them.

Jordan's growth as a writer, activist, and educator parallels her focus on the lives of young people. In Chapter 5, "The Voice of the Children," I address the poet's texts for children and young adults and their concentration on the use of black English and black cultural forms, quality educational opportunities, the significance of safe spatial designs in urban communities, and the importance of young people in the fight for civil rights. A look at Jordan's children's and young-adult books, including *The Voice of the Children* (1968), *His Own Where* (1971), *Fannie Lou Hamer* (1972), *Dry Victories* (1972), *New Life: New Room* (1975), and *Kimako's Story* (1981) demonstrates her attention to the lives, languages, and literacies of young people. Such themes were important to her teaching and activist efforts.

Discussion of her writing for an audience of young people leads into the final two chapters of this book. Chapter 6, "Affirmative Acts: Political Essays," explores Jordan's professorship at the University of California, Berkeley, her creation of *Poetry for the People Collective,* and her sentiments concerning the role of the poet and the importance of quality, democratic forms of education. While at the University of California, Berkeley, Jordan published several popular essay and poetry collections—*Technical Difficulties: African American Notes on the State of the Union* (1992), *Haruko/Love Poetry* (1993), *Kissing God Goodbye* (1997), *Affirmative Acts: Political Essays* (1998), and, posthumously, *Some of Us Did Not Die: New and Selected Essays of June Jordan* (2003) and *Directed by Desire: The Collected Poems of June Jordan* (2005). Reflecting on her writings and teachings in California, this chapter responds to the following inquiries: In what ways do Jordan's poetry, essays, and commentaries speak to the fundamental element of democratic education for students of color in public schools? How can the writer and her works be brought closer to the work of secondary classes? What are the connections between the *June Jordan Poetry for the People Collective* and other writing initiatives, including Teachers & Writers Collaborative (NYC) and Writers-in-the-Schools (Houston, TX)?

"Kissing God Goodbye," the final chapter in the book, opens with a look at the journey Jordan began after being diagnosed with breast cancer and undergoing surgical procedures, and thereafter recommitting herself to life and love. In exploring this journey, I respond to the following concerns: How did Jordan confront her breast cancer, mastectomy, and cancer treatments? In what ways did she muster the energy to both battle cancer and fight for human justice through writing, teaching, and activism? How did her family, friends, and colleagues honor her life upon her death? What is the power of the written word and how does this power live on after years of struggle, even after death? In short, why did we love June Jordan and why should we remember her? This last chapter asks these questions in order to explore Jordan's undying commitment—in the face of her eventual death—to human justice and the eradication of oppressive conditions for all people.

Taken altogether, then, *June Jordan: Her Life and Letters* presents brief, but poignant, aspects of her extraordinary life, visionary power, and political writing. It is this life, and its poetic sensibility, that makes June Jordan an important political poet whose legacy must be studied and cherished.

ONE

Soldier: A Poet's Childhood

As a Black woman living with change and beset by continuing situations of peril,
I am the same and I am different, now. For me, winning has become the point. I
have known and I have seen too many people dead, absolutely dead and gone, to
settle for resistance or struggle: I am working to win.[1]

June Millicent Jordan, in life and in memory, proves that it is crucial to
engage in fights for freedom and equality when groups of people are
denied human rights, when political refugees are forbidden civil liberties,
and when unjust conditions threaten the existence of any group of people, at
any time, anywhere. Over the course of her life, June Jordan became known
for her incessant drive to win, whether in the face of disagreement and alleged
rage within her parents' Bedford-Stuyvesant household in Brooklyn, New York;
during the violent Harlem Riot of 1964; throughout battles for civil rights legislation in Southern states such as Mississippi; or against the United States'
interference in the Palestinian peace process. Jordan's visionary power and
political writings indicate a perpetual search for a justice connected to language, freedom, progress, and love, a search that often occurred at the expense
of her own familial history—particularly the histories of her mother and
father. Nevertheless, the poet deftly crafted works representative of the lives of
young people on the streets of Harlem, Brooklyn, and the Bronx, as well as in
the San Francisco Bay area and throughout the Diaspora and developing
nations considered Third World countries. Jordan often referred to what was

then known as the Third World as "First World" because of the political implications of language and freedom struggles that oftentimes define people's
resistances to injustices. For these reasons, June Jordan is considered by scholars and critics in various literary and political circles to be an American hero,
a dissident lover of words, and a people's poet whose struggle to live is embedded in one's struggle to win.

This latter message, especially, is evident in the creation of the June Jordan
Poetry for the People Collective at the University of California, Berkeley in the
early 1990s. Meanwhile, the struggle which Jordan observed, participated in,
and documented for more than forty years—that of local, national, and international justice for people kept on the outside of privilege and power—did not
die with her. Her love of justice, freedom, and words has had lasting effects on
human relations, educational research, and the communicative engagements
people have with one another. Jordan was, by any sense of the imagination, a
complex human being who demonstrated her lifelong desire for social
progress; she also expressed her desire for passionate love through joyful and
tumultuous interactions with family members, friends, and colleagues, as well
as in her published writing. Jordan's "GREATEST GIFT," according to poet and
longtime friend, Sara Miles, "was falling in love. She fell in love over and over
during her life, with a kind of reckless momentum, that defied everything
else—fear, boredom, rage, and disappointment."[2] In the poem, "Directed by
Desire," Miles describes Jordan's cycle of falling in and out of love, a cycle that
connects well with Jordan's political and literary strivings. Miles states:

> June fell in love, first, with words. She fell in love with Kipling and Shakespeare
> and Isaiah and Neruda and Whitman and with all the astonishing ways black
> people talk in America. June fell in love with thinking, with the thrill of intel-
> lectual life and the irresistible pull of half a dozen disciplines: architecture,
> music, poetry, journalism, teaching, theatre, politics. June fell in love with
> poets—living and dead—with artists, with musicians, with her students, with
> her friends, with a cute girl she saw at the copy shop, with a shy guy she met at
> a reading. She fell in love with Belfast and with Palestine.[3]

Indeed, Jordan encountered many loves throughout her lifetime. The cyclic
experiences of the poet falling in and out of love can be connected to the trajectories of her professional career—poet, essayist, dramatist, activist, journalist, librettist, educator, and seeker/lover of knowledge and social justice. Such
trajectories, as introduced in this opening chapter and discussed in more detail
throughout the other chapters of this book, make way for a critical inquiry
into the reasons why both Jordan's life and work should be remembered, studied, and critiqued.

June Millicent Jordan was born on July 9, 1936 during a heat wave in
Harlem, New York. In 1942, her family left the Harlem River Public Housing
Projects and relocated to the neighborhood of Bedford-Stuyvesant in Brooklyn
to the dismay of the poet's mother, Mildred Maude Fisher. Mildred complained

about the filth left behind by the previous tenants of their Brooklyn brown-stone, and at first wondered who would be responsible for cleaning it up. She quickly realized that it would be her. It was in this brownstone on Hancock Street that Jordan spent her adolescent, young adult, and some of her adult years, and it was in this neighborhood where, according to her father, "white people lived. . . . *Me no gwine to stay in a ghetto, you see?!*"[4] His sentiments, in many complex ways, signify a degree of success, privilege, and power based in a black–white dynamic that Jordan would later interrogate in her political writings and activist work. Her adult life was a living testament to this inquiry into racial dynamics, as marked by extraordinarily significant events: she married a white man during the height of the Civil Rights Movement and she dropped out of Barnard College. Yet having never officially received an undergraduate degree, she went on to become a professor at several American universities. Jordan was also caught in the Harlem Riots and she marched, picketed, demonstrated even more for the rights of people who could not readily fight for themselves. Jordan fought, literally, for her life in her parents' Bedford-Stuyvesant house as well as out in the racist world that she sought to change—and that sought to change her.

She was the only "soldier-child" of West Indian immigrants, Granville Ivanhoe Jordan and Mildred Maude Fisher. Jordan has written of her parents' impoverished origins and their unrelenting desire for social and economic prosperity. With individual missions and paths that did not intersect before they immigrated to the United States mainland, Granville and Mildred, as Jordan documents in *Soldier: A Poet's Childhood*, each left their "barefooted," substandard living conditions, strapped with hope and aspirations for improved living situations and increased opportunities in America.

Granville celebrated the political ideologies of survival and nationhood preached by Black Nationalist Marcus Garvey and wrote meticulously crafted letters to government officials. He also took pride in engineering household projects and was devoted to "Negro" poetry and political thought. His celebrations of the beauty of black life—black people reading and acquiring an education, black culture and the arts, black people working hard and achieving success—can be attributed to the influence of Garvey's teachings. In "Intelligence, Education, Universal Knowledge, and How To Get It: Lesson I," Garvey writes, "You must never stop learning. The world's greatest men and women are people who educated themselves outside of the university with all the knowledge that the university gives."[5] In Garvey's intellectual likeness, Granville came to America with a poor education, barely proficient in reading and writing, and his journey toward becoming an educated man took place outside of the structures of university training. He eventually taught himself the "hows" and "whys" of surviving in a new and foreign land, America, and in a new and foreign city, New York. His education did not stop there, for he used his newfound knowledge to delve into the beauty and the depths of poetry—a cultural point well advanced by Garvey, and one passed on from Granville to his daughter.

On poetry, Garvey writes the following sentiments:

> You should also read the best poetry for inspiration. The standard poets have always been the most inspirational creators. From a good line of poetry, you may get the inspiration for the career of a lifetime. Many a great man and woman was first inspired by some attractive line or verse of poetry.[6]

Granville agreed with many of Garvey's social and political beliefs, and took great pleasure in exposing young June to inspirational writing such as poetry. His personal celebrations of the beauty of black life are marked by his active engagement with knowledge, political ideologies, and poetic thought-celebrations that transferred themselves into his expectations of, and disappointments with, success, freedom, and American democracy.

Granville's expectations of and for American democracy remained high, even in the face of many unfulfilled dreams and opportunities. For if democracy signifies the essence of freedom and equality, then Granville was bent headstrong on its possession. His limited opportunities in Jamaica, the mystery surrounding his departure from his birth land of Panama, and his preoccupation with progress and ownership are all embedded in larger, multilayered struggles for equality across racial boundaries and class affiliations. Granville, who resembled a white man enough that he probably could have passed as such, was often dismayed by the socioeconomic and sociopolitical struggles

Granville Ivanhoe Jordan, June Jordan's father, date unknown. Courtesy of Valerie Orridge.

black people were forced to endure. Yet such struggles did not outweigh the prospects afforded by hard work and perseverance promised by American democracy—the confounding belief in which was the basis of Granville's strength. Tracing his connection to Panama and Jamaica, one discovers a young Granville, bullied and insulted by grade-school peers; later one finds a self-determined Granville who was his own reading and writing teacher. Both connections led to a painful reality: life in America for this black immigrant husband and father meant a life without immediate access to quality resources or an abundance of public respect and honor. Thus, his life was often filled with a combination of rage, fear, anger, love, and hard work. He does not merely represent the struggles of one black and interracial man in America, but that of a multitude of black men throughout the Diaspora searching for the truth and justice of a democracy that does not represent them experientially, and that does not readily acknowledge their racial, economic, and educational struggles.

Unquestionably, Granville could very well have been James Weldon Johnson's fictional "ex-coloured man" who passes as a white man until the emotional disconnection from his black mother's ancestry becomes intolerable and too much of a moral burden to ignore.[7] Then again, Granville could have been an "invisible man." In the epilogue to *Invisible Man*, Ralph Ellison's classic novel about a black boy's travels through white America—from a Southern town where he and other black boys battle in front of drunken white men to the boy's expulsion from a Southern college and brief participation in the Communist Party—is written the following:

> And my problem was that I always tried to go in everyone's way but my own. I have also been called one thing and then another while no one really wished to hear what I called myself. So after years of trying to adopt the opinions of others I finally rebelled. I am an *invisible* man. Thus I have come a long way and returned and boomeranged a long way from the point in society toward which I originally aspired.[8]

In many ways, what is known of Granville—his close resemblance to racial whiteness; his travels to, and life in, the U.S. mainland; his interactions with his wife and daughter; his reasons for moving from Harlem to Brooklyn— signifies the desires of many black men, particularly those who are naturalized black American citizens. Their desires are often embedded in their determination to create a safe life in a mostly racist, hostile, and undemocratic state that beckons, often quickly and forcibly, their invisibility.

In another way, what is known of Granville, such as his alleged abusive behavior toward his daughter or his silence upon discovering the supposed suicide of his wife, reflects a level of submission that rendered him *invisible* and that presumably forced him to rebel.[9] Does this explain why Jordan accused Granville of beating or punishing her for not quickly memorizing the lines of great poems, which she eventually learned to do with great speed and sophistication? Does this explain why he became confused or appreciative, or a

Mrs. Marie Taylor, June Jordan's grandmother, immigrated to the United States from Jamaica and settled in New Jersey. Courtesy of Valerie Orridge.

combination of both or neither at all, when his daughter, June, a child, memorized the great lines of poetry and recited them back to him with as much passion and energy as Granville himself had on coming to America, this new land of opportunity? Discovering the most authentic representation of Granville is very difficult to do, for there is no readily available documentation of his own familial past in Panama and Jamaica. One can only rely on the narratives offered by June Jordan—narratives that appear detailed, but that may, in fact, be one-sided.

> West Indian in kitchen exile
> alone between the days
> and studying the National Geographic Magazines
> white explorations and
> excitement
> in places you were forced to leave
>   no shoes
>   no teeth
> but oxlike shoulders
> and hazel eyes that watered
> slightly
> from the reading you did teach yourself to do[10]

Valerie Orridge, June Jordan's cousin, and Valerie Kinloch (left to right), are pictured here in Orridge's home on January 1, 2006. Courtesy of Orridge and Kinloch.

The life of Mildred Maude Fisher, the poet's mother, is equally difficult to understand. Unlike her husband, who taught himself to read and write, Mildred had completed her high-school studies before moving to the U.S. mainland at the request of her mother, Mrs. Marie Taylor, an entrepreneur who was initially employed as a domestic worker for a wealthy white family in New Jersey. Concerning the poet's mother and relatives, Jordan's first cousin, Valerie Orridge, informs me of her family's impoverished living conditions in Clonmel, a tiny, high-altitude mountain village in Jamaica. Growing up in Clonmel, Mildred, her sister Lynne, and other family members resided in a small, dirt-floor cabin that was not equipped with either running water or electricity. In *Soldier: A Poet's Childhood*, Jordan describes how young Mildred and the other mountain-village residents traveled on the "goat tracks" at night and were met with frightening shadows of scary banana-tree leaves. During the day, they were burdened with the task of getting pails of water from the local river.[11] Mildred left this destitute place to immigrate to the United States mainland years after her mother immigrated there with the assistance of a wealthy white family for whom she had worked on the island.

To further understand the journeys of Mildred and her eventual relationship with Granville, one must consider the familial struggles and choices of Mildred's mother. According to Orridge, years before Mrs. Taylor left Jamaica and immigrated to the United States, she experienced two out-of-wedlock teenage pregnancies that resulted in the births of Mildred and Lynne. On the experiences of working and caring for her two children, Orridge indicates that Mrs. Taylor became "a very, very hard working woman; I mean she could work. She was working for a white woman." Orridge continues:

> There were many rich white people there in the island who had big homes . . . and some very wealthy woman . . . came there and asked [Mrs. Taylor]

if she wanted to come to the States and she said yes. And she left her children there: Lynne was left with someone that she called her godmother and June's mother was left with June's mother's father's sister [June's great aunt]. Now this is not to detract from any of June's work because I am very proud of her accomplishments and what she has done in her literary contributions, but she has misrepresented the family in many ways. And I have never been very happy about that.[12]

Orridge's unhappiness has a lot to do with Jordan's readings of the events of her familial history, beginning with the reasons why Mrs. Taylor left Jamaica without her children to why she decided to bring Lynne to the states before Mildred.

In many of her political writings, Jordan refers to her grandmother's departure from both Jamaica and her family as an act of abandonment. However, Orridge provides a different reading of the departure, explaining that her grandmother immigrated to the States without her children in order to secure employment and the necessary finances that would afford her family a better life. Soon after Mrs. Taylor, a woman of dark complexion, arrived in New Jersey and began working in the household of a rich, white family, she married the butler, a Jamaican who could pass for a white man himself. Together, they purchased a home in Orange, New Jersey, with the financial assistance of their employer, and requested that Lynne join them. Orridge states:

After they married [Mrs. Taylor and her husband], she went back to Jamaica . . . on a boat. She brought my mother [Lynne] here. Why she brought her first, I don't know. I feel that she had a preference for my mother who was the second child. June's mother was older. . . . So Lynne came here and lived with her stepfather and her mother, June's mother having been left in Jamaica. Now my mother was a very, very brilliant woman. She went to school . . . in Orange, New Jersey.[13]

Mildred Maude Fisher Jordan, June Jordan's mother, date unknown. Courtesy of Valerie Orridge.

Orridge goes on to discuss how Mrs. Taylor was "very enterprising," having paid for the beautifully large home that was originally financed by her employer and having rented out rooms to needy tenants. Orridge also describes how Mrs. Taylor cared for her husband and for Lynne, and how she eventually sent for Mildred to join them in New Jersey a while after Lynne had arrived and formed a bond with her mother and stepfather.

Mildred soon joined the family in the States and, according to Jordan's published accounts, became a domestic worker in New Jersey. She later became employed as a full-time maid in order to support Lynne's efforts at completing her studies at Hunter High School in New York City, where she graduated class valedictorian. Ironically, Lynne was not allowed to deliver the valedictorian's speech at the graduation ceremonies because school officials feared that the audience would not understand her heavy West Indian accent. Jordan's account of Lynne's educational experiences and Mildred's support of her sister's academic pursuits is highly questionable. Orridge recalls a different story, one that begins with her mother, Lynne, attending Orange High School in New Jersey before attending Hunter College (not high school, as Jordan recounts) in New York City where she became pregnant and married her first husband to the dismay of Mrs. Taylor.[14]

Regardless of which account is accurate, Orridge does agree with Jordan's documentation that Lynne did go on to college and successfully earned several academic degrees. After Mildred and Lynne immigrated to the States, Mildred met and married Granville, and gave birth to their only child, June Millicent Jordan. Around this same time, Lynne divorced her husband and asked Mildred to care for young Valerie. Mildred agreed, Valerie moved into the Jordan's Brooklyn brownstone, and they—Mildred and Valerie—forged a strong "mother-daughter relationship that Jordan never had with Mildred." Their relationship had everything to do with their outsider identities: Mildred felt like an outsider, an

John Taylor, Marie Taylor's husband, is pictured here at a family member's wedding celebration, date unknown. Courtesy of Valerie Orridge.

Ethelynn Mulholland Orridge, June Jordan's "Aunt Lynn," is pictured here upon her graduation from Columbia University in New York City, date unknown. Courtesy of Valerie Orridge.

Other, who did not quite belong in the established familial circle that Mrs. Taylor, her husband, and Lynne had formed; Valerie felt like an outsider when her parents divorced and her mother left her to be raised by Mildred. In addition to the outsider and Other identities, both women appreciated the challenges presented by hard work so much that they dedicated their professional lives to the healthcare profession, a decision that further strengthened their "mother-daughter" bond.[15]

Mildred's belief in hard work can be traced to her ability and perseverance to leave Clonmel and begin another life in New Jersey and then in New York City. At the dissent of Orridge, Jordan recounts that Mildred eventually fell into, or accepted, a life of submission and silence. For Jordan, her mother's silence was not just a part of her devotion to God and the Holy Spirit, but also a consequence of Mildred's familial interactions, especially with her supposedly abusive husband. Interestingly, one can extrapolate from Jordan's personal reflections on her parents that Mildred's silences enabled Granville to take control of his daughter's life, especially when it came to the lessons Jordan would come to learn and the rhymes and poetry she would memorize. According to Jordan, "As he [Granville] assumed control, he advised my mother that she, in effect, had been dismissed. He knew what had to be done. He'd do it. I'd do it. She'd see, very soon, that his decision was the right decision."[16]

Mildred's "dismissal," or silence around the in-house lessons her husband taught their young daughter, did not stop there. There were times that Mildred,

June Jordan, her first cousin, Valerie Orridge (left to right), and the family dog sit in the backyard of Jordan's childhood home in Brooklyn, New York, circa 1942. Courtesy of Valerie Orridge.

offering no explanatory remarks, allegedly knocked young June down upon her late arrival home from school. As Jordan herself recalls,

And sometimes, just as I'd be
coming in right past my mother, she'd
just knock me down. And I'd
cringe there on the concrete, waiting for the next blow.
But with my mother, there was never
a second or third attack.
I was down.
It was over.
And I never knew why about the whole thing.[17]

In addition to her silent and sometimes harsh physical treatment of her daughter, Mildred often remained quiet as Granville inflicted physical harm on their only child. Of her father's violence, Jordan writes, "It seemed he needed to frighten me first with his words and his voice. Then he'd rush at me, either by himself or with something he'd pick up as he lunged."[18] To reiterate his authority, Granville once ran down their Brooklyn neighborhood streets after her, seeking to punish and to beat her into submission. According to Jordan,

Once I ran out of the house for several blocks in my pyjamas [sic]. And he chased after me and, at last, caught me and beat me—in public. . . . I took to sleeping with a knife under my pillow. So when my father rumbled those mahogany doors open and started to beat me in the middle of the night, I pulled my knife and I asked him, "What do you want?" And I meant, "I'll kill you!" And soon after that my father stopped waking me up.[19]

Young June recognized the necessity of defending herself against her father. From that point on, Jordan realized that she had power and a voice, even as a child—a realization that she would later come to articulate in many of her published books for children and young adults. Nevertheless, in this relationship of alleged violence perpetuated by Granville and received by both his wife and daughter, Mildred often stood by as a silent observer. Even with her occasional gestures of "stop it" or "don't speak that way to *him*,"[20] her silence, according to Jordan, was never transformed into either action against her husband or physical protection of her daughter.

In "The Transformation of Silence into Language and Action," feminist writer Audre Lorde writes of the need for women to engage in self-revelation and to speak, even if their speaking occurs in light of possible threats from an unforgiving public. Lorde writes, "Of what had I *ever* been afraid? To question or to speak as I believed could have meant pain, or death. But we all hurt in so many different ways . . . and pain will either change or end." She continues by writing of how "death . . . is the final silence" even if one never speaks what one so desperately needs to.[21] Was Mildred waiting to speak? Was she waiting to be asked to speak and thus, waiting to be heard? Was she speaking to and with herself about Granville's physical and verbal attacks, or was she praying that her silences would protect her and her daughter from some larger sociopolitical and sociopsychological pain? Or, was Jordan's reading of her familial past fictionalized, even to some extent, in comparison with the accounts offered by Valerie Orridge?

In her poem "Ghaflah," Jordan poetically writes of the pain associated with passiveness, acceptance, protection, and forgetfulness, points that are reiterative of aspects of Mildred's life and points that allow one to question the level of hostility present, or not, in the Jordan household:

> Or how I strut
> beside her walking anywhere
> prepared for any lunatic
> assault
> upon her shuffling
> journey
> to a bus stop
>
> I acknowledge nothing
>
> I forget she taught me
> how to pray
> I forget her prayers
> And mine[22]

The presence of forgetfulness in "Ghaflah" can be interpreted in a number of ways. Jordan's forgetting that her mother "taught me/how to pray" can be associated with the relinquishing of religious hope and the spiritual power of

June Jordan and Valerie Orridge (left to right) lie on the grass of a wide-open yard, date unknown. Courtesy of Valerie Orridge.

patience that insist on the eventual ending of difficult, painful experiences, such as verbal and physical abuse, feelings of abandonment, neglect, and forced loneliness. On the other hand, Jordan's forgetting may be symbolic of how her supposed violent and volatile experiences in her parents' home are remembered and dismembered in ways that suppress alternative truths, thus allowing Jordan to "acknowledge nothing." Then again, given the divergent *rememberings* of the familial past that Jordan and Orridge recount, one might speculate that Jordan's forgetting is an act of fictionalizing the past so as to re-create, reconstruct, and re-present it: Was Jordan really abused as a child? Were her interactions with Granville so painful that she can only remember, understandably but unfortunately, the abuse and yet still consider Granville to be "amazing" and her "literary inspiration"? Why do the remembrances of Jordan and Orridge, first cousins who lived in the same household for years, differ so drastically?

Orridge remembers a different history, one that derives from her experiences as a young child in the Jordan household when June Jordan was born. Soon, "there was some resentment" from Jordan, who did not understand her cousin's role or presence in her mother's life. For Orridge, Mildred was not particularly a silent or submissive woman; instead, she was not understanding of the early personal and professional choices Jordan made. Unlike Jordan, Mildred "was no revolutionary" and "didn't understand June had talent and she wanted to write." Orridge continues: "All my aunt understood was that you go to college and get an education and you come out and you get a job."[23] Jordan, however, often understood Mildred's behavior as representative of silence and submission that derived from Granville's strong-willed nature and Mildred's unfilled dreams.

Even with Mildred's presumed silences and Granville's strong-willed nature, together they were determined to form a better life for themselves and their daughter in New York City. Although their commitments were fashioned differently, they both believed in the ideals of hard work and faith. In 1933, a short time after the married couple moved into a rather small, uptown Manhattan apartment and three years before their daughter was born, Granville found a job as an elevator operator, and he excitedly "ran the whole length of Manhattan . . . to shout, 'A job! A job! I got a job!'"[24] Some years later, he became employed as a postal worker and eventually "earned the traditional gold watch as a retiring civil servant."[25] During his married life, he often volunteered to teach boxing classes to black youths at the Harlem branch of the YMCA on West 135th Street, believing that black people had a responsibility to acquire strength of mind and body. Throughout his lifetime, Granville's strength of mind and body showed itself in his disruptive relationship with his daughter, whom he treated as a boy and a soldier son, and whom he raised to function in the world as white men do. The insistence by Granville that his daughter function as white men do can be connected to how he encountered the world as a nonwhite, or raced, immigrant man who could have traveled between the limiting worlds of black and white based on appearance. In her popular memoir, Soldier: A Poet's Childhood, dedicated to her father, Jordan narrates some of her father's daily experiences with race, power, and struggle.[26]

In an interview with David Barsamian, journalist, author, and founder of Alternative Radio in Boulder, Colorado, Jordan remarks of her father:

> We were as close as father and son. . . . It [the connection] was problematic and without any question extraordinarily positive for me. . . . At the time he came here, there were no resources available to him at all as a black immigrant man. I know that he did better than he could trying to raise a family, be a good husband. I feel without question that his inordinate ambitions for me have everything to do with most of the really happy, productive aspects of my life that I continue to honor in his memory.[27]

In various interviews, personal and self-reflexive writings, and political commentaries and poems, Jordan has described her relationship with her father in loving ways. The complicated nature of their daughter/son-father bond stemmed from several factors: her father's treatment of young June as a boy, his son, and a soldier; his insistence that June study and memorize great literary and poetic works from the Bible to the writings of Paul Laurence Dunbar, Shakespeare, and Edgar Allen Poe; Granville's love of music, which Jordan, as a young, budding pianist, studied and quickly learned to appreciate; and his temperamental behavior, such as chasing his daughter down the street or waking her from sleep to punish her, many times in her mother's presence.

One can appreciate the poet's interpretative construction of her relationship with her father as being connected by the closeness of a father and a son, for Granville served as Jordan's intellectual and literary inspiration. She attributed her entrance into the literary world as highly influenced by the lessons taught to her by her father; it is significant to note that she was partially influenced by Mildred's desire to become an artist. Even the validity of Jordan's suggestion that her mother wanted to become an artist is uncertain. Orridge indicates

Mildred's lifelong desire to be a nurse, and her enthusiasm upon discovering that young Valerie also wanted to become a nurse: "I became a nurse like my aunt, who was like a surrogate mother. Even when I went to the Harlem Hospital School of Nursing . . . my mother [Lynne] didn't take me, she [Mildred] took me."[28]

Even if Mildred wanted to become an artist instead of a nurse, Jordan does not reveal the reasons behind Mildred's reluctance, if any, to share more of this information with her. This may be a result of her mother's silence about the very things she desired, but did not believe she could rightfully experience or accomplish during her lifetime. Or, this could be a result of Jordan's inaccurate reading of her mother. Nevertheless, Jordan's attention, as recounted in *Soldier: A Poet's Childhood*, is deflected from her mother's life, as she, June, became her father's exclusive possession. Praising her father's influence on her literary teachings, Jordan claimed that her father "was an amazing human being." This proclamation further complicates one's understanding of how and why Granville, a man who bravely immigrated to the U.S. mainland, could both love and physically abuse his very own daughter and name her as his soldier son. One must wonder: How could Granville live on in the memory of Jordan—that abused female child and that politically astute adult—as "an amazing" person? How can Jordan consider Granville to be "amazing" in light of his supposed abusive behavior? Was she really abused?

Jordan's loving and questionably passive mother, Mildred, was a dedicated nurse who cared for the sick and worked to heal the ailments of others, even though she, herself, has been portrayed by her daughter as profoundly unhappy and internally disturbed. Mildred attended the Lincoln School of Nursing, where she served as president of the first graduating class of black practitioners. As a resident of Harlem, she attended the West 125th Street Universal Truth Center church and openly shouted her religious annunciations to the congregation members. She also attended and regularly volunteered in church-related activities. In Granville's absence, Mildred and young June attended weekly church services. It was here that Jordan began singing melodies and hymns at the prompting of her mother and the women of the congregation; her musical performances in the church parallel her interest in becoming a classically trained pianist during her young adult life. In response to an interview question asked by Barsamian, "Did your mother nourish you intellectually in any way?" Jordan admits that the nourishment that she received from her mother was different from Granville's nourishment. She states:

> She did, but not in the same way my father did. My father was serious about it, testing me everyday. My mom was more religious. So much of the Bible and the biblical lore and values that she continuously immersed me in raised so many questions that in that way it was intellectually provocative.[29]

Jordan sympathized with her mother's dreams, or her own self-imposed dreams for her mother, of becoming an artist and she sympathized with her life

of unfulfilled longings, but rejected Mildred's submission to silence and eventually, to suicide. This is yet another point of contention: while Jordan admits
that Mildred committed suicide, Orridge disagrees and insists that Mildred
"was sick with hypertension . . . at that time, there were not the medications
that exist now—anti-hypertensions and the like. She [Mildred] was ailing with
. . . hypertension or heart disease and June insists my aunt killed herself."[30]
Orridge continues:

> I said to her, "June, I said your mother didn't kill herself." And she kept insisting
> that she took an overdose of digoxin, she took an overdose. My aunt did not kill
> herself. She was sick and she probably died of a heart attack. . . . And that's how
> I suggest she [June] has misrepresented the family.[31]

Although Jordan and Orridge's recollections of Mildred's death differ, one thing
that is certain is that Mildred and Granville, brave as they were, cared for their
extended family and provided their daughter with an intellectually and reli-
giously stimulating, as well as a debatably violent childhood.

While the events surrounding Jordan's interactions with and readings of her
parents are speculative, it is clear that Mildred and Granville shared a belief in
literacy and intellectual sophistication just as much as they did in American
democracy. However, Mildred's belief in democracy had less to do with political and social mobility and more to do with religious prosperity and prayer.
Granville's belief, however, had more to do with political, economic, and social
mobility for black people and less to do with waiting on salvation. Their different approaches led to a family life blended with love and rage, pleasure and
violence, and at the center of this maelstrom were issues encountered by all
immigrants and people of color: the lack of civil rights, the recognition of
political injustices, a desire for economic prosperity and educational advancement, access to quality resources and jobs, and survival in both the segregated
communities and the white institutions where they lived, worked, and struggled for advancement.

Granville and Mildred's individual departures from their native lands during the Roaring Twenties signified an escape from their West Indian birth-
places with their attendant socioeconomic barriers and inaccessibility to
educational resources; however, these departures also showed their pursuit of
another type of life enhanced by the hope and longing for more positive situations in America, the land of opportunities. Jordan, herself, often questioned
the individual strengths of her parents as they journeyed to the U.S. mainland:
"How did my parents even hear about America, more than half a century ago?
In the middle of the Roaring Twenties, these eager black immigrants came, by
boat. Did they have to borrow shoes for the journey?"[32] Her parents probably
had to borrow more than shoes for the journey; they needed to borrow the
strength and energy of brave ancestors who had previously ventured from their
native lands and immigrated to America. While Granville's form of arrival to

the States is unknown, Mildred's arrival is connected to her mother's and sister's immigration.

In order to understand the journeys of Jordan's immigrant parents from their homelands to the U.S. mainland, one must situate their travels in the context of the 1920s. The decade of the 1920s opened with the passage of the Constitution's 18th Amendment/Prohibition Act (1919), which declared the following:

> Section 1: After one year from the ratification of this article the manufacture, sale, or transportation of intoxicating liquors within, the importation thereof into, or the exportation thereof from the United States and all territory subject to the jurisdiction thereof for beverage purposes is hereby prohibited.[33]

United States legislative powers and lawmakers believed that by making consumption and possession of alcohol illegal, the crime rate would decrease and the general conditions of life would improve. However, crime increased—illegal bars and speakeasies flourished, and gangsters such as Al Capone profited from smuggling and distributing alcohol into the United States. The 1920s, often called "The Roaring Twenties," the "Jazz Age," the "Age of Intolerance," and the "Age of Wonderful Nonsense," was a decade of cultural conflict. On the one hand, this period represented prosperity and optimism for American-based businesses: the emergence of bathtub gin, the first transatlantic flight, the $5 workday, and the movies. On the other hand, the nation also saw the rise of the Ku Klux Klan, prohibition, the Tulsa Race Riot of 1921, restrictive immigration laws, and antiradical panic and hysteria around the Palmer raids.

In the midst of this all, Granville and Mildred ventured to this new place and created lives of optimism wrapped in American prosperity. One speculates that the struggles of this strong, curious, and eager couple, particularly during their separate immigrations in the 1920s, influenced the ways that June Jordan struggled—as a young girl, as an adolescent, and as an adult—to define herself and her voice in light of these American and immigrant identities. Was her mother really silent, and if so, then from where did her silence come? What social and political forces motivated Granville's violent behavior? Can violence be tempered by the cultivation of an intellectual life? In what ways did their immigrant identities become lost or displaced in master narratives of whiteness and privilege, power and access? And how was young June really to understand such complicating dynamics at the same time that she was supposed to understand the beauty of life and living, the beauty of language and music, the beauty of love and freedom, and the Beauty of Blackness? What did it mean to be born in 1936 to immigrant parents who had ventured to America only a decade earlier?

It is obvious that from the beginning, Jordan, like most young girls, loved her father. She enjoyed the times when he swung her by the arms as they crossed the Harlem River Bridge or held her hand as they walked the streets of downtown Manhattan. For Jordan, these were monumental times that demonstrated the father-daughter connection she had with Granville in the absence of such a connection with her mother. Jordan believed that her courageous father really cared about her and wanted the very best for her despite any hardships and disagreements that may have occurred. In her many writings, the poet acknowledges her parents' level of difficulty raising, caring, and providing for her, their girl-child, in 1936, years after they had immigrated to the States and attempted to find their way in the City. As noted in *Soldier: A Poet's Childhood* (2000), and in essays found in *Civil Wars: Observations from the Front Lines of America* (1981), Jordan was always her father's little boy and male warrior, and Granville would stop at nothing to teach her the value in defending one's self and in being well versed in the poetic disposition of language. He showed his daughter the beauty of language, as illustrated in this poem by Paul Laurence Dunbar:

> You bid me hold my peace
> And dry my fruitless tears,
> Forgetting that I bear
> A pain beyond my years[34]

Granville also showed Jordan the language of beauty, as embodied in work by William Shakespeare:

> O that you were yourself! but, love, you are
> No longer yours than you yourself her live:
> Against this coming end you should prepare,
> And your sweet semblance to some other give[35]

Jordan recalls memorizing and loving the poetry of Dunbar and Shakespeare just as much as she remembers establishing profitable and trusting interpersonal relationships based on her love of the written word. As a child living in Brooklyn, Jordan wrote and sold "break-up" poetry, infatuation poems, and other emotionally provocative writings to innocent youngsters her age. Documenting and capturing the honesty of language on paper for others was one of her favorite pastimes. Writing for other people at such an early age allowed Jordan to understand that human feelings provide invaluable exposure to the beauty and usability of language.

As a youngster, the burgeoning poet recognized how her father employed language to punish her and to silence her mother, lessons that she describes in vivid detail in *Soldier: A Poet's Childhood*. Writing in the voice and with the heart of a child, Jordan chronicles how the fighting, arguing, and disagreements between her father and mother began when she was barely two years old. She also remembers how Mildred allowed her to dress in pastels, learn childhood rhymes, and play with toys. Granville, on the other hand, insisted on taking control of everything, including her development and learning. This insistence particularly resulted from an assessment by the Ethical Culture School in Manhattan that young June was a genius. According to Jordan, she and her father "went inside the Ethical Culture School. . . . I'm not sure what happened there, but I guess it was a test situation of some sort." Jordan continues by admitting, "And my test score and the teachers who assessed me there evidently persuaded my father that he had a genius—or a monster—on his hands."[36] From then on, Granville worked with his daughter to prove that she was, in fact, a little genius. He dedicated time to teach her various learning techniques that could help her to become attentive, focused, and trusting. Her mother, however, encouraged her daughter to have teatime, doll time, and to engage in the childhood pleasures of make believe.

In addition to her father, Jordan's early upbringing was influenced by her maternal grandmother, Mrs. Marie Taylor or, as Jordan referred to her, "Nanny." Jordan writes that her grandmother was a special woman who always appeared in beautiful dresses and shoes: "she was the first lady of my life."[37] Unlike Mildred, who always wore flat shoes, Jordan indicates that "Nanny" would wear heels and would always be dressed as if she was prepared for the coming of the Lord: "She never wore anything besides immaculate church dresses and church dress-up shoes: Lace-ups with a one-and-a-half-to-two-inch heel."[38] Jordan often wondered why her mother was not as attentive to her appearance as "Nanny" was, given that she and her father often purchased fancy outfits for her.

Jordan's focus on her mother's ordinariness was quickly replaced by a serious need for protection in her Brooklyn neighborhood; not only was Jordan required to defend herself in her parents' home, but also from the neighborhood bullies on the streets and in the schoolyards. She found herself fighting all the time. Fights and bullies just somehow came looking for young June—from the confrontations with her father and onward. She was so happy when her Uncle Teddy, or Theodore Roosevelt Rutledge, who was cousin Valerie's stepfather and aunt Lynne's second husband, came to live with them in Bedford-Stuyvesant. He was Jordan's savior, teaching her how to fight back and how to defend herself against bullies, even if her defense was not enough to win the battle. According to Jordan, he taught her how to maintain faith and optimism; many times, he stopped Granville from hitting her. Such lessons followed Jordan into her neighborhood and school, and people quickly realized that they should not mess with her more than once, for Jordan was a fighting machine who would fight like crazy if prompted.

Jordan's uncle was an American-born black man, and her West Indian father had no problems letting her and everyone else know this fact: "Something about my Uncle Teddy really got on his [Jordan's father] nerves."[39] For some undisclosed reason, Jordan speculates that her father resented black Americans. Jordan writes that there were just as many black Americans as West Indians who lived on Hancock Street in their Brooklyn community. Nevertheless, Granville was quick to point out the differences between the two groups, and he took special pleasure in highlighting the differences when it came to Uncle Teddy.

Based on textual analyses of Jordan's writing, one might assume various reasons for Granville's attitude. He may have blamed black Americans for allowing white people to treat them as inferiors. It is also possible that Jordan's father blamed Uncle Teddy for not taking more responsibility for his stepdaughter, Valerie, and for being "very mean to Lynne."[40] Thus, Granville probably expected a better "catch" for Lynne, a woman with more than four advanced degrees, a math teacher, and "the first black female principal in Brooklyn."[41] Theodore Roosevelt "Teddy" Rutledge, according to Jordan, was a nonpracticing law school graduate who worked as a probation officer, was a self-taught storyteller, a natural-born talker, and a black American citizen who was not a West Indian. Orridge, however, provides a different picture of her stepfather, saying that he "was a lawyer with a thousand degrees, but was never the gentleman my father was." She then admits that her stepfather "had several law degrees. . . . He graduated from, I think, NYU and had another law degree from Fordham University and a third one," and was "a judge and a lawyer."[42] It is clear that the facts surrounding Uncle Teddy's profession and his tumultuous relationship with Granville are arguable. One thing, however, is certain: despite Granville's dislike of Uncle Teddy, the two men did have some things in common: fighting, reading, cooking, dressing up, and loving June Jordan, for whom each stressed the importance of educational pursuits.

Jordan's formal education occurred amidst the mainly black student body of the New York City Public School System, beginning with her studies at P.S. 26 elementary school. Every day after school, she was met with a fight by some little boy or girl, or even a group of girls. In *Soldier: A Poet's Childhood*, Jordan writes of her childhood school fights: "Another little girl, or a group of other little girls, would insult or jump me, and pretty quick I'd be banging away with my fists and keeping my chin tucked down."[43] It was not until her high-school years that the well-known routines and racial safety and sanctity of her educational situation changed. Granville removed his daughter from the environment that she had come to live in and love—the environment that housed the cute boys on the block, her first "wanna-be-boyfriends," and her fighting, "crazy girl" reputation in the neighborhood. He enrolled Jordan in a private preparatory school that was known for its academic rigor.

Despite her protests, Jordan became the only black student among over 3,000 total students at Milwood High School in New York. She was probably the youngest student at the school: having skipped two grades, Jordan was a twelve-year-old sophomore. She traveled for over an hour one way to get to the school only to be met with a homogeneously white population of students and the accompanying pressure to excel. After one academically successful, but emotionally difficult year at Milwood, Jordan's parents consulted Father Coleman, their neighbor, minister, and the first black man to serve on the New York City Board of Education. Together, they decided that Jordan would apply to Northfield School for Girls, a preparatory school in Northfield, Massachusetts. Her successful interview and high IQ scores garnered her a full academic scholarship. On the experience of Jordan attending Northfield, Orridge remarks:

> She went there, I don't know how she felt about going there. I think she was the only black person there. She had to do some work assignment as part of the scholarship, . . . washing the dishes . . . and doing the same thing my grandmother was trying to get away from. Anyway, when she left there she came back to New York and she went to Barnard.[44]

Northfield School proved to be even more hostile to Jordan's racial and cultural identities than Milwood High School. However, her three intensive years of training at Northfield School for Girls positively cultivated her love for boys, language, and words. This love was later fostered in her undergraduate studies at both Barnard College and at the University of Chicago, as well as in her publications, speaking engagements, and international activist efforts.

In 1953, Jordan matriculated to Barnard College in New York City (1953–1955), with the intention of studying music, applied piano concert preparatory techniques, and English. It should be noted that Jordan studied under Professor Frank Sheridan at The Julliard School in New York City and became a classically trained pianist. During her undergraduate studies, the poet continuously searched for "the connection between the apparently unrelated worlds of white and Black."[45] While not finding this connection at Barnard College, Jordan became unrelentingly active in one of the college's literary publications, *Focus,* which was in circulation from 1948 to 1969 and where many of her early writing appeared. The connection Jordan established with the literary publication was not enough to keep her at Barnard, for she officially dropped out some years and experiences later. During an anti-McCarthy petition signing, Jordan, a then eighteen-year-old freshman, became acquainted with Michael Meyer, a twenty-four-year-old white undergraduate student enrolled at Columbia University. Of meeting Meyer, Jordan writes:

> In between classes and in the middle of campus, I met him on a very cold day. He stood, without shivering, behind a small table on which an anti-McCarthy petition and pages of signatures lay, blowing away. . . . He looked like a hero to me.[46]

They married in 1955, although both Jordan's and Meyer's parents utterly opposed their union, and despite Meyer's parents' refusal to attend the ceremony. In an interview with writer Alexis De Veaux for *Essence Magazine,* Jordan defended her nuptials by declaring: "'When I married Michael, that was defiant' . . . 'In the fifties the central thrust against racism was in this country was [sic] to integrate, whether it was the schools or getting married. I didn't feel that marrying interracially was any kind of copout.'"[47]

Orridge, however, reads more into Jordan's interracial marriage by drawing attention to "the competition among the women in the family regarding [skin] color."[48] She notes the near-white complexion of her grandmother's husband and of Mildred's husband, and insists that "the family was all mixed up with this color business,"[49] including Jordan, whose marriage to Meyer occurred around the time of the Civil Rights Movement in America. Nevertheless, Jordan's marriage and participation in the Civil Rights Movement proved monumental to her social activism, emerging stance on universal freedom fights, and political writing on race, sexuality, and love.

The newly married couple eventually moved to Illinois where Meyer studied anthropology at the University of Chicago and where Jordan enrolled (1955–1956) before leaving Chicago for New York City. Upon her return to New York, she re-entered, albeit briefly, Barnard College (1956–1957), and became involved in the Civil Rights Movement and in urban planning. Then she moved to "the projects in Long Island City [and] she absolutely refused to work. She told her mother she was going to be a writer."[50] But in 1958 Jordan gave birth to her only child, Christopher David Meyer, and shortly thereafter, she and Meyer officially separated and Jordan began to seek steady employment. Five years after her son's birth, Jordan became an assistant to the producer for *The Cool World*, a Shirley Clarke film adaptation of Warren Miller's novel about Harlem. Then in 1965, after two years of separation and ten and a half years of marriage, Jordan and Meyer divorced. On their divorce, De Veaux writes: "When pressed, it is difficult for her [Jordan] to articulate a reason. She absolutely refuses to call it racial, or to give it any name at all."[51] But in some ways, Jordan does allude to it in her attempt to give it a name. In "Letter to Michael (1964)," she writes, "My husband was away at the University of Chicago, finishing up his graduate studies in anthropology. Or so I thought. . . . Michael was in Chicago but he could have been on Mars."[52] And in "Love is Not the Problem: February, 1983," Jordan admits:

> I went on that freedom ride as the wife of a white man and the mother of a Black child. . . . I was working out a disjuncture between my personal life and my social situation, for myself. None of this means that any marriage is a great idea or a terrible thing. All I'm saying is that *love* is not the problem.[53]

Love was not the problem in Jordan's love-fight relationship with her father, in her daughter-mother connection of silence and sacrifice, or in her interracial marriage to, and subsequent divorce from, Michael Meyer.

Love was not the problem. Love! The problem was not June Jordan. The problem was, in some ways, wrapped in Jordan's desire to live her life according to her own beliefs, values, and standards in the face of a racist society that was experiencing an increase in civil rights protests, rallies, and freedom fights. From the memories of a supposedly violent and silent childhood, one that the adult poet always described as loving, and from the hard-won realization that race, in this society, does matter, Jordan committed herself to a life of change that involved a search for freedom and acceptance—for her father, mother, husband, son, larger artistic and political communities, and ultimately for herself. For this lover, emerging poet, activist, and intellectual, love for the people in her life, and those yet to enter it, was not, and would never be, the problem, which is, in many ways, a highly contentious point. Jordan's childhood in her West Indian parents' home, in her surrounding Brooklyn neighborhood, and in the educational spaces that did not quite resemble her family's cultural history is directly connected to her adult life of activism and political writing. From her father's strictness to her forced presence in predominantly white educational institutions, to her ten-year interracial marriage and her mother's silencing and alleged suicide, Jordan realized that it, life, is "a bully. It's not about fair."[54]

TWO

Who Look at Me

I n the 1960s and 1970s, Jordan's familial relationships in New York City had just as much to do with her understanding of intimate struggles as they had to do with her growing acceptance of the complications and politics of love, as indicated by her interracial marriage to Michael Meyer. Life for the poet was never easy nor absent of challenges, a message that she delivers in the opening pages of *Civil Wars: Observations from the Front Lines of America*. Here, Jordan declares, "I learned, in short, that fighting is a whole lot less disagreeable than turning tail or knuckling under. It feels better. . . . I lost a lot of fights as a kid in Bedford-Stuyvesant. But nobody fought me twice."[1] The poet, telling of her love of words and her hatred of fights, admits, "But if, as a Black girl-child in America, I could not evade the necessity to fight, then, maybe, I could choose my weaponry at least."[2] Throughout her life, she attempted to do just that: select the "weaponry" and employ the techniques needed to successfully engage in battle. Meanwhile, she stood in direct opposition to other people even as she opened herself up to experiencing the unlimited love of her 1950s interracial marriage.

In 1963, Jordan and Meyer separated. Just a short two years later in 1965, their marriage ended in divorce. As a single mother in New York City, Jordan assumed full parental responsibility for her growing seven-year-old son, Christopher, since Meyer "didn't do a . . . thing for him. June did it all."[3] This full-time responsibility was, in fact, short lived because in order for Jordan to survive as a single, working mother and artist, she needed the assistance of friends and family to help care for Christopher. Mildred was often "taking care of him . . . and actually helping while June was going back and forth in the city trying to . . . [get] literary contacts."[4] As Jordan sought to form a new identity without her ex-husband, she began work at various jobs: an assistant to the producer of the film, *The Cool World*; a freelance reporter and journalist; a participant on freedom rides; and a volunteer for organizations that formed as a result of the Civil Rights Movement. During this time, she completed her first poetry collection, *Who Look at Me* (1969), and her first novel, *His Own Where* (1971).[5] Such personal and professional events proved that Jordan's life was never really easy. Her life signified battles with familial and intimate love as well as ongoing struggles over the civil rights, liberties, and freedoms of disenfranchised people, including herself, her son, and her parents. The 1960s and 70s can attest to the beginning of Jordan's battles over and for various rights.

In the 1960s Jordan reported on the struggle for civil rights in Southern states, particularly in Mississippi, for various newspapers including the *New York Times* and the *Herald Tribune*. The poet visited black communities that were heavily afflicted by violence, segregation, and racism; she was committed to her work with black Southerners fighting these conditions and striving to gain and ensure their civil rights. Jordan eventually joined the freedom rides and became a protégé of Mrs. Fannie Lou Hamer, organizer of the Mississippi Freedom Party and Field Secretary for the Student Nonviolent Coordinating Committee (SNCC).

Then Jordan witnessed firsthand the violence of the 1964 Harlem Riot. Shortly thereafter, she worked on the architectural redesign of Harlem with engineer, inventor, poet, and mathematician, W. R. Buckminster Fuller. Committed to human rights, Jordan insisted that one must always resist injustice of any kind, by any name, and against any person; she was not afraid to do battle. In the introduction to *Civil Wars: Observations from the Front Lines of America*, Jordan powerfully declares,

> In 1964, I believed I was fighting hard in the middle of an enormous argument about America and anybody's right to be here, specific and nondissoluble. I perceived myself to be surrounded and outnumbered by enemies. I accepted media notions of my "minority" status in a "naturally" white America.[6]

Was it when Jordan saw the rising flames in Harlem that she accepted her minority status? Was it upon becoming a single parent that her status as a minority officially became her "minority status"? Or was it a combination of events such as her eventual divorce, Harlem on fire, Mississippi burning, and the events surrounding her mother's death that convinced the poet, however temporarily, that she was outnumbered by her enemies, known and unknown, most of whom were not black? In her 1968 book, *Who Look at Me*, Jordan writes a powerful poem about being viewed as "Other." Her words, guiding the discussion of this chapter, are as relevant today as when they were first penned:

Who would paint a people
black or white?
*

For my own I have held
where nothing showed me how
where finally I left alone
to trace another destination
*

A white stare splits the air
by blindness on the subway
in department stores
The Elevator
        (that unswerving ride
where man ignores the brother
by his side) . . .
*

Is that how we look to you
a partial nothing clearly real?[7]

Indeed, Jordan crossed many rivers and won many battles in the period leading up to and following the Harlem Riot of 1964. Before that time, she regularly entertained "Huck," a friend from her student days at Barnard College,[8]
who engaged Jordan on many topics, especially architecture. Jordan soon
began to explore the world of the Donnell Library, located at 20 West 53rd
Street in Manhattan, reading books dedicated to the topic of architecture and
paying attention to the architectural design of the buildings, rooms, and arti-
facts. At the same time, Huck convinced Jordan to "write scenarios, and
thereby, combine poetry and architecture in a medium accessible to most people."[9] Jordan agreed, and from 1963 to 1964 in New York City, she became the
assistant to Frederick Wiseman, "a white man" and the producer for the film,
The Cool World. Directed by "a white woman,"[10] Shirley Clarke, the film is an
adaptation of the book of the same title, and stars local black Harlem teenagers
confronting racism, hatred, black-white conflicts, and identity formation in
America. Jordan was taken by the idea behind the film and the book it was
based on, and began working on "a frame for the reality of *The Cool World.*"[11]
Included in her "frame" are interviews, statements, and personal reflections
from cast members on life in Harlem and in America for black males. Jordan
successfully completed and titled the frame, and subsequently the first chapter in *Civil Wars,* "Testimony," just as the film opened in 1964. Soon thereafter,
she left Wiseman's film group to dedicate more time to freelancing.

Jordan freelanced for the *Herald Tribune* and became even more involved in
the politics of Harlem. She met and interacted with black civil rights leader
Malcolm X, whose Temple Number Seven was located in the heart of Harlem,[12]
author Louis Lomax, activist James Farmer who was the National Director of

the Congress Of Racial Equality (CORE),[13] and a slew of news reporters, writers, editors, and political figures. Around this time, tension in Harlem was
coming to a head. The 1964 Riot, provoked by a white police officer's fatal
shooting of James Powell, a fifteen-year-old unarmed black male, spanned the
course of two nights before spilling into Brooklyn's Bedford-Stuyvesant community where the poet grew up. Jordan and her friend Dorothy Moscou were
there in Harlem.[14] Jordan stood, ran away, and then returned to, before eventually leaving, Harlem's 132nd Street and 7th Avenue. This was the area where
police officers with guns and anxious fingers filled the sidewalks and streets,
and also where Powell was being eulogized by masses of black people gathered
to pay respects to this fallen child. Gunfire could be heard in the midst of gathered family and friends who tearfully bid farewell to Powell; Jordan was there
as a witness to these events.

On the streets, a group of teenage males continuously shouted, "WE WANT
MALCOLM," as Jordan reports in her book, *Civil Wars*. [15] These youngsters
were unwilling to back down from face-to-face confrontations with police officers; even more, they were unwilling to silently endure the unlawful and continual violence perpetuated by those who were sworn to protect them. Their
refusal to back down and the refusal of other black people to *go home*, *leave the
area*, or *stop doing what they were doing* cycled into rounds of gunfire, grenade
throwing, verbal and physical abuse, and many injured, innocent bystanders.
Jordan retreated to the headquarters of the Congress Of Racial Equality
(CORE) with Bostic Van Felton, her friend and a cast member from *The Cool
World*. Together, Jordan and Van Felton assisted the director of CORE, James
Farmer, and the CORE staff with various duties, from tallying up the number
of the injured admitted to hospitals to determining the number of black people who had been jailed and charged with criminal activities and/or resisted
arrest. This work, along with the rioting and protesting on New York City
streets, went on into the early morning hours and lasted for two days.

The Harlem Riot of 1964 was not the first instance of civil unrest to knock
on the city's door. In March 1935, a sixteen-year-old black male, accused of
department store shoplifting, was accosted by store employees and beaten by
police officers. Fueled by this incident, and by rumors that a black woman who
had tried to stop the beating was violently attacked by police officers, angry
Harlem residents protested by marching against police violence. In August
1943, another Harlem-born rebellion occurred after a white police officer shot
a uniformed black serviceman. In addition to residents protesting the murder,
they also organized against price gouging by white-owned businesses in
Harlem, mainly along the popular West 125th Street. These rebellions were not
isolated to the community of Harlem, though, for such police induced riots
occurred in Southern and Northern cities across America: Chicago, 1919;
Oxford, Mississippi, 1962; Watts, 1965; Miami, 1980; and Detroit, 1943 and
1967. After the 1943 riots in Detroit, Thurgood Marshall, who was Assistant
to Special Counsel for the National Association for the Advancement of

Colored People (NAACP) and who was later nominated by John F. Kennedy to the Second Court of Appeals, produced a report that condemned major cities like Detroit for ignoring the brutal treatment of black Americans. Then, in 1968, the National Advisory Commission on Civil Disorders, popularly known as the Kerner Commission, confirmed what black people had already known for many years: the existence of a large social divide and institutionalized unfairness toward black people in major American cities.

The war zone in Harlem energized people to do what Jordan herself was beginning to do: "to stand on the picket line, to march in the demonstration, to speak at the rally, to write and read the poems, to remember not to forget any of the minutes of the meetings of my one life among so many lives, at risk."[16] Being center stage at the 1964 Harlem Riot pushed the poet into creative ventures. Nearly two weeks after the riots, Jordan accepted her first collaborative venture with architect W. R. Buckminster Fuller, whom she had initially met through viewing and examining photographs of his architectural work at Manhattan's Donnell Library. Later, they agreed to co-author an article for *Esquire* magazine on Harlem's architectural reconstruction. The reconstruction took into consideration the placement and viability of hospitals, schools, and housing—safe living conditions and affordably priced homes for Harlem residents. It also considered residents' access to the shoreline, recreational sites, and green spaces, such as Harlem's Morningside and Mount Morris Parks, and to transportation, such as a new bridge that would connect New Jersey to New York with direct access into Harlem. This plan for Harlem's urban renewal was carefully devised so as to not remove and displace black residents from their very own community. Jordan and Fuller fully acknowledged that other plans for urban renewal and gentrification had been quickly devised without thoughtful consideration of the dangers imposed on residents and long-standing community businesses. According to musician and close friend of Jordan, Adrienne Torf, the collaboration between Fuller and Jordan sought to increase the level of safe and affordable living conditions for Harlem residents. Torf informs me that designs of safe space that promoted communal interactions were major concerns for the poet.[17]

Jordan and Fuller worked on the plan and drafted the article, and in December 1964, *Esquire* accepted the article and published it in April 1965. On receiving payment from the magazine in December 1964, Jordan was able to move her son, Christopher, back into her apartment from his grandparents' house just in time for Christmas. Up until this point, Christopher regularly stayed with his grandparents because Jordan could not financially support the two of them, especially since she was no longer with her husband, Meyer, and was struggling financially.[18] Mildred, who "was working at night," made conscious efforts to care for her family, Jordan and Christopher included. Of her payment from *Esquire,* Jordan writes, "On our way home, we kept stopping to buy food, a Christmas tree, presents for Christopher, presents for friends who would come by, and that Christmas Eve I was a millionaire in love."[19] When the article was published in *Esquire*, to Jordan's dismay, Fuller received full credit for it, from its ideas to its proposed plans for Harlem's redesign. This, however, only motivated Jordan to continue to produce important writings; work in, for, and with the community; and live, love, and advocate for social and political change for people considered disenfranchised and silenced.

Over the next few years, Jordan, often under her married name of June Meyer, continued to freelance. She wrote various short stories, poems, and critiques for periodicals such as *Esquire*, the *New York Times*, the *New York Times Magazine*, *Essence*, *Urban Review*, *Black Creation*, *Evergreen*, *Partisan Review*, *Black World*, and *American Poetry Review*. From 1965 to 1966 she worked as a writer and research associate for the Technical Housing Department of Mobilization for Youth in New York City, and in 1967 Jordan began a slightly untraditional teaching career. She taught and worked with young writers at the insistence of Herb Kohl, a founding member of Teachers & Writers Collaborative. This nonprofit organization, established in 1967 in New York City, pairs poets and writers with public-school teachers and students to provide in-school writing sessions and workshops, after-school and weekend poetry programs, and literacy initiatives for youngsters. Jordan joined the initiative and collaborated with educator Terri Bush. Together they held Saturday writing workshops for Puerto Rican and black teenagers in East Harlem and then in Fort Greene, Brooklyn. In much of her writing on her experience with the Teachers & Writers Collaborative, Jordan tells of her commitment to the student-writers: after the workshop, she, along with Bush, took them to "Prospect Park, museums, Jones Beach, and to the Chock Full O'Nuts near Columbia which we picketed" for undisclosed reasons.[20] Jordan and Bush later compiled *The Voice of the Children* (1970), a book of the students' creative writings published by Holt, Rinehart, and Winston that I will discuss in greater detail in a later chapter.

Upon ending her work with the student writers in 1968, Jordan wrote a letter to the director of Teachers & Writers Collaborative that describes how she, Bush, and the dedicated students all survived the larger learning experience of the program. The poet states,

> We have somehow and sometimes survived the systematic degradation of America. And therefore there really are Black children who dream, and who love, and who undertake to master such "white" things as poetry. There really are Black children who are *children* as well as victims. And one had better be pretty damned careful about what one will "accept" from these children as their own— their own honest expression of their dreams, their love, and their always human reality that not even America can conquer.[21]

Oh, how beautiful are these words by Jordan, an activist who believed in honesty, human rights, and freedom of expression, particularly for young people. These sentiments are still necessary in this present-day state of racism, violence, and police brutality—a state named by many people during the 1960s as Harlem, New York; Detroit, Michigan; or Jackson, Mississippi; and a state later named by June Jordan to be America, USA.

Jordan's work with Teachers & Writers Collaborative led to her first university teaching appointment, and as with the poet's previous teaching experience, Herb Kohl was behind the initiation. In the fall of 1967, she was hired to teach English and college composition to freshman students at City College of the City University of New York, located at 138th Street and Convent Avenue in Harlem. On the faculty in the college's English department were the poets and writers, Audre Lorde, Toni Cade Bambara, Adrienne Rich, Mina Shaughnessy, and Barbara Christian. This was a fruitful time for Jordan, her colleagues, and her students, for City College was experiencing major disputes and upheavals, particularly around the Open Admissions Policy.[22] Supporters of the Open Admissions Policy at City College argued for a university welcoming of all people prepared to learn on a collegiate level. They believed that an open university would enhance efforts to create a more humane and free society. However, critics of the policy insisted that the university be guided by standards, which are measurements of excellence and higher learning. In 1970, in the omnipresence of the Vietnam War *and* six years after the 1964 Harlem Riot *and* five years after Malcolm X's assassination *and* two years after Martin Luther King's assassination *and* after rallies and protests on the campus for changes in admissions' policies and student representation, City College finally became an Open Admissions University. According to Jordan and her students, City College was finally, "A Free University at Harlem's I.S. 201."[23]

In 1969, Jordan published "Black Studies: Bringing Back the Person," a position paper that first appeared in *Esquire Magazine*. In it, she decries poverty and exploitation, and praises the students who committed themselves to work against hatred and violence in order to acquire a quality education. She argues,

> Poverty is a bloodbath. Exploitation of human life, for material gain, is unfor-givable-letting-blood-flow for the sake of other currencies. Perforce, the natural element of Black children has been the American bloodbath. We know American violence, power, and success. Is the university prepared to teach us something new?[24]

Jordan's question was answered when the students insisted that City College adopt "new college admission policies"[25] and when the school's administration approved the Open Admissions Policy. For Jordan's colleagues, specifically the ones teaching freshman composition and college-level literature, the policy allowed more academic freedom in the curriculum, reading materials, and instructional approaches. According to poet and former City College instructor, Adrienne Rich,

> These were classes, not simply in writing, not simply in literature, certainly not just in the correction of sentence fragments or the redemptive power of the semi-colon; though we did, and do, work on all these. . . .At City College all Basic

> Writing teachers have been free to choose the books they would assign. . . . There
> has never been a set curriculum or reading list. We have poached off each oth-
> ers' booklists, methods, essay topics, grammar-teaching exercises, and anything
> else that we hoped would "work" for us.[26]

City College, from its faculty and student bodies to its academic curriculum,
became radicalized in its approach to teaching, learning, and educational
access. People from various ethnic, religious, cultural, and linguistic backgrounds, from all age and socioeconomic groups, and from differing learning
levels, were invited to enter and study in the college's classrooms. Jordan was
able to witness and document this occasion:

> There has been no choosing until now. Until the university, there is no choice.
> Education is compulsory. Education has paralleled the history of our Black lives;
> it has been characterized by the punishment of nonconformity, abridgement,
> withered enthusiasm, distortion, and self-denying censorship. Education has
> paralleled the life of prospering white America; it has been characterized by rev-
> erence for efficiency, cultivation of competence unattended by concern for aim.
> . . . Students everywhere must insist on new college admission policies that will
> guide and accelerate necessary, radical change, at all levels of education.[27]

Jordan was not only teaching and fighting for students' rights in New York
City during the late 1960s and early 1970s; she was also writing. Her literary
career, marked by a 1969 Rockefeller Grant in Creative Writing, was already
under way, and her work was being widely read and critically reviewed in literary commmunities. In 1969, Thomas Y. Crowell Company published
Jordan's first poetic collection, *Who Look at Me*, originally a project that the
poet Langston Hughes worked on until his unfortunate death on May 22,
1967. After his death, Jordan asked permission from the publishing company
to work on *Who Look at Me*, and two years later she completed the project. In
an undated *New York Times* piece (obviously published around the time of
Hughes' death), titled "What Happens to a Dream? This One Lives," journalist David Vidal mentions Jordan's attendance at Hughes' funeral: "Others
attending included June Jordan, the poet, who said she considered herself a
'daughter' of Mr. Hughes because she had drawn a book from work he was
doing when he died."[28] Historian, scholar, and prize-winning author Milton
Meltzer encouraged Jordan's work on, and completion of, *Who Look at Me*.
According to Jordan "Gratitude is owing to Milton Meltzer; in response to a
book idea conceived by him, and thanks to his encouragement and respect, I
undertook the creation of *Who Look at Me*. The pictures for the book were cho-
sen from a collection assembled by him."[29]

The book that "she had drawn" became *Who Look at Me*, which, according
to Jordan, "was the text of a poem I wrote when I was in Atlanta for Dr. King's
funeral."[30] In this magnificent and poetically rich text, Jordan uses poetry to
depict the strength and beauty of black and interracial lives, experiences, and
identities by telling the stories of twenty-seven colorful paintings that portray

aspects of black life. Jordan opens with "Who would paint a people black or white."[31] She then moves into a rhythmic response to oppression; the contemptuous stares of white people; the beautiful removal of a white mask by a young boy; and the search for fatherhood, motherhood, and family by including the paintings of highly skilled artists, such as Romare Bearden, Ben Shahn, Thomas Eakins, Charles Alston, Hughie Lee-Smith, Andrew Wyeth, and others. The paintings display a variety of black people: slaves, sailors, artists, revolutionaries, civil rights protesters, and young children. The juxtaposition of paintings with highly sophisticated and original poetry presents a fine opportunity for the book's readers to question the complexities of humanity, the nature of differences, and the unfairness of stereotypes. Such an interrogation, for Jordan, was necessary. In closing, she writes:

> I trust you will remember how we tried to love
> above the pocket deadly need to please
> and how so many of us died there
> on our knees.
>
> Who see the roof and corners of my pride
> to be (as you are) free?
>
> WHO LOOK AT ME?[32]

Around the same time that Jordan was completing *Who Look at Me* and teaching at City College, she began traveling to Mississippi as part of her freelance assignment for the *New York Times*. Her first visit to Mississippi was in the summer of 1969. As documented in her 1970 *New York Times* newspaper story, "Mississippi 'Black Home,'" Jordan wanted "to shake some warm black hands and glimpse some live black people who are determined to stay, and to direct their own survival in that place."[33] She met a lot of black people who were committed to Mississippi. Jordan's commitment to the sacrifices of the people in Mississippi should be remembered for the lasting effects they had on her as she ventured into local and international movements for the rights of people throughout the world; her later writings on Nicaragua and Lebanon attest to this point.[34]

For her freelancing assignment on "Mississippi 'Black Home,'" Jordan spent her first week in Jackson, Mississippi with Dr. Aaron Shirley, husband, father, pediatrician, and cochair of the Mississippi United Front, "a coalition originally formed to defend Head Start programs against the opposition of the Governor."[35] His wife, Mrs. Ollye Shirley, was a coordinator of social services for the Hinds County Head Start program. Charlie White was a junior-high-school science teacher who owned and rented affordably priced apartments in the town, and his fiancée, Frankie Walton, was a university professor by training—she had studied at Tougaloo College and the University of California, Los

Angeles, and taught at Wellesley College. Mel Leventhal, originally from Brooklyn, New York, was a white lawyer for the National Association for the Advancement of Colored People (NAACP) Legal Defense Fund, and an activist in the movement for civil rights. Alice Leventhal, his wife, is the now-famous Pulitzer Prize-winning writer and Civil Rights activist, widely known as Alice Walker. During her travels in Jackson, Mississippi, Jordan was confronted by black people's ongoing struggle to receive equal protection and rights in a historically unjust land—from their demands for fair employment practices and equal pay, to civil and political rights. Seeing the solidarity across socioeconomic lines among Jackson's black and white activists kept Jordan hopeful that changes were coming, even if by force and perseverance.

During the second week, Jordan went to Coahoma and Clarksdale County, Mississippi and visited with Dr. Aaron Henry, chairman of Mississippi's Democratic Party, and owner of a drugstore where freedom fighters often congregated to initiate activities. The communal feel of Dr. Henry's drugstore fascinated Jordan. Freedom fighters gathered at the store to discuss the changes America must undergo if black people are ever to receive fair treatment, governmental representation, equal opportunities, rights, and privileges. Establishing and maintaining "Black Home" in Mississippi was an important conversation of the Mississippi freedom fighters.

Jordan spent the third week with Mrs. Fannie Lou Hamer in Ruleville, Mississippi. Mrs. Hamer was founder of the nonprofit Freedom Farm Cooperative, an organization that was committed to cultivating acres of vegetables and providing for poor families. It was in Ruleville where fourteen-year-old Emmett Till was taken from his relatives' home and brutally tortured and murdered by white men who accused him of whistling at a white woman. The murder and subsequent trial was national news in 1955. In this same town, years after the Till murder, Jordan met Mrs. Hamer who had testified at the 1964 National Democratic Convention about the physically brutal beating she received from white men in Mississippi because of her voter registration work there. Jordan came to admire and deeply respect Mrs. Hamer and her commitment to black life, survival, and financial independence in Mississippi. She eventually became an important leader and female figure in Jordan's personal, political, and creative life, a leader Jordan would emulate.

Jordan went to Mound Bayou, Mississippi, during week four. She met Earl Lucas, the young black mayor of Mound Bayou and director of the Systematic Training and Redevelopment (S.T.A.R.) adult-literacy program. She also met Richard Crowe who had returned to Mississippi after working for nine years on the Chicago police force. In Mound Bayou, Crowe unofficially worked in a makeshift police headquarters that was housed in his mother's barbeque restaurant. At John F. Kennedy High School, Jordan also met Mrs. Minnie L. Fisher, who was the town librarian, clerk, and tax collector, and Willie Gates, the high school principal. Gates believed that the educational progress of the town's children was dramatically slow. Of her experiences during week four, Jordan writes:

> The poverty of Mound Bayou is such that the Mound Bayou Community Hospital, with only 150 local people among its employees, qualifies as a primary source of revenue and jobs. In descending significance, the others are the public-school system, S.T.A.R. and two seasonal cotton gins.[36]

Week five, Jordan's final week, was spent in the city where her explorations began: Jackson, Mississippi. Here, she met Ed Cole, Director of Economic Development, in the town of Fayette, and Charles Evers, the mayor of Fayette who was popularly known throughout the city of Jackson, his second home, and who was the brother of slain civil rights leader Medgar Evers. Jordan recognized the strength of black people in Mississippi, and appreciated how they did not forget those people who died actively fighting for rights and those innocent people who were killed simply because of their dark skin. "Black Home" was slowly happening in the city of Jackson and across the entire state of Mississippi, and according to Jordan, "Perhaps it is true that the more white violence threatens the existence of black life, the stronger will grow black love—self-determination toward survival."[37]

At the end of her five weeks in Mississippi, Jordan returned to New York City with the experience of facing and interrogating some of her fears as related to her black female, mother, poet, and activist existences in a "racist" world. Poetically, Jordan ends her *New York Times* article with the following:

> I think all the way back to the labor of slave toil that made this earth a farmland sweet with food. I remember the gardens and the flowers, even in Jackson. There is no fence; the yards lie open to the sunlight and the passer-by. The dead have been remembered. The children grow in love. It is Black Home.[38]

Jordan's month-long visit to Mississippi in 1969 was not her last venture to the state. Before her return to Mississippi in the early 1970s, Fuller nominated the poet for the Prix de Rome award in Environmental Design. At Fuller's insistence, Jordan accepted the award for her novel, *His Own Where* (1971), and spent a large portion of 1970–1971 in Rome studying the structures of cities, examining human interactions in public spaces, and writing projects on urban design. While in Rome, she reflected on her experiences in Mississippi and on her encounters with Dr. Aaron Henry and Mrs. Fannie Lou Hamer. Her reflections resulted in her early return to New York City from Rome, as well as the completion of an unpublished manual for land reform in Mississippi and her unpublished second novel, *Okay Now*. Jordan was disappointed that her manuscripts, particularly the land reform manual, were not accepted for mainstream publication. The poet's disappointment temporarily subsided upon realizing that her first novel, *His Own Where*—selected as one of the "Most Outstanding Books" (1971) by the *New York Times* and nominated for the National Book Award (1972)—was receiving high praise from supporters as well as unfavorable criticism from angry black parents. The novel's popularity was, in fact, a result of its employment of Black English.

In the essay, "Black English as a Linguistic System: A Statement about Our Rights" (2004), I summarize Jordan's novel:

> In 1971, June Jordan's award-winning young-adult novel, *His Own Where*, was written entirely in Black English, a first in this country! In this love story of political protest, Jordan sophisticatedly establishes connections between language and space, or Black English and the urban redesign of Harlem, through the central characters, sixteen-year-old Buddy Rivers and fourteen-year-old Angela Figeroa. Throughout the plot and narrative of this story is weaved a most significant message: Black English is a vital language, a necessary communicative form, that allows its users to confront and/or make sense of a world full of abandonment, violence, social inequality, and asymmetrical power dynamics that insist, "You be really different from the rest, the resting other ones."[39]

In one way, Jordan's insistence to an audience of young adults, especially young black readers, to "be different from the rest, the resting other ones"[40] signifies her desire for them to embrace the beauty of their identities—their black skin, linguistically rich languages, communities and cultures, and all other forms of black life that historically have been under fire for decades upon decades. In another way, Jordan's insistence stems from her reflexive ability to examine the spaces of her very own childhood in Harlem and in Bedford-Stuyvesant with West Indian parents who attempted to make her into *their own where* instead of nurturing her to become *her own where*.

Both interpretations of Jordan's novel point to the same conclusion: in order for positive change to replace inferior living conditions in America, and in Harlem, in particular, people of color must always work, write, and collaborate against a dominant and one-sided political system that attempts to disempower them and diminish their rich cultures. *His Own Where* is one of many attempts by Jordan to eradicate this system and its codes by allowing the voices of young black people who speak Black English to be heard and respected, and by encouraging them to create a new world, "living spaces," of love and safety in place of the current world of abandonment and neglect. Adrienne Torf indicates that *His Own Where* is a text that not only questions the employment of Black English and black cultural practices, but also one that "questions space and spatial designs of where one could and could not walk and where cars could and could not park." Torf continues by highlighting how Jordan, through the publication of *His Own Where*, and through professional collaborations with Fuller during the 1960s and composer Peter Sellers in the 1990s, "always called for the creation of people's power and determination to change things. Her commitment to young people and their voices is proof of this."[41]

Jordan made the declaration to protect the voices of young people because she understood the power of language; this understanding allowed her to connect personal experience with political analysis. Examples of this connection can be found in the death of Jordan's mother with the police murders of young

black and Puerto Rican males in New York City, or in the abusive language of
the poet's father with the international language of systemic domestic violence.
The poet uses language to insist on the power of people's experiences and the
way that it coalesces the personal with the political. Some of the best examples
of this may be *His Own Where* and Jordan's political essays.

In "White English/Black English: The Politics of Translation," Jordan
alludes to the beauty of language that is free from restrictive codes of power
and standards of white privilege. She writes, "In America, the politics of language, the willful debasement of this human means to human communion has
jeopardized the willingness of young people to believe anything they hear or
read."[42] Jordan goes on to inquire, "And what is anybody going to do about it?
I suggest that, for one, we join forces to cherish and protect our various, mul-
tifoliate lives against pacification, homogenization, the silence of terror, and sur-
render to standards that despise and disregard the sanctity of each and every
human life."[43] *His Own Where*, despite the negative criticism that it has
received from many black parents and teachers, represents a radically creative
text that cherishes black life, language, and living spaces. Even so, it was
banned from many public-school libraries and reading lists—"Black parents in
Baltimore joined together to ban the book."[44] In response to this negative criticism, Jordan met and talked with parents, teachers, and naysayers, and published articles on Black English in various professional journals such as the
Library Journal, *Black World*, and *Leaflet*.

The politics of language has always been a main theme in Jordan's writings
and activist efforts; she was greatly influenced by writer George Orwell's 1946
essay "The Politics of the English Language."[45] Orwell's essay, commenting on
political writing and outlining what he considers to be rules for good writing
and effective style, encouraged Jordan to examine the political implications of
language and its employment, a theme that was at the forefront of her work
near the end of the 1960s and into the 1970s. It can be assumed that Orwell's
text, among others, had a powerful influence on Jordan's writing of *His Own
Where* and her further explorations into the validity of Black English
Vernacular. In addition to meeting with parents and educators who were critical of the linguistic form of *His Own Where* and writing articles that discuss
the significant systematic structure of Black English,[46] Jordan was busy with
many other responsibilities. She was caring for her son, with the dedicated
support of Mildred and other family members, in a single-parent household,
advocating the Open Admissions Policy at City College, declaring herself a
Black Nationalist, paying close attention to the Women's Movement, and
returning to the Mississippi Delta. She led an undoubtedly busy and sacrific-
ing life that, in my opinion, was often at the expense of her relationship with
her family, especially in the absence of her former husband. Jordan, however,
never really addressed that aspect of her family life in her published writings.

On the poet's return to the Delta, she stayed at the home of Mrs. Hamer and
her husband, Mr. Perry "Pap" Hamer, a tractor driver. Under the guidance of

Mrs. Hamer, Jordan witnessed what it meant to be a dedicated, conscious activist. Mrs. Hamer rallied for local and national action on discovering the killing of Joetha Collier, "the young Black girl shot down by white beer-drinking teenagers on the afternoon of her graduation from high school. When her body was found, Joetha's hand still held her diploma."[47] Jordan's poem, "May 27, 1971: No Poem," originally published in *The Village Voice*, honors the life and brings attention to the death of young Joetha:

> Joetha Collier she was
> killed
>
> at eighteen only
> daughter
> born to Mr. and to Mrs. Love
> the family
> Black love wracked
> by outside hogstyle hatred
> on the bullet fly
>
> Joetha Collier she was
> young and she
> was Black and she was
> she was
> she was
>
> and
>
> blood stains Union Street in Mississippi[48]

Mrs. Hamer continued to increase her political involvement so as to help establish peace and equality in Mississippi. She served as a representative on the Democratic National Committee (1968–1971), sought election to the Mississippi State Senate (1971), and became a Delegate to the Democratic National Convention (1972), all after she campaigned for a congressional seat in the Mississippi State Democratic Primary (1964).

During Jordan's visits to the Hamer household, Mrs. Hamer recounted the story of her life, from her political campaigns and activism, to the violent beating she endured from a solid-lead blackjack used by two black prisoners at the orders of a white State Highway Patrol Officer in a Winona, Mississippi jailhouse. As Mrs. Hamer waited on a bus, members of her voter registration team went into a Trailways food stop and were arrested for seeking service. She was taken off of the bus, arrested, beaten, and denied hospital treatment for three days. The activist also told Jordan about her involvement in the Mississippi Freedom Democratic Party, her work with the Freedom Farms Cooperative, and her early years as the youngest of twenty children born to poor sharecroppers,

Jim and Ella Townsend. With this information, Jordan later wrote the children's biography, *Fannie Lou Hamer*, published in 1972.

Fannie Lou Hamer is an illustrated biography of Mrs. Hamer's commitment to political equality and black life in Mississippi, including her quest to register black voters across Southern states and her insistence that black people learn to be self-sufficient; Mrs. Hamer's Freedom Farms Cooperative serves as an example of self-sufficiency. The biography opens with information on Mrs. Hamer's mother, Ella Townsend, a domestic worker on a plantation, and how she protected her children from the abuse and violence of white Southerners. The story moves into a discussion of young Fannie Lou Hamer's work in the cotton fields with her parents, her singing talents, and her school experiences that ended after sixth grade because she needed to work full time with her family in the fields. From there, Jordan informs readers about the denial of voting rights for both black people and women in Mississippi, Fannie's marriage to Perry Hamer in 1945, and how she bravely registered to vote in 1962, despite threats from white people and her white "Bossman." The book concludes with an account of the political leader's beating in a jailhouse and Martin Luther King, Jr.'s insistence that the officers release her; Jordan also documents Hamer's political campaigns and her Freedom Farm Cooperative. In words that mean just as much today as they meant in the 1960s, Jordan asserts,

> But there are thousands and thousands more people still living in Mississippi. And so Mrs. Hamer has not finished her fight. The problems of hurt and hunger are huge problems, but Mrs. Fannie Lou is just too busy fighting to be afraid of failure. . . . People everywhere know that Mrs. Fannie Lou Hamer has helped to make human freedom real, for everyone.[49]

Jordan was highly influenced by Mrs. Hamer's activism and committed herself to learning from the political activist and from other black residents of Mississippi. She would later use her lessons to continue the fight for justice and equality, beginning in her hometown of New York City.

Mrs. Hamer, her husband, and the people of Mississippi clearly taught Jordan valuable lessons about living, fighting, and the struggle for human rights. Jordan came to understand that the struggle for rights cannot begin and end with the individual; it requires dedicated visionaries who are willing to sacrifice themselves, stand against threatening forces, and challenge the status quo. Mrs. Hamer convinced Jordan not to accept defeat in her work for human rights. For the poet, this message would prove significant, given the challenges she encountered throughout her life: her strained relationship with her father until his death,[50] her mother's unexpected death, her divorce from Meyer, and her professional demands at major universities in juxtaposition with her literary career and parental responsibilities.

In Jordan's view, and in the view of many others, Mrs. Hamer's brutal beating in June 1963 parallels, in some ways, the history of violence perpetuated against black people in America. One need only turn to the history of the 1923

Rosewood Massacre and the 1921 Tulsa Race Riots for documented examples of larger, organized attacks on black communities. Given these continual violent acts against black people and communities, Mrs. Hamer bravely fought for the Civil Rights of people. For Jordan, the courageous political leader was like "a mother . . . protective, earthy, fearless, and blessed by an hilarious and deadpan sense of humor."[51] The poet needed Mrs. Hamer in her life, particularly as she struggled to raise an interracial son in New York City and even more so after the 1966 death of her mother in their Brooklyn brownstone. On her mother's alleged suicide, Jordan admits that she wondered about the larger implications of living in this world—the battles one must fight, the unfair representation that one experiences, and the white power structures that are visible everywhere. She contemplates the reasons for her mother's untimely death: Did Mildred really kill herself, or did the violence within her home and in New York City kill her? Was she too weak to give in to a natural and slow death, or so strong that she decided to capture death before death captured her?[52] Did Mildred really commit suicide as Jordan claims, or did she die of hypertension and heart complications as Orridge insists?

In *Moving Towards Home: Political Essays* (1989), the poet openly and descriptively writes of her mother's supposed suicide. Jordan begins her chronicle by describing the stroke that prohibited Mildred from fully taking care of herself and other people; she was forced to retire from nursing. Around this time, Jordan, with the assistance of her longtime hairdresser and advocate, Mrs. Hazel Griffin, moved back into her parents' brownstone for financial reasons. According to Orridge, Jordan moved out of the projects and back into her parents' home and lived "on the top floor of the brownstone."[53] Orridge then speculates: "I never understood whether she moved out the projects because she and her husband separated; I never understood whether she moved out or whether she was evicted."[54]

Regardless of the reasons, it was within a few days of Jordan's move that she found her mother dying: "'Momma?!' I called, aloud. At the edge of the cot, my mother was leaning forward, one arm braced to hoist her body up. She was trying to stand up! I rushed over. 'Wait. Here, I'll help you!' I said."[55] Jordan was too late. Her mother was already dead and Jordan believed that her father, Granville, had done nothing about it except to shout, "Is she dead? Is she dead?" Jordan continues, "At this, my father tore down the stairs and into the room. Then he braked. 'Milly?' he called out, tentative. Then he shouted at me and banged around the walls. 'You damn fool. Don't you see now she's gone. Now she's gone!' We began to argue."[56]

At the adamant disagreement of Orridge, Jordan believes that her "mother had committed suicide."[57] The poet retreated to Orridge's apartment "and then [June] revealed to me that she had had an abortion." Orridge claims that Jordan was so sick that she "was taking care of her for a couple of days, and she was bleeding. Bleeding!" In the middle of the night, Orridge and her boyfriend struggled to physically "hold Jordan up" as they flagged down a cab on 6th Avenue in Harlem to take Jordan to the Harlem Hospital located at 506 Lenox Avenue. When they arrived at the hospital, the hospital staff,

Gave her an extremely difficult time. The funeral [for Mildred] was on a Sunday and the burial on a Monday. June begged those people . . . to please do the DNC—the dilation and curettage—and those people were so mean, they told her if she was so concerned about her mother's funeral, she wouldn't have had the abortion.[58]

Jordan had missed the funeral and burial services because she was in the hospital hemorrhaging, "and that [missing the funeral] was something that June never got over. And she wouldn't particularly talk about it. There was a lot of guilt there. [Granville] never forgave her. Of course, we couldn't tell him June had an abortion."[59]

Years later, Jordan wrote and dedicated the poem, "Getting Down To Get Over" (1972) to her mother: "help me/turn the face of history/*to your face.*"[60] The poem opens with a list of signifying labels commonly, and unfortunately, directed at black women:

MOMMA MOMMA MOMMA
momma momma
mammy
nanny
granny
woman
mistress
sista

luv

blackgirl
slavegirl

gal[61]

Jordan arrived too late to help her mother and to attend her funeral, but not too late to help others. She promised herself to be there for women, for the people she loved, and for the people whose lives depend on her timely arrival: "I know there is new work that we must undertake. . . . That new work will make defeat detestable to us. That new women's work will mean we will not die trying to stand up: we will live that way: standing up."[62]

In life and in memory, Jordan awakens a sense of urgency in her readers. This urgency is measured by the need for people to be on time—to be at the rallies and protests, at the meetings and debates, on the streets and in the communities, in the schools, and in our families' homes whenever asked and whenever needed. According to Jordan, we are all needed. We must, somehow, be there on time.

While Jordan was unable to save her mother from death and her father from anger at her absence from Mildred's funeral, she vowed never to be late again; this became, unfortunately, a vow that she was not always able to keep. She traveled to the Mississippi Delta in the 1960s and 1970s when black people were denied voting rights and when freedom fighters were riding buses, boy-cotting on the streets, and insisting on rights and fair representation for black people. Jordan was not late in her meetings with Mrs. Hamer, whose children's biography is as important today as it was in 1972. Jordan was not late for the 1964 Harlem Uprising, for the Civil Rights movement, for falling in love with Michael Meyer, or for the birth and rearing of their son, Christopher. Some might debate Jordan's dedication to her son, given the many professional and political affiliations of this virtually single parent. Nevertheless, she was quite close to him.[63] How was Jordan able to fulfill her many obligations and foster a close relationship with her son? Clearly, Jordan was beginning to swim in many rivers: Black Nationalist, Freedom Fighter, Instructor, Poet, and Mother. One can only imagine the strain such affiliations eventually had on their rela-tionship; Jordan never really addressed the strains and tensions publicly even as she tried to keep the personal and the private affairs of her life in balance.

During these years back in New York City, the poet began to advocate the building of a multicultural America within a cultural pluralist framework, an idea reminiscent of the dream of one of her aesthetic and political models—Langston Hughes. In "On Bisexuality and Cultural Pluralism," Jordan writes that she was about to enter into "serious trouble here":

> I am swimming in too many rivers. . . . How can I fail to accept the simple truth/the natural state of affairs/the divine order of whatever prevails, whatever dominates? Especially when whatever prevails, whatever dominates, protects its power through cautionary folk tales, primitive law, and state-initiated or state-sanctioned violence.[64]

Jordan did not accept "the simple truth" of anything, including suicide and death, child abuse, language, human rights, discrimination, or mainstream sexuality. She swam in many rivers, even if alone. Jordan challenged racial, gender, and sexual stereotypes, making it a point to argue that "you [people] be different from the dead. . . . You be really different from the rest, the resting other ones."[65] She was definitely different.

She believed that the problem involved many patriarchal laws that pre-vented people—mainly people of color, women, and children—from exercis-ing their civil liberties in a democratic state. This latter point is clearly presented in Jordan's political works *Civil Wars: Observations from the Front Lines of America* and *On Call: Political Essays*, and in her literary recognitions, including *Who's Who of American Women*, *Who's Who of Children's Book Authors*, and the *International Who's Who of Women*. Meanwhile, the poet's cre-ative engagements, keynote addresses, and poetry readings, having begun in New York City in the 1960s, served as the foundation for later writing and teach-ing appointments; they also blurred the categories of devoted, full-time mother and dedicated, full-time poet and activist.

THREE

New Days:
Poems of Exile and Return

The previous chapter details how June Jordan filled her life with political and creative work, including participating in the 1960s Civil Rights Movement, traveling to Rome as the recipient of the 1970 Prix de Rome in Environmental Design, and working with activist groups in New York City and Mississippi to campaign for the civil rights and liberties of people of color. Jordan was also employed by Teachers & Writers Collaborative, a nonprofit educational organization, and the Technical Housing Department of Mobilization for Youth in New York City. Eventually, Jordan became a faculty member at City College and later at Connecticut College and Sarah Lawrence College before becoming a professor at the State University of New York at Stony Brook, among other institutions. Meanwhile, her writing became increasingly popular as it found homes on the pages of the *New York Times*, the *Nation*, *New Republic*, *Essence*, *Village Voice*, *Ms.*, *Partisan Review*, *New Black Poetry*, *Mademoiselle*, *Newsday*, *American Poetry Review*, *Chrysalis*, *Callaloo*, and *American Dialog*. Jordan's literary success and activist agenda continually reiterated her decision to work toward the eradication of discriminatory political and educational practices. She continued to draw attention to the inadequacy of governmental structures that maintained, quite unfairly, a status quo that directly harmed poor and nonwhite people. She also recognized the need to honor the struggles of black people who have been fighting "all the hurdles

that the murdering/masterminds threw up to stop/the comings of/Black
Love."[1] Jordan asserts this message in her "Poem: On the Black Family":

> *we came*
> we came and we come in a glory of darkness
> around the true reasons for sharing
> our dark and our beautiful
> name
> that we give to our dark and our beautiful
> daughters and sons
> who must make the same struggle
> to love
>
> and must win[2]

June Jordan used every available resource to fight for the rights of her con-
stituency, from writing political essays and poems to teaching at public institutions, always insisting on the legitimacy of black "love" and cultural forms.
Jordan was full of rage at the conditions that threatened the lives of people of
color relegated to substandard living conditions; she channeled her anger, her
rage, into meaningful political writing, speeches, and teachings. Jordan never
stopped interrogating the harsh life lessons afforded to her by her father, the
death of her mother, or the lessons in activism learned from Mrs. Fannie Lou
Hamer. Jordan was determined to learn from her past, familial and historical, as
she, along with other activists, forged into political action communities joined
by a common good: justice. This ideal of the common good surfaced in many
of Jordan's writings and activities during the late 1960s and the mid-1970s.

For example, some of Jordan's political writings were published in
Chrysalis, a quarterly publication that began its operations in February 1977
and was wholly devoted to feminist perspectives about the experiences of
women.[3] The magazine was successfully controversial in its publication of
writings on female erotica, sexual identities and experiences, and on the politics of the feminist movement in America. June Jordan, along with various
other writers and poets such as Marilyn Hacker, Audre Lorde, Mary Daly,
Marge Piercy, Jodi Braxton, Sara Miles, and Honor Moore, viewed the magazine
as an outlet for the dissemination of information about the contemporary feminist cultural critique and identity politics. Lorde, who was poetry editor of the
quarterly and who did not feel she owed anything to Jordan, did support
Jordan's literary pursuits. In *Warrior Poet: A Biography of Audre Lorde*, biogra-
pher Alexis DeVeaux writes that Lorde "admired her as a poet, having met
Jordan when the two were teaching in the SEEK program at City College during the sixties."[4] Although Lorde and Jordan were never intimate friends, they
were former university colleagues and important literary figures who valued
writing as a powerful medium for explorations into feminist thought and

political discourse. Writing for *Chrysalis* was one way for Jordan to publicly engage issues of justice, freedom, national representation, and women's rights during the 1970s.

In her drive to complicate the homogeneity, or one-sidedness, of American political values along lines of national representation and belonging, Jordan joined groups that rallied for change through action. From her "Freedom Rides" to Mississippi in the 1960s, her *Chrysalis* writings and crowded classrooms in the 1970s, to the packed cafés and community spaces that sponsored her poetry readings in the 1980s—including the Donnell Library and the Studio Museum of Harlem—Jordan displayed political commitment and an activist spirit.

The poet protested and picketed at every possible opportunity, and she also stood with her students at rallies. Jordan spoke against scientist William Shockley's research that supported the notion of black inferiority and urged minority women's sterilization.[5] She challenged former senator Daniel Moynihan's report that alleged an increase in black out-of-wedlock births and suggested a connection between unemployment rates and the absence of black husbands and fathers. She crafted a poem "Memo to Daniel Pretty Moynihan," in response to Moynihan's claim. In the poetic memo, Jordan writes:

You done what you done
I do what I can
Don't you liberate me
from my female black pathology

I been working off my knees
I been drinking what I please[6]

To close, Jordan offers Moynihan some advice: "Clean your own house, baby-face."[7] Instead of accepting the findings of Moynihan as evidence of the inferior status of black people, which Jordan vehemently refuted, she makes an authoritative assertion: "I got a [sic] idea something's wrong/with you."[8] "Memo to Daniel Pretty Moynihan" is another example of how Jordan's writings continually resist injustice even when she stood alone.

Jordan's political resistances and outspoken poetic voice are directly connected to her teaching, writing, and activism of the 1970s and 1980s. In her essay "Thinking About My Poetry, 1977," Jordan writes about her decision, near the end of the 1960s, to work "for the achievement of a collective voice . . . to speak as a community to a community, that to do otherwise was not easily defensible, nor useful, and would be, in any case, at variance with clarified political values I held as my own."[9] Jordan wanted to speak to and for black communities, a desire that stemmed from her active involvement in the revitalization of black communities in both New York and Mississippi. Her political beliefs reinforced her desire to be part of a serious collective, or a politically conscious community; nevertheless, she soon realized how limiting her beliefs were for what she sought to accomplish as an activist, an artist, and a black woman living in America. Entering the 1970s, she reexamined her beliefs and concluded that she was, in fact, just an "ordinary" person whose desires "toward a collective voice" were "conceitful." Jordan writes:

> I came to know the idea of myself as ordinary. As I came to know other poets as friends . . . it did seem to me that we were all of us working on the same poem of a life of perpetual, difficult birth and that, therefore, I should trust myself in this way: that if I could truthfully attend to my own perpetual birth . . . that then I could hope to count upon myself to be serving a positive and collective function, without pretending to be more than the one Black woman poet I am, as a matter of fact.[10]

While this particular passage demonstrates Jordan's poetic and individual growths, it also shows her personal struggles with the politics of community and with the idea of being "ordinary," which she was not. Throughout the poet's life, she affiliated herself with multiple communities, whether civil rights activists, academic groups, poetry collectives, or a cadre of personal friends and activists including, among others, Malcolm X, Terri Bush, Angela Davis, Alexis De Veaux, James Farmer, Laura Flanders, Sara Miles, E. Ethelbert Miller, Toni Morrison, Adrienne Rich, Ntozake Shange, Adrienne Torf, and Alice Walker. Jordan embraced ideas of radicalism not readily accepted by U.S. conservatives. She envisioned, and sought to create, a United States governed by diversity, multiculturalism, multilingualism, justice, and sexual freedom; her desire to help create communities that work for justice parallels her discovery of herself as an "ordinary" person, poet, and teacher. In this way, Jordan can be considered a daughter of Walt Whitman, the father of American poetry and one of her literary models. Whitman's experiences as a Civil War nurse compelled him to poetically document what he viewed as the spirit of America: the strength of the common man against the backdrop of war, suffering, death, and the making of a new, and hopefully different, self and country.

In "Song of Myself," Whitman confronts themes that Jordan addresses over a century later in her collection of poetry *Moving Towards Home*. Whitman considers an understanding of self as a spiritual entity existing as a signifier of both the individual and the universe. In other words, as Whitman debated ways to nurture the individual (mind and art), he considered the relationship of self to others, mainly community. Jordan contemplates this point in her aforementioned essay, "Thinking About My Poetry, 1977." Whitman, in "Song of Myself," declares:

> Stop this day and night with me and you shall possess the
> > origin of all poems,
> You shall possess the good of the earth and sun....
> > there are millions of suns left,
> You shall no longer take things at second or third hand....

nor look through the eyes of the dead....nor feed
  on the specters in books,
You shall not look through my eyes either, nor take things
  from me,

You shall listen to all sides and filter them from yourself.[11]

In these lines, Whitman's voice, full of wisdom, song, and figurative speech, adopts "oracular qualities"[12] supported by the repetition of "You shall" and the invitation for readers to "listen to all sides." Jordan, like many other poets, emulated and utilized many of Whitman's literary techniques, as is evident in her "Poem About My Rights," "Something Like a Sonnet for Phillis Miracle Wheatley," and in her essay "For the Sake of People's Poetry: Walt Whitman and the Rest of Us." These writings and Jordan's claim of her ordinariness expose a Whitmanesque wisdom, a "Song," that seeks to distinguish the individual from the world and that then attempts to nourish the connection and responsibility the individual has to the world—to the universe, to nature, to ideas, and to communities. Jordan was never ordinary, a point that becomes obvious as one investigates how she located lessons learned from Whitman inside her own writing and teaching so as to "serve a positive and collective function."[13]

This point can be further debated by examining aspects of Jordan's professional life. Just before joining the faculty at City College, Jordan worked as a research associate and writer for the Technical Housing Department of Mobilization for Youth in New York City (1965–1966). Attorney and judge, Dorothy Kenyon (1888–1972), founded Mobilization for Youth, a social program that provided legal services and counseling assistance for young and poor people, and advocated for civil rights legislation, women's rights, and other forms of social and political reform. Kenyon also fought for equitable housing laws, minimum wage legislation, and the establishment of public relief funds for those in need. As a research associate and writer for Kenyon's Mobilization for Youth organization, Jordan came into contact with many people whom she later described as serious allies, or "multitudes working together, around the world, if radical and positive change can be forced upon the heinous status quo I despise in all its overwhelming power."[14] Working for many progressive causes, people came together to organize for the issues to which they were committed.

During this time, Jordan's affiliations with Mobilization for Youth and with other allies led her into the company of professor and civil rights activist, Frances Fox Piven, who was also a research associate for the organization. With similar political missions, it was natural that Frances Fox Piven and June Jordan became good friends. Piven was interested in rehabilitating urban communities, often called "ghettos," and in rallying political action by working-class people within U.S. cities as a way of fighting for housing rights, homelessness, starvation, reform, and community development. Jordan was more interested in examining the effectiveness of integration; she wrote that

Piven, "a white intellectual, [needed to] to mind her own damn business" inso-far as urban restoration was concerned.[15] In the final essay collected in *Civil Wars: Observations From the Front Lines of America*, Jordan writes of what she considered to be essential in the rehabilitation, or revitalization, of black com-munities: "And I was advocating a push for integration because I thought that, otherwise, you might achieve better housing for Black families but you would still lack supporting community services such as reliable garbage collection, police protection, and ambulance response."[16] While Jordan and Piven's differ-ences over community restoration issues and politics did not initially end their growing friendship, it did cause Jordan to become silent on issues of personal importance, from religion to sexuality. Eventually, their disagreements on inter-pretations of gay rights and civil rights strengthened.

For example, when Piven and Jordan discussed "the impending referendum in California" that would support the firing of "a teacher who expressed the opinion that sexual preference was not the business of the state," Piven argued that it was about gay rights while Jordan counterargued that it was about civil rights.[17] They also disagreed over issues of sexuality: Jordan informs *Civil Wars* readers that Piven considered the poet's "loving a woman" as "deviant behav-ior" that was a distraction from the more important work of "radical human-itarian concern."[18] Their differences did not stop there; other debatable topics included Hasidim, Zionism, Palestine, human rights, and violence. Piven and Jordan's conflicting positions led to the end, however temporarily, of their friendship.

At the insistence of her son, Christopher David Meyer, who was a student and a literacy tutor at Harvard University in Cambridge, Massachusetts[19] at the time, Jordan read with excitement the 1978 publication of *Poor People's Movements: Why They Succeed, How They Fail* by Frances Fox Piven and Richard Cloward. The book examines four prominent protest movements in the history of the 20th century: the mobilization of unemployed people dur-ing the Great Depression; the workers' movement and industrial strikes of the Great Depression; the movement for Civil Rights; and the movement for Welfare Rights. At the center of the book is the question of representation and benefits: how have poor people been affected and influenced by their partici-pation in the politics of the American system? Impressed by Piven and Cloward's groundbreaking research and argument, Jordan decided to call Piven, her old adversary. This served as the beginning of a new relationship, one marked by the development of strategies to eliminate unfair living condi-tions and to unite the people in a shared struggle for change.

Shortly after her newfound friendship with Piven and her involvement with the Technical Housing Department of Mobilization for Youth in the mid-to-late-1960s, Jordan entered the 1970s and 1980s influencing communities of learners as an instructor of English Literature and Composition at several educational institutions, including City College, City University of New York (CUNY), Connecticut College, Sarah Lawrence, and Yale. As she worked with college-aged students, she realized that there were many more allies than enemies campaigning for universal justice, love, literacy initiatives, democracy, and quality health care. Upon discovering allies, Jordan also discovered something about the politics of academic institutions.

As a visiting lecturer in the Departments of English and Afro-American Studies at Yale University in New Haven, Connecticut (1974–1975), she noticed the obvious disparities between female and male professors of the same rank. Male professors were paid substantially higher than female professors and there was a particular unvoiced, but noticeable code of appearance for female professors that reinforced gender differences and power dynamics. This experience helped to revive Jordan's consciousness of inequality and of the need to question systematic structures that support the relegation of women to levels allegedly unfit for men.

Teaching at Yale also encouraged Jordan to reflect on her life, work, and time with Mrs. Fannie Lou Hamer in the Mississippi Delta and on her burgeoning commitment to Black Nationalism. Jordan considered the value of her presence during the 1970s Open Admissions Policy at City College and on her status as a divorced black mother raising a biracial, bicultural son in New York City. What was happening? What was going on with the necessary work of the Civil Rights Movement and of the Women's Rights Movement insofar as advancement, particularly at the institutional level, was concerned? For Jordan, what was going on did not adequately address the gender differences and power dynamics at institutions like Yale, which was an unsettling point for her.

Even so, Jordan was not content without critiquing the disparities between, for example, female and male professors, and black and white students. She turned her classrooms into spaces where critical analysis informed critical thinking, reading, and writing skills just as much as they informed elements of American literature and history, theories of race, and questions of social responsibility. According to Jordan, this time was both special and significant because at Yale, she "encountered every traditional orthodoxy imaginable" and was thrilled that "the hallowed halls [would] echo to the fact of a woman, a Black woman, passing through!"[20]

In her writing immediately prior to her Yale experience, Jordan tells readers that her friend and the well-known author, Alice Walker, introduced her to folklorist and novelist, Zora Neale Hurston, and to Hurston's text *Their Eyes Were Watching God*.[21] Jordan became fascinated with Hurston's writing style, voice, and plot development; she eventually decided, as other scholars at Yale had already done, to include the text in her university courses. Jordan contributes to the longstanding argument for the study of black authors such as Hurston by insisting against the manipulative ways black male and female authors are pitted against one another, and by focusing on the dangers of ignoring the literary contributions of black women writers. On the value of black literature, Jordan writes that "we have lost many jewels to the glare of white, mass-media manipulation" before explicitly referring to the scholarly overemphasis on literature by selected black male authors. She continues:

> [Richard Wright] has been presented as a solitary figure on the literary landscape of his period. But, right along with him, and six years his senior, there was Zora Neale Hurston. And the fact is that we almost lost Zora to the choose-between games played by Black Art . . . So we would do well to carefully reconsider these two, Hurston and Wright.[22]

Jordan's critical approach to black literary figures such as Hurston defined her classroom teaching style post-1974. She eagerly included the writings of understudied authors in her curriculum, debated with students the necessity of civil rights and fair representation, and challenged students to consider the multiple perspectives, or "realms of responsibility,"[23] of historical oppression including enslavement, genocide, rape, and police brutality. Moreover, Jordan's commitment to the students at Yale extended outside of the classroom: with students and participating faculty members, she co-founded and directed "The Yale Attica Defense Group" (1975), lectured at various student-sponsored events, and rallied against unjust conditions of people afflicted by war, abuse, and other acts of violence. She was, by any definition, an extraordinary teacher, activist, and humanitarian. Before joining the faculty as a visiting lecturer at Yale, Jordan's visionary model of communal interaction had already begun. In this model, people supported and critiqued one another's ideas and worked to create equitable living and learning conditions; her work as co-founder and director of the Afro-Americans Against the Famine in Africa (1973) serves as an example of this. Arriving at Yale, she had already established a "track record."

As discussed earlier, in the late 1960s at City College in New York City, Jordan rallied with students to support open admissions. She, along with other instructors, was responsible for the academic preparation of black and Puerto Rican students who may otherwise have been admitted to college on the sole basis of standardized tests scores.[24] Next, at Connecticut College in New London, Connecticut, Jordan directed the Search for Education, Elevation, and Knowledge (SEEK), a program that continues to provide assistance to students who need financial, academic, and counseling support. She also taught English and worked with the Upward Bound Program before leaving to teach literature and writing at Sarah Lawrence in Bronxville, New York in the early 1970s. Her teaching appointments, many of which appear to overlap in dates, are important because they inform her approach to rethinking the responsibilities of the poet as a revolutionary artist whose political involvements are overtly connected to larger educational and personal concerns.

For instance, Jordan's reading of "Getting Down to Get Over: Dedicated to My Mother" to a room of well over 500 black women at the National Gathering of Black Women Conference at Radcliffe College in 1973 was monumental in its politicization of the personal. In this case, the personal was the glamorization of female identity. The poem, opening with a series of historical references to motherhood, such as "Momma," "sista," "mistress," "woman," "granny," "nanny," and "mammy," chronicles the many travails, degradations, and demands placed upon the black woman who, at once, can have her

hand on her hip
sweat restin from
the corn/bean/greens' field[25]

At the same time, according to Jordan's poem, a black woman is often required to mediate the demands of the domestic sphere (the family and the household) and the outer world (the "bossman"):

she fix the cufflinks
on his Sunday shirt
and fry some chicken
bake some cake
and tell the family
"Never mind about the bossman"[26]

Such mediation has political implications for how women are viewed in constructed narratives of national identity, citizenship, and belonging. Jordan's reading of the poem signified that her voice would not be silenced in debates on the rights of women; it also intensified her commitment to fostering connections between the personal and political lives of historically underappreciated people, including her West Indian mother. Additionally, this commitment surfaced in Jordan's desire to visit Cuba. In 1976, she applied to the Center for Cuban Studies located at 220 East 23rd Street in New York City, and by the early 1980s, the poet began recognizing, in her essays and teaching experiences, the efforts of "women" and "raced" revolutionaries in Cuba and Angola. As Jordan considered the value of international peace struggles and mended the divide between the political and personal aspects of her work, she came to view teaching as an outlet that would allow her to debate such significant issues to a large population of young students.

From 1978 to 1982, Jordan taught at the State University of New York (SUNY) at Stony Brook as an associate professor of English. She also worked with students outside of the classroom by initiating an antiapartheid group and spearheading teach-ins on South Africa before and after being promoted to full professor in 1982. While still on faculty at Stony Brook, in 1983 Jordan was a Visiting Mentor Poet for the Loft Mentor Series in Minneapolis, Minnesota, and then from 1986 to 1989 she was the director of Stony Brook's Poetry Center and Creative Writing Program. Her tenure there was met with several national awards. In 1979, while Jordan was a Yaddo Fellow[27], she wrote *The Issue*, a full-length, two-act play "about freedom, police violence, and Black life."[28] It was performed in the 1980s and directed by close friend and play-wright Ntozake Shange. Shortly thereafter, in 1982, Jordan received a National Endowment for the Arts Fellowship in Creative Writing and a few years later, in 1985, the poet was awarded a New York Foundation for the Arts Fellow-ship in Poetry, an Award in Contemporary Arts from the Massachusetts Council on the Arts, and, in 1987, she became a MacDowell Colony Fellow.[29]

Between 1980 and 2002, Jordan was a visiting poet, artist-in-residence, and playwright at several institutions and organizations, including Macalester College (1980), the New Dramatists in New York City (1987–1988), the Walt Whitman Birthplace Association (1988), Swarthmore College (2001), University of Pennsylvania (2001), and New York University (2002). In 1976, she was one of two Reid Lecturers at Barnard College in New York City,[30] and in 1986, she served as the Chancellor's Distinguished Lecturer at the University of California, Berkeley. During the summer of 1988, Jordan was a visiting professor in the Department of Afro-American Studies at the University of Wisconsin, Madison. In 1978, she became a member of the Board of Directors for Teachers & Writers Collaborative, a New York-based organi-zation that the poet had worked with in the late 1960s. Then in 1986, Jordan became a member of the Board of Governors for the New York State Foundation for the Arts.

The poet returned to teach at the University of California at Berkeley from 1989 to 2001. During this time, she served as a Professor of Afro-American Studies and Women's Studies, and she founded and directed the Poetry for the People Collective, an educational program with a large student and faculty fol-lowing. As I will discuss in a later chapter, the Poetry for the People Collective continues to enable emerging poets to lead workshop on their writings, par-ticipate in political readings and academic events, and work with other stu-dents, some prison inmates, and service organizations in and around the San Francisco Bay area.

In June 2002, the world lost June Jordan when she succumbed to breast cancer at her home in Berkeley, California. Whole communities of writers and activists mourned her death. In the same year, Jordan's book *Some of Us Did Not Die: New and Selected Essays of June Jordan*, was released after much antic-ipation. Bookstores across America were receiving phone calls from eager sup-porters of Jordan's work. After e-mail reminders for the publication of *Some of Us Did Not Die* were sent out, university students in Texas, New York, and California bought, read, and discussed the book. They read the published reviews and concluded that Jordan, once again, had restored the public's faith in the good fight for justice in a world of homelessness, injustice, and war. She encouraged readers to believe in their own strength and in the strength of the collective forces working for human justice throughout the world. In this book, Jordan adamantly insists that the protesting, picketing, and fight-ing *for* equality and *against* violence are never over. The poet died writing and fighting energetically, and campaigning for universal peace, as witnessed in the opening passages of *Some of Us Did Not Die*. The poet begins:

> ONCE THROUGH the fires of September 11, it's not easy to remember or recognize any power we continue to possess.
>
> Understandably we shrivel and retreat into stricken consequences of that catastrophe.
>
> But we have choices, and capitulation is only one of them.
>
> I am always hoping to do better than to collaborate with whatever or
> whomever it is that means me no good.
>
> For me, it's a mind game with everything at stake . . .
>
> Luckily, there are limitless, new ways to engage our tender, and possible responsibilities, obligations that our actual continuing coexistence here, in
> these United States and here, in our world, require.[31]

This passage summarizes Jordan's political stance and activist efforts during the last thirty-five years of her life. She participated in a perpetual search for "new ways to engage" people in a discourse of difference that would rebuild a world that embraces all perspectives, including women's and children's.

But before her teaching appointments, numerous publications, and awards, Jordan experienced personal conflict, especially in her divorce from Michael Meyer in 1965 and her mother's death the following year. Following these events, the poet embarked on trips to Mississippi and forged a professional and personal relationship with Mrs. Hamer. By 1974, she had buried her father, Granville, in Jamaica to the dismay of family members who still insist that he wanted to be buried next to his wife in a New Jersey cemetery.[32]

Jordan's commitment to freedom may well have come from her acceptance of what she once referred to as "the responsibility that love implies,"[33] and from her desire to make a fair playing field for people like her mother and father, both intelligent workers who idolized American democracy without receiving its full benefits. Or maybe Jordan's devotion came from her experience as a single mother solely responsible for her growing son. Either way, her involvement in these activities proved transformational for both herself and those around her.

In working to unite communities, Jordan learned that it was important to identify both allies and enemies in the rally for freedom and peace. In a published interview with writer Karla Hammond (1981), Jordan discusses her involvement within overlapping communities of struggle by addressing this responsibility:

> It is impossible to be inside the struggle that concerns and governs all of our lives—whether we recognize that to be true or not—unless you recognize that you have an adversary and you undertake, in the most direct and effective way

possible, to address that adversary—either to conquer him or her through persuasion or to eliminate that adversary.[34]

Here, Jordan refers to the overt violence of domination and the passive violence of subservient living conditions for all women and children, and especially for women and children of color. Contextually, such violence threatens the lives of people through channels of war, genocide, poverty, and inequitable educational opportunities and living spaces. Jordan wrote of such conditions in her many published collections of poetry and essays, including *Soulscript: Afro-American Poetry*, *Some Changes*, *New Days: Poems of Exile and Return*, *Things That I Do in the Dark: Selected Poetry*, *Passion: New Poems*, and *Living Room*.

Soulscript: Afro-American Poetry (1970), dedicated to Jordan's parents, is a collection of poems by young and established black writers, ranging from unknown poets like Vanessa Howard and Phillip Solomon to established writers like Jean Toomer, Gwendolyn Brooks, and LeRoi Jones (hereafter referred to as Amiri Baraka) among others. In this text, Jordan honors the literary voices of young black children alongside widely published professional adults. These voices of sophistication and talent demand fair representation in the national discourse of identity and rights; they refuse to be censored by the dominant political system and an indifferent mass media. Addressing this indifference, according to spoken-word poet and political activist Staceyann Chin, represents "courage and commitment to difficult truths."[35] In the "Foreword" to the revised edition of *Soulscript* (2004), Chin relates the importance of the collection to the courage of the *Soulscript* poets and to the powerful employment of words to document the "human struggle" for freedom. She states, "*Soulscript* is a toast to all the poems, novels, and essays that have stirred us toward action. It is a challenge to those of us left holding the torch of change, an invocation to disarm our own narrow agendas." In closing, Chin asserts, "it is a mandate for all those living to put pen to paper and march the masses toward a more meaningful collage of life."[36] This collage, as echoed by Chin and lived by Jordan, must, by definition, include the voices of black writers.

It is no surprise then, that beginning in the late 1960s Jordan became aware of the lack of attention given to black writers and their words. In the opening pages of the 1970 edition of *Soulscript: Afro-American Poetry*, the poet writes of the importance of this anthology:

> The poetry of Afro-America appears as it was written: in tears, in rage, in hope, in sonnet, in blank/free verse, in overwhelming rhetorical scream. These poems redeem a hostile vocabulary; they witness, they create communion, and they contribute beauty to the long evening of their origins.[37]

Soulscript also contributed to the already existing base of a developing community of black poets, and according to Jordan, "Coast to coast, on subways, in bedrooms, in kitchens, in weekend workshops, at parties—almost anywhere except the classroom, as a matter of fact—Afro-Americans are writing poetry. It's happening now, and it's wonderful, fine, and limitless, like love."[38] Black people had been writing poetry for decades upon decades only to have their writing dismissed as uncritical, underdeveloped, and overly hostile in the eyes of many publishers and editors. In the face of this literary disenfranchisement, bookstores, homes, and community centers became communal sites of articulation where the words, thoughts, artistic creativities, experiences, and voices of black writers and thinkers flourished: "the cultivation of *own voice* became a workaday occupation, an unrelenting protest, and an ultimate social triumph."[39]

In the monumental publication of *Soulscript: Afro-American Poetry*, Jordan demonstrated the power of community building, activism, and an articulate black voice. She sparked fire and excitement by challenging the silencing of black writers, activists, intellectuals, and children. Still fighting for children, she also challenged racist classroom conditions in which children of color were sometimes viewed with hostility and even contempt. Jordan underscored the urgency of representing black writers to students: "And when American classrooms switch from confrontation to communion, black poetry will happen in the schools as well."[40] The confrontation alluded to is one in which black writers, along with other raced writers, are marginalized in, or absent from, the literature curriculum of public schools. Jordan continued to urge students, teachers, administrators, and parents to examine the complexities of this marginalization. For Jordan, the banning of her young-adult novel *His Own Where*, as well as the absence of progressive works by other raced writers, speaks to "the struggle to determine and then preserve a particular, human voice [which] is closely related to the historic struggling of black life in America."[41]

This "historic" struggle comes through vividly in the poems included in *Soulscript*. For example, in the poem "Reflections," a young Vanessa Howard writes,

> If the world looked in a looking glass,
> It'd see back hate, it'd see back war and it'd see
>   back sorrow,
> it'd see back fear.
> If the world looked in a looking glass, it'd run
>   away with shame, and hide.[42]

Connecting this poem with Michael Goode's "April 4, 1968" and Linda Curry's "death prosecuting" demonstrates the struggle to make sense of young and beautiful black lives prematurely and indelibly marked by racist contempt and hatred. Goode's poem is a perfect example of this. Before referencing the life and assassination of civil rights leader Martin Luther King, Jr., Goode writes, "war war/why do god's children fight among each other/like animals."[43] Almost as if in response, Curry writes, "death prosecuting life born/freedom slave today tomorrow/yesterday day before/O what a life i have lived."[44] These poems by articulate young writers address issues of contemporary violence and

hatred just as much as they speak to historical struggles; they are both profound and timeless.

What is even more powerful is that Jordan was aware of these youthful
voices, embraced them, and included them among the voices of writers such
as Langston Hughes, "The night is beautiful,/So the faces of my people;"[45] Paul
Laurence Dunbar, "We wear the mask that grins and lies,/It hides our cheeks
and shades our eyes;"[46] and Claude McKay, "Like men we'll face the murderous, cowardly pack,/Pressed to the wall, dying, but fighting back!"[47]

The obvious intensity of the *Soulscript* poems obliterates the linear
approach of representation of the mainstream "canon" to the benefit of the
powerful political writing of nonwhite writers; this point, however, is not limited
to *Soulscript*. In 1971, Jordan's ferocious collection of new poems *Some Changes*,
was published. Much like *Soulscript*, published a year before, *Some Changes* is a
provocative text in that it acknowledges the complex relation of words to language and of language to struggle. In the book's "Introduction," General Editor
Julius Lester asks readers and listeners to participate in the musical experience
of Jordan's intensely lyrical poems. He writes:

> She wants the listener to feel what she feels, see what she sees, and then do with
> it what he may. Hopefully, he will become more human, more caring, more
> intensely alive to the suffering and the joy. Her poems only begin to live in the
> space around the words, that space representing the spaces inside the listener.[48]

According to Lester, Jordan uses words figuratively to communicate experiences of "a black woman poet" who argues for the legitimization of black cultural forms and experiences. Jordan's poems enter into a public space that
encourages people to utilize the language of their lives in forging intersecting
and overlapping relationships with others. The poems in *Some Changes*, which
signify a wealth of experiences including death, life, and activism, contribute
critiques on justice, freedom, and shared social responsibility and insist that
"no one should feel peculiar living/as they do" and that "no one should feel
peculiar living well."[49]

This peculiar feeling that permeates the spaces of human lives is also presented in Jordan's "Not a Suicide Poem." The poet writes:

next door the neighbors rent their windows

formerly a singing
shatters toneless shards
to line an inmost holdup . . .

terrific reeking epidermal
damage
marrow rot . . .

no one should feel peculiar living well.[50]

Jordan's attention to the peculiarity of living well and her decision to draw on language, human encounters, and personal strength to obtain political freedom, as presented in "Not a Suicide Poem," coincide with her focus on the musicality of life, and hence, of poetry. For instance, Jordan's attempt to make sense of the lives of her parents and of the silencing, violence, and love that filled her childhood, parallels her belief in love and her personal decision to love both men and women while surrendering herself to the good fight for justice. Her declaration that love was limitless, and hence her self-identification as a bisexual, has everything to do with the politics of identity and her commitment to civil rights movements that insisted upon adequate living spaces and universal love among human beings. Jordan's fight for justice, clearly connected to her belief in love and sexual freedom, demonstrates the level at which she sacrificed personal relationships with her parents: her father, wishing Jordan had been a boy, wanted her to become a doctor instead of a political artist; her mother wanted Jordan to marry a doctor; and her son, at the time being cared for partially by Jordan, but mainly by Jordan's parents, wanted her to be a mother.[51] Without a doubt, the poet's quest for universal love and "living well" was beset with complications.

In "For My Mother," Jordan points to love's complications by indicating what she would do for her parents. In the poem's opening stanza, Jordan rhythmically indicates what she would do for her mother, Mildred:

> for my mother
> I would write a list
> of promises so solid
> loafing fish and onions
> okra palm tree coconut
> and Khus-Khus paradise

As the poem continues, Jordan writes the following lyrical sentiments for her father, Granville:

> for my father
> I would decorate a doorway
> weaving women into the daytime
> of his travel also
> season the snow to rice and peas[52]

For her unnamed love, she insists on getting rid of the existing silence:

> for my only love
> I would stop the silence
>
> one of these days

wouldn't come too soon . . .
loving.[53]

Jordan's list of promises for her mother symbolizes Mildred's silent desires and sacrifices she made in her daily quest for survival and freedom—first in Jamaica and finally in New York City. Likewise, Jordan's desire to "weave" women into her father's journey symbolizes his failure, from Jordan's perspective, to recognize the significant value of women in the daily interactions of life, work, social and political activities, and love. The mere recognition of something, of someone, outside of the self requires knowledge and an appreciation of that person or thing. In many ways Jordan's desire to show this to her father coincides with a desire to "stop the silence"[54] that permeates the physical, political, emotional, and sexual realms of human existence. This point is related to the peculiar sensations of "living well" in "Not a Suicide Poem," "For My Mother," and the other poems in *Some Changes*.

Through uncensored, democratic, and always political language, Jordan made serious attempts to stop the silence from infiltrating her adult life, her memories of her mother and father, and her work to dismantle the very structures that maintain inequality and human silence. The poet used convincingly sophisticated language in crafting "What Would I Do White?," another poem included in *Some Changes*. The thematic connection of this poem to "Not a Suicide Poem" and "For My Mother" is an example of the figurative way Jordan questions life through the lens of her black and female identities and through the problem of invisibility. What would Jordan do? What powers and privileges, acceptance and (mis)understandings would be made possible by whiteness? In a poetically powerful, yet subdued tone, Jordan declares,

What would I do clearly full
of not exactly beans nor
pearls my nose a manicure
my eyes a picture of your wall?"[55]

She argues that she would be afforded looks of "foreignness" as she enters into the streets, as she ignores service employees, and as she accumulates ways to increase her material worth. Actually, if she were white, if we were all white, it would be possible to "do nothing./That would be enough."[56]

June Jordan, however, was not white. As the only child of West Indian parents, she was intensely aware of her diminished status in the eyes of the dominant group; this awareness compelled the native New Yorker to journey around the globe to fight for rights, representation, and equality. Not being white, Jordan was able to critique the principles of whiteness along lines of identity, race, and privilege, which proved that doing nothing could never be enough. Doing nothing would not allow the poet to "write a list/of promises" for her mother or "decorate a doorway"[57] for her father, or not "feel peculiar living well."[58] Writing was her meaningful work; she used her words and experiences to demonstrate how the social construction of whiteness and of being white implies the social and cultural differences that are so often absent from talk of life and living.[59] Such themes are prominent in "My Sadness Sits Around Me," "Not Looking," "Solidarity Day, 1968," "A Poem for All the Children," "Last Poem for a Little While," and many other poems in *Some Changes*.

As a collection, *Some Changes* is indicative of where Jordan chose to locate herself in society during the late 1960s, 1970s, and into the early 1980s. She positioned herself in political movements for freedom, in the company of social activists and intimate friends, Marilyn Hacker, E. Ethelbert Miller, Adrienne Torf, and Alice Walker, in rallies in New York City and Mississippi, and in debates over black pride and representation. Jordan also located herself in the memories of being raised by Mildred and Granville and in the conflicting demands of university teaching. In "Poem for My Family: Hazel Griffin and Victor Hernandez Cruz," Jordan writes,

> Here is my voice the speed and the wondering
> darkness of my desire is
> all that I am here
> all that you never allowed:
> I came and went like meat not good enough to eat
> remember no remember
> yes remember me
> the shadow following your dreams
> the human sound that never reached your ears[60]

The intensity of the poet's voice as she remembers her "family members," Hazel Griffin and Victor Hernandez Cruz, against the backdrop of slavery, American history, and unforgotten historical struggle, will not be silenced even as she inquires, "America/I mean America how/do you intend to incinerate/ my slavery?"[61] Jordan's vibrant voice, as witnessed in the aforementioned poem, is present in the poems in *Some Changes* just as much as it is in the poems collected in *New Days: Poems of Exile and Return* (1970), *Things that I Do in the Dark: Selected Poetry* (1977), *Passion: New Poems* (1980), and *Living Room* (1985).

For example, the poem "Ah Momma," published in *Things That I Do in the Dark*, reads like a lamentation, a song of praise and regretful worry, and a love poem of sorts from a child's diary. While "Ah Momma" honors and employs the prose form as it explores an imaginary "momma," Jordan evokes the poetry and letter-writing style of Langston Hughes as she asks what happens to "dreams deferred." She does this by simultaneously observing, multidimensionally, topics of womanhood, motherhood, blackness, and working-class angst, using her own mother's life to create a multilayered portrait-poem that reveals her innermost thoughts on how struggle can permanently defer one's dreams:

> Ah, Momma!
> You said this had been your wish when you were quite as young as I was then: a twelve- or thirteen-year-old girl who heard your confidence with terrified amazement: what had happened to you and your wish? Would it happen to me too?[62]

Here, Jordan alludes to her fear that her own dreams would be deferred. Would she follow the path of silence that had allegedly swallowed her mother, preventing her from becoming the artist that she wanted to be? Would June Millicent Jordan be able to do better than her mother? Would she be able to stand strong and fight the good fight and remain the daughter of Mildred Maude Fisher Jordan? Accordingly, Jordan reflects, "it was there that I came, humbly, into an angry, an absolute determination that I would, one day, prove myself to be, in fact, your daughter/Ah, Momma, I am still trying."[63]

Jordan's writing demonstrates her complicated relationship to love, life, and living, which in many ways is a result of her complicated personal and familial history. The poet's varied relationships did not prevent her from embracing the power of language and political action in order "to resist abuses of power and violations of dignity in—and beyond—her country."[64] Poet Adrienne Rich writes in the "Foreword" to *Directed by Desire: The Collected Poems of June Jordan* (2005), that Jordan believed it was necessary to live and teach the poetry that she created, especially during tumultuous times. On June Jordan, Rich declares, "Keeping with vibrations of hope on the pulse through dispiriting times was part of the task she set herself. She wanted her readers, listeners, students to feel their own latent power—of the world, the deed, of their own beauty and intrinsic value." Rich continues by indicating how Jordan wanted people to understand and critique "how isolation can leave us defenseless and paralyzed. She knew, and wrote about, the power of violence, of hate, but her real theme, which infused her style, was the need, the impulse, for relation."[65]

All of Jordan's poems, in some distinct way, emphasize what Rich calls "relation" as they create vivid images that either attract a supportive audience or run off a potential audience in the other direction. Jordan's poem "For My Brother," published in *Things That I Do in the Dark*, is an example. She opens the poem,

> Teach me to sing
> Blackman Blacklove
> sing when the cops break your head
> full of song[66]

On the one hand, Jordan's desire to be taught how to sing could parallel with her plea for black people to rebel against violence and complacency: "cops break your head," "bullets explode in the back/you bend over me," and "needles killing you."[67] On the other hand, singing could offer a creative nonviolent response to violent actions: Jordan invokes the use of songs and the historical connection of black people to songs—chain gang work songs, Negro spirituals, the blues, and shared words—to continue the struggle to obtain civil rights. So why not sing so as to continue to live? This question points to the poem's employment of "Blackman Blacklove" and "Blacklove Blackman" in ways that acknowledge "my brother," the historical struggle for freedom, and the joy that comes from a rebellious song full of energy and "Blacklove."[68]

Similar messages are conveyed in other poems in *Things That I Do in the Dark*, such as "Some People," "Getting Down to Get Over," and "For Ethelbert"—poems of struggle and love, hope and desire. It is important to note that Jordan wrote the last poem in response to a poem that E. Ethelbert Miller wrote to her, titled "FOR JUNE."[69] Miller opens his poem:

if I had met you
in '60 or '61
I would have given
you Valentine cards
made out of construction
paper and cut into
apple shaped hearts . . .

baby—I would have
loved you

given you everything

all this
and more[70]

Jordan's response to Miller's poem begins:

if I cda known youd be real
back in them supreme court
gonna rule all evil out
days
I wda rushd to judgment
(lordy lord)
rushd thru
to the fiery seat itselve
and stayd there
cool as any momma madeup[71]

Miller and Jordan's relationship, which was as political as it was amorous, contributed, as had other intimate relationships that Jordan experienced, to her fierce desire to establish connections among themes of "Blacklove,"[72] activism, and "living well."[73]

In Jordan's *Passion: New Poems, 1977–1980*, a combination of love, living, and urgency rings forth from the first page through the last. In an interview with writer Karla Hammond in 1981, Jordan described *Passion* as "a collection of the poems produced in three years by this particular poet who has come to an evident clarity of world view and of determination to be who she is in a completely self-respecting, truthful way."[74] Readers entering the text not only experience the poet's honesty, but also her rage, excitement, and the sounds of sweet music. Many become infatuated with Jordan and her subjects. Some of these lively subjects include Walt Whitman, one of Jordan's literary models, other writers, like poets and close friends Alexis De Veaux and Ntozake Shange, and political activist Mrs. Fannie Lou Hamer. Jordan also writes about the police, rape, South African women, and Isabella Baumfree, who is widely known as Sojourner Truth. In "Rape is Not a Poem," Jordan opens with a reference to the destruction of a garden that held beautiful life, colors, and sweet sensations:

> One day she saw them coming into the garden
> where the flowers live . . .
> they stamped upon and tore apart
> the garden
> just because (they said)
> those flowers?
> They were asking for it[75]

"They" destroyed the garden, and its flowers, stripping it of its virginal charm. From this opening, Jordan names the violation of the garden, "rape," by explicitly writing about her own rape:

> I let him into the house to say hello . . .
> "Well, I guess I'll be heading out, again,"
> he said.
> "Okay," I answered and, "Take care," I said.
> "I'm gonna do just that," he said.
> "No!" I said: "No! Please don't. Please"[76]

But he did not leave her alone, and the poem's victim, the woman, was left, however temporarily, physically defenseless and full of "hatred consequent to that."[77]

"Rape is Not a Poem" and "Poem About My Rights" are thematically connected and have powerful messages. In the highly popular and anthologized

"Poem About My Rights," Jordan opens by talking about the feeling of danger that oftentimes results from her perceived "status as a woman alone in the evening."[78] She begins:

> Even tonight and I need to take a walk and clear
> my head about this poem about why I can't
> go out without changing my clothes my shoes
> my body posture my gender identity my age
> my status as a woman alone in the evening/
> alone on the streets/alone not being the point/[79]

Being alone, or rather single, according to Jordan, is not the primary point of debate or interrogation. The point is that Jordan has been—like many women, particular groups of people, and particular countries—historically marked as "Other" in the larger narratives of national identity, place making, and ownership. The historical demarcation of people as "Other" means that narratives of survival for people of color have taken a back seat to popularized notions of belonging and the myth of someone else's American dream. Jordan continues:

> I am the history of rape
> I am the history of the rejection of who I am
> I am the history of the terrorized incarceration of
> my self[80]

She ends by resisting labels of "wrong," and substitutes political action of her own naming and freedom of choice:

> *I am not wrong: Wrong is not my name*
> My name is my own my own my own
> and I can't tell you who the hell set things up like this
> but I can tell you that from now on my resistance
> my simple and daily and nightly self-determination
> may very well cost you your life[81]

In this poem, as in her other politically charged poetry and essays, Jordan challenges the reading and listening audience to contemplate the intensity of her argument and to contest the restrictions imposed on the female body by patriarchy. For Jordan, theorizing about the many injustices faced by groups of disenfranchised people was pointless if action did not follow.

In relation to "Rape is Not a Poem," Jordan's "Poem About My Rights" focuses, in large degree, on the inability of any woman to think in solitude, to be mesmerized by the silence of the night, and to embrace her skin, her identifying qualities, the way she desires to because "I can't do what I want/to do with my own body,"[82] without the impending danger of physical rape and systemic violence. This way, "Poem About My Rights" is also about the violence that prevents peoples and countries from existing democratically and that prevents choices and mutual relationships from being fostered across lines of difference, "which is exactly like South Africa/penetrating into Namibia penetrating into/Angola."[83]

According to E. Ethelbert Miller, Jordan's poem denounces a public attitude toward women "not having the freedom of movement" in its articulation of a politics of inclusion that values the civil liberties of women.[84] It is this framework of inclusion that creates the poem's intimate quality. Its strength derives from how Jordan establishes sociopolitical connections among womanhood, sexism, rape, politics, geography, history, economics, and identity so as to critique abuses of power. Additionally, Jordan successfully makes the point that many countries and peoples, especially women and children of color, are prevented from experiencing life in a democratic world because they are considered "wrong" by operating power structures that are inscribed with patriarchal behaviors. "Poem About My Rights" deconstructs physical and geographical boundaries that threaten the existence of humanity by participating in a larger narrative of resistance, which includes critiques on gender identity, female safety, and political rights. In this way, the poem is reiterative of messages presented in Jordan's "Rape is Not a Poem" and "To Free Nelson Mandela."

In the latter poem, published in *Naming Our Destiny: New and Selected Poems*, Jordan declares the following:

> Have they killed the twelve-year-old-girl?
> Have they hung the poet?
> Have they shot down the students?
> Have they splashed the clinic the house
> and the faces of the children
> with blood?
>
> Every night Winnie Mandela[85]

"To Free Nelson Mandela," a poem that reads like a powerful ritualistic chant and that builds on Jordan's theme of being "wrong" as presented in "Poem About My Rights," uses repetition to assault dominant beliefs that "the twelve-year-old," "the poet," "the students," and "the children" are undesirable and thus, not valuable. This message parallels the poem's focus on apartheid, Mandela's long imprisonment and subsequent freedom, and the strength of his wife and the community not to succumb to the atrocities and victimizations of a political system: "Every night Winnie Mandela/Every night the waters of the world/turn to the softly burning/light of the moon."[86] Jordan's poem goes a step further to detail how injustices can result in the organization of communities that resist silence and dehumanizing acts. The poem concludes with a memorialization by "the carpenters," "the midwives," "the miners," "the diggers of the ditch," and other community members[87] for the murders of several South African activists in the township of Lingelihle. Documenting this act of remembrance speaks volumes to Jordan's attack on institutional silence through a politics of inclusion that values and validates the multiple experiences of people.

The poet immersed herself in the experiences of people considered disenfranchised. The police murders in South Africa and the ensuing violence around the world—whether the murder of Victoria Mxenge (in "To Free Nelson Mandela") or the violence in "Namibia," "Angola," or "Zimbabwe" (in "Poem About My Rights")—were events that Jordan felt the need to write about, publicize, and share with others so as to provoke political activism, moving her anger into action.

Furthermore, Jordan's writings represent a desperation to know what is happening, to be in the world, and never to be late because other lives depend on the responsible presence of dedicated leaders. Clearly, this is but one of many messages in "Poem About My Rights" and "To Free Nelson Mandela," poems that combine lyricism with narrative and free verse in a journalistic story form. These writings capture the intensity of lives destroyed by systematic racism, classism, and violence. They also capture the complicated nature of Jordan's life in America: daughter of West Indian parents, mother of Christopher David Meyer, ex-wife of Michael Meyer, protégé of Mrs. Fannie Lou Hamer, and lover of words, people, and activism. Such intricate detail was captured in "POEM: On the Black Family" and her series of "Roman Poems" published in *New Days: Poems of Exile and Return*; and in "Richard Wright Was Wrong," "Brooklyn," and "Poem for Nicaragua" collected in *Living Room: New Poems*. In "Poem for Nicaragua," Jordan writes:

> So little I could hold the edges
> Of your earth inside my arms
>
> Your coffee skin the cotton stuff
> The rain makes small
>
> Your boundaries of sea and ocean slow
> or slow escape possession[88]

In "If You Saw A Negro Lady," published in *Things That I Do in the Dark* and in *Naming Our Destiny*, Jordan begins:

> If you saw a Negro lady
> sitting on a Tuesday
> near the whirl-sludge doors of
> Horn & Hardart on the main drag

of downtown Brooklyn . . .

she would not understand
with spine as straight and solid
as her years of bending over floors
allowed . . .

would you turn her treat
into surprise
observing
happy birthday[89]

Although the two poems are for different occasions, they tell important stories: the first reflects on the poet's experiences in Nicaragua, which she visited in 1983, and the latter observes a woman who, while not interacting with the narrator, informs spectators of life stories through her appearance. The poems also epitomize Jordan's political engagements and commitments during the 1980s, a time that redefined how Jordan's "commitment," according to poet Marilyn Hacker, "is as seamlessly joined to her work as it is to her life." Hacker continues by discussing the political poetry of Jordan by writing,

> [It] is, at its best, the opposite of polemic. It is not written with a preconceived, predigested agenda of ideas and images . . . the process of composition is, or reproduces, the process of discovering how events are connected, how oppressions are analogous, how lives interpenetrate.[90]

Hacker's sentiments show themselves in Jordan's "Poem for Nicaragua," "If You Saw a Negro Lady," "Poem for Nelson Mandela," and "Poem About My Rights," all of which are political, personal, and controversial. The poems have as much to do with Jordan's racial solidarity as with her lifelong concern for the universal protection of human life.

Jordan wrote on controversial topics to increase attention on issues of the heart and the soul, and on freedom and civil rights. She was an outspoken political voice who used words to rally people into action. In her collections of poetry, in her published commentaries in *The Progressive*, which I discuss in detail in Chapter 6, and in her lyrical essays, Jordan's words scream off of the page with a silent, palpable anger. This anger can be felt as one reads her poems, "Calling on All Silent Minorities," "One Minus One Minus One," or "War and Memory." It is June Jordan's anger over the absence of rights for disenfranchised people that motivated her to script such powerful poems, and it is this anger that allows others to continue in the Whitmanesque tradition of poetically documenting and organizing for change. This latter message comes through quite clearly in Jordan's poem "Calling on All Silent Minorities:"

HEY

C'MON
COME OUT

WHEREVER YOU ARE

WE NEED TO HAVE THIS MEETING
AT THIS TREE

AIN' EVEN BEEN
PLANTED
YET[91]

In response to Jordan's plea for "silent minorities" to meet at an unplanted tree, I often wonder if "we" will ever gather together to make use of the poet's message: to transform a "tree" that has never really been planted, or a movement that has not been fully actualized, into a discourse on a rhetoric of rights for disenfranchised people. As I read "Calling on All Silent Minorities," I repeatedly hear, in the not so far distance, poet Amiri Baraka's voice delivering his telegraphic message to black people—those who are conscious activists invested in the struggle for liberation—in the poem "SOS":

Calling black people
Calling all black people, man woman child
Wherever you are, calling you, urgent, come in
Black people, come in, wherever you are, urgent, calling
You, calling all black people
Calling all black people, come in, black people, come
on in.[92]

I also hear the magnificent, urgent, and demanding music of poet, Gil Scott-Heron, in "The Revolution Will Not Be Televised," particularly when he announces,

You will not be able to stay home, brother.
You will not be able to plug in, turn on and cop out.
You will not be able to lose yourself on skag and skip,
Skip out for beer during commercials,
Because the revolution will not be televised.[93]

The aforementioned poems, indicative of the importance of civil rights movements, are startling in their political directives for people to gather, take action, and insist on change. Jordan's words, in particular, are even more necessary today than they were in the 1960s, especially as debates continue to occur over language rights and censorship, education and access, corporate America and bankruptcy, foreign policy and war. Her perpetual search for community, fights for freedom, writings, teachings, and belief that "hatred kills people,"[94] as addressed in more detail in the next chapter, serve as reminders that the right to live, love, and contribute to the welfare of society is contingent upon how people organize for change. "I'm not crazy," wrote Jordan in *Affirmative Acts: Political Essays*. "I am seeking an attitude."[95]

FOUR

Moving Towards Home:
Political Essays

Prior to the 1980s, June Jordan was actively influenced by, and involved in, movements for and over rights: the Civil Rights Movement, the Women's Rights Movement, the Black Arts Movement, and movements against war. These are but a few of the many political causes that, in some way, influenced her art and politics. Even with her connection to these movements, Jordan never considered herself controversial, but rather an activist unwilling to contain her frustration and anger. Jordan's unwillingness to suppress the feelings that made her a participant is a result of her honest confrontation with the past. She learned to recognize the struggles of her past: the challenges her immigrant parents faced in America; the violence perpetuated by her father; the difficulty of a 1950s interracial marriage; the physical abuse incurred by Mrs. Fannie Lou Hamer during a freedom ride/voter registration campaign; and discriminatory practices encountered by countless men, women, and children of color everywhere. Her involvement was always grounded in her politics as much as in her art, for Jordan always believed that the two—politics and art—were inseparable and from this belief, revolutionary work resulted.

Clearly, Jordan's writing embodies the principles and ideals of the influential Black Arts Movement, which is highly indicative of the connection between art and politics.[1] Poet-critics Amiri Baraka, Ed Bullins, Harold Cruse, Nikki Giovanni, Ron Karenga, Askia Muhammad, Larry Neal, Sonia Sanchez, and notable others spearheaded a grassroots-turned-national collective of black artists who supported black cultural traditions and artistic innovations in the black community. These artists sought to affirm the black aesthetic: the existence of a powerful artistic and culture-based political collective that strives to reform current understandings of beauty and privilege, culture and power, and the philosophical principles of a black genius, or imagination, as related to black life, politics, and work through art. To establish and affirm this aesthetic, groups of black people—musicians, dancers, poets, writers, film-makers, dramatists, educators, working-class laborers—denounced what they saw as oppressive conditions in America: from U.S. imperialism, police violence, and black rejection from mainstream white publishing markets to apartheid. They marched in the streets, protested at rallies, publicly decried Eurocentric values, and, most importantly, created venues for the dissemination of scholarship on and by black people. Journals and magazines such as *Soulbook*, the *Liberator*, *Black America*, *Black Dialogue*, *Journal of Black Poetry*, and *Black Theater* flooded the streets and circuits of political action and social reform. Black visionary artists who sought an understanding of black people, cultures, politics, and communities supported the work of this cultural movement. Their work helped to establish a black aesthetic grounded in art and politics, words and actions—the fabrics of their poetry, the poetry of their lives.

According to writer Addison Gayle, Jr. in the "Introduction" to writer-editor Woodie King, Jr.'s book *The Forerunners: Black Poets in America* (1975), the artists of the Black Arts Movement worked to create "a true racial poetry" that has at its center "the creation of a new people and a new nation and the destruction of images and symbols that enslave." Gayle goes on to declare that the poets of the Black Arts Movement produced "a poetry that demands a revolution of the mind and spirit, that calls, with Baraka, for the greatest of man's creations: 'We want a Black poem. And a Black world/Let the World be a Black Poem.'"[2] Gayle acknowledges an important idea in relation to the work of the Black Arts Movement: that the black aesthetic imagined by Baraka, Muhammad, and Neal, for example, is one that has as its basis the creation of "a true racial poetry" unencumbered by the vices and values of mainstream poetry and established by the artistic work and political principles of an older generation of black poets—from Wheatley, Hughes, and McKay to Hurston and Wright. For Gayle, "The perceptions of the younger poets, therefore, were sharpened by the works of their predecessors." Gayle continues:

> These are the poets who came to prominence, mainly, after the Renaissance years, who bridged the gap between poets of the twenties and those of the sixties and seventies. They began the intensive questioning of the impossible dream, the final assault upon illusion that produced the confrontation with reality, the search for paradigms, images, metaphors, and symbols from the varied experiences of a people whose history stretches back beyond the Nile. With a few exceptions, they are the literary godparents of today's black poets.[3]

Remembrance and acknowledgment of the work of previous generations of poets and writers played a central role during the Black Arts Movement. For example, writers Toni Cade Bambara, June Jordan, Audre Lorde, Essex Hemphill, and others sought to "bridge the gap" between previous black writers and contemporary writers by investigating long-standing issues of classism, racism, and sexism in both the literary and critical mainstream and civil rights efforts in America. Their work contributes to how black artists and activists learn "to step outside the parochialism of the American society" at the same time that they discover "that to be a good poet as well as a relevant poet entails as great a concern for race as it does for the mastery of craft."[4]

As the cultural component of the Civil Rights Movement and the successor of the Harlem Renaissance and the New Negro Movement of the 1920s, the Black Arts Movement stimulated black-owned businesses, including theater troupes, magazines, journals, bookstores, and publishing companies, as well as historically black colleges, universities, and communities of people who would later proclaim, "I'm black and I'm proud." Likewise, Baraka's founding of the Black Arts Repertory Theatre/School (BART/S) in March 1965 serves as a significant contribution to educational and artistic initiatives for black people. Such efforts support Baraka's call for a poem and a world that is black, and for a black aesthetic that is a poem and a world (see Addison's "Introduction").

Additionally, the creation of viable black businesses and educational programs during this time encouraged writers such as John Blassingame, Alex Haley, Ernest Gaines, June Jordan, Gerda Lerner, and Toni Morrison to produce literature that acknowledges the multiplicity of black identities and the richness of cultural practices that are connected to the history of slavery, segregation, and protests in this country. Blassingame's anthology *Slave Testimony* (1977), Lerner's edited volume *Black Women in White America* (1973), and Morrison's editorial commitment to *The Black Book* (1974) represent increased attention to the significance of history, identity, art, and politics in black communities before, during, and after the Black Arts Movement.

The work of the Black Arts Movement specifically influenced the direction June Jordan would take with her art and politics. During this movement, Jordan to come of age as a writer who completed editorial assignments for various New York-based magazines, witnessed the 1964 Harlem rebellion, embraced many of the principles of the Black Power Movement, and increased her commitment to Mrs. Fannie Lou Hamer and her political agenda for the state of Mississippi. It would be false to assume, however, that Jordan fully accepted Amiri Baraka, or any other leader of the Black Arts Movement, as her mentor or model. She had developed a voice of her own, one that would be tested many times over. Also, her work began to appear more frequently around the same time that other Black Nationalist writers began to articulate "a black aesthetic." Jordan's presence in New York City during the Civil Rights Movement—when people were collectively campaigning for rights, violently and nonviolently, and when the Voting Rights Bill of 1965 was passed—is fundamental to her commitment to sustaining national conversations about civil rights, political opportunities, quality education, and affordable housing for black people. She was committed to improving the living conditions for black people in America, which shows itself in Jordan's analysis of human rights as based on the philosophical teachings of Martin Luther King, Jr. and the Civil Rights Movement, and Malcolm X and the Black Power Movement. Jordan critiqued the work of both leaders in ways that complicated her relationship with the Black Arts Movement and its politics and activist agenda; she questioned its leadership through her published writing and social activism.

During the Civil Rights Era, Jordan did not readily align herself with the ideals of Martin Luther King, Jr., nor did she quickly embrace King's belief in nonviolence, benevolent love, integration, and the "Beloved Community." She believed that acts of violence perpetuated against black communities in America required immediate action not met by turning the other cheek. In fact, Jordan's rejection of "turning the other cheek" is illustrated by her reaction, during the late 1960s, to a white Marine who insisted that she, a black woman on a freedom ride, give up her lunch counter seat to a male officer of the law. In response, and to the dismay of other freedom riders who considered themselves nonviolent, Jordan aggressively elbowed the man. Jordan's act demonstrates her unwillingness to confront violence with love or to tolerate white contempt. Jordan's willfulness points to her rejection of nonviolent pleas and demonstrations, as well as her resistance to fully accepting the philosophical teachings of King. She wanted to see immediate results from her political actions.

In her 1997 essay "Update on Martin Luther King, Jr., and the Best of My Heart," Jordan admits her ambivalence toward the leader by noting how she did not always embrace his political disposition. She writes, "In the sixties I could not understand his reaching beyond race to stand on principle. I could not understand, or support, his own example of 'nonviolence.' There was so much I didn't know!"[5] Jordan offers an explanation of King's use of "the Beloved Community"—that "everybody is sacred. Nobody is excluded from that deliberate embrace"—as well as King's commitment to nonviolence— "'nonviolent' did not mean cowardly."[6] Jordan's eventual embrace of King's philosophy, grounded in love and nonviolence, did not occur until after King was assassinated in 1968. Her commitment to those goals further increased during the 1980s, as is reflected in the poet's statement about King's devotion to equality:

> By enlarging his concern for Blackfolks to a concern for universal equality, Dr. King heightened the likelihood of equality in all of our lives. The more people you could hinge to the principle of equality, the more people you could rally together in that fight—on the basis of common self-interest.[7]

Jordan's lessons on universal equality, community, and love had a lot to do with her resistance to King's political philosophies. In some of her published writings, Jordan refers to many of King's philosophical principles and activist work such as his participation in the December 1961 demonstrations over desegregation and voting rights for black residents in Albany, Georgia; his participation in the April 1963 civil rights campaign in Birmingham, Alabama;[8] and King's support of the new proposed Civil Rights Act in August 1963.[9]

In "The Mountain and the Man Who Was Not God," Jordan articulates King's belief in freedom, the sanctity of human life, and the importance of non-violent resistance in fighting for rights. She also writes about desegregation, voting rights, and the Vietnam war. The essay always returns to Jordan's reflection on the life and legacy of King. For example, she passionately remembers the radio coverage of the Civil Rights demonstrations in Birmingham, Alabama in 1963. She grounds her reflections on the coverage by saying that King "was not a god," and continues by indicating how she was seriously beginning to consider the liberation of black people according to the principles articulated by King as a possibility. Jordan writes:

> And when, one afternoon, that fast talking, panic-stricken newscaster in Birmingham reported the lunging killer police dogs and the atrocious hose water and I could hear my people screaming while the newscaster shouted out the story of my people, there, in Birmingham, who would not quit the streets,— when he described how none of that horror of nightsticks or torrential water pressure or mad dogs on the attack could stop the children of Birmingham from coming out again and again to suffer whatever they must for freedom, I remember the positively stunned sensation that engulfed me.[10]

She experiences this sensation—based on the realities of groups of people demonstrating for rights—as a sign of victory. These signs, for Jordan, were met by the "magical calm voice leading us, unarmed, into the violence of White America."[11] That voice belonged to Martin Luther King, Jr. It was a voice of reason and the voice of a body that had been "clubbed and stabbed and shoved and shot at and jailed and spat upon."[12] Yet Jordan was disturbed by King's declaration, "If any blood will flow in the streets of Birmingham let it be our blood and not the blood of our white brothers."[13] Jordan was never to embrace fully Martin Luther King, Jr.'s doctrine of nonviolence; she always wanted to fight back.

Later in the same essay, Jordan tells of her awakening—the beginning of her understanding, if not full embrace—to the principles of King only after his assassination: "And so, when the news came, April 4, 1968, that Dr[.] King was dead, I thought, I felt, along with millions and millions of other Black Americans, that so was love and so was all good will and so was the soul of these United States."[14] On King's assassination, Jordan expressed her feelings of anger and her desire for universal peace. She promised to remember King's life work and to work with others to foster King's vision of the "Beloved Community."

Perhaps because of the sense of urgency he exuded, Jordan was moved somewhat more by the forceful, immediate strategies of Malcolm X. She admired his magnificent oratorical skills and his heated speeches on the need for social action, his love of black people, his insistence on black pride, and his belief in black cultural consciousness. Jordan met with Malcolm X and other black political leaders, writers, journalists, and activists to discuss the conditions of black life in America; these important encounters further strengthened Jordan's desire to work for social, political, educational, and economic changes in the black community. Initially, she was solely concerned with the denial of civil rights for black people, but in some cases, this concern later metamorphosed into a concern for the rights of all people treated unjustly in America and elsewhere.

In many ways, Malcolm X's later political philosophies supported Jordan's thinking about the need to extend civil rights efforts for black people from a local to an international context. After his pilgrimage to Mecca, visits to the Congo, and eventual separation from the Nation of Islam and the teachings of Elijah Muhammad, Malcolm X began to preach his philosophy of Black Nationalism and freedom. According to writer James H. Cone in his 1992 essay "Malcolm X and Black Nationalism," Malcolm X "wanted to join the civil rights movement in order to expand it into a human rights movement, thereby internationalizing the black freedom struggle."[15] Malcolm X's growing interest in a larger, more international civil rights movement connects well to Jordan's increasing dedication to expanding the fight for rights to include the realities of people of color throughout the world.[16]

Prior to the assassinations of Malcolm X and Martin Luther King, Jr., Jordan found herself caught between the philosophical teachings of both leaders. While she disagreed with Martin Luther King, Jr. on issues of nonviolence, she did consider him a hero. In the 1999 published interview "Poetry is a Political Act" with Julie Quiroz, former Associate Director of the Coalition for Immigrant Rights in Northern California, Jordan discusses her attitude toward nonviolence and freedom fights in relation to social and political activism. During this time, Jordan was caring for her son, Christopher, in a New York City housing project when she met freedom fighter and activist Evie Rich and Rich's husband, Marvin Rich, who at the time was the National Director of CORE. Jordan admits:

> CORE was committed to nonviolence, but I was not. But, based on my friendship with Evie as young mothers, I started going on freedom rides in 1966. The purpose of my first freedom ride was to try to desegregate the bus route from New York to Maryland. I said I'd go, but I didn't say I'd be nonviolent.[17]

According to Jordan, her first freedom ride came almost a year after the assassination of Malcolm X (February 21, 1965), and it was met with a tempered level of anger that, for Jordan, did not have to be calmed in nonviolent ways. She continues the interview by indicating how she officially decided to be "in," but on her own terms, terms that did not exclude the possibility of violent action. Jordan determined early on that responding to violence with nonviolence was a philosophy she could not completely commit to.[18]

Jordan's decision to be "in" speaks to how her experiences during the 1960s and 1970s, highly influenced by the activism and legacies of Martin Luther King, Jr. and Malcolm X, helped her to visualize a different kind of America in which everyone would receive equal rights without the threat of violence and hate. Their work also impacted the political direction Jordan followed during the 1980s. In many published interviews and writings, Jordan has admitted that the closing of the 1960s was an intense time for her: she cared for her son, with the assistance of family members and friends, became a Black Nationalist, participated in the Black Power Movement and criticized it for its gender bias and its politics-before-art beliefs, became involved with CORE, and talked with Malcolm X after his departure from the Nation of Islam. She also reported on the grassroots freedom movements of black people in Mississippi, gained increased awareness of the Women's Movement, cofacilitated poetry work-shops for youth in Brooklyn and Harlem through Teachers & Writers Collaborative, accepted a teaching position at City College, and participated in the college's Open Admissions battle.

The effects of the assassinations of Malcolm X and Martin Luther King, Jr. continued to affect the political direction of human rights movements throughout the world. With their assassinations, Jordan began to wonder about the struggle for black people's liberation in relation to international civil rights struggles. Around this time, her poetry and political essays increased in intensity and became even more full of rage. Jordan's presence in the literary, political, and educational scenes of the 1960s continued to demand her atten-tion years later because of long-standing, institutionalized systems that per-petuated unequal treatment for poor and working-class people of color.

In particular, she approached the 1980s fighting against everything she knew to be wrong and loving everything she believed was right. For example, Jordan fell in love with a powerful black man whom she thought was commit-ted to the struggle for black liberation until "he lied" to her by telling Jordan, after a long day of working with black parents in Englewood, New Jersey on ways to desegregate the school system, that what he wanted all day was to be with her sexually, a comment that for Jordan minimized his activist efforts.[19] According to Jordan, this man was no longer a lover whom she wanted nor a hero of the people she could trust: "He was my introduction to the idea that you have sex, love, or both, on the one hand, and you have politics or princi-ples on the other."[20] Jordan, however, wanted both at all times—to fight and to love the fights, honestly and collectively—a point highlighted in her discus-sion of black love and sexuality in *Affirmative Acts: Political Essays* (1998).

Jordan enjoyed collaborating with people whose focus was on community-building, love, and the inclusion of multiple voices in public discourses on equality. In her 1997 published keynote address delivered at the National Black Lesbian and Gay Conference, Jordan recalls her introduction to many black political leaders and spokespersons during and immediately following the height of the Civil Rights Movement in the 1960s. In particular, she writes of how she fell in love with a woman who relocated to Harlem, New York from Hazlehurst, Mississippi "about ten years after my hero episode"[21] and just before Jordan went to Mississippi to complete a freelance assignment for the *New York Times*. They were both in love with the political and ideological constructions of Blackness as well as with "Black People," "Black Power," and "Black Fights;" they bravely accepted a most defining slogan of the arts movement: "Black is Beautiful." Jordan indicates that she and this woman fell in love with one another and remained partners "for several, unforgettable years."[22] This relationship, among others, encouraged Jordan to explore the absence of sex and sexuality in political efforts. It also forced her to question the lack of attention given to "Black and gay and lesbian and bisexual" rights, especially since there were many people who believed as she did: that "there was no conflict between the political and the personal chambers of my political and personal heart."[23] Jordan was angry that the movements of the 1960s advocated freedom and identity at the sheer neglect of sexual identities and gay rights. Years later, she and socially conscious writers such as Audre Lorde, articulated the importance of including the movement for gay rights in progressive efforts for civil rights. Jordan's insistence for a more universal rights movement that represented various people and their differing experiences showed itself in her numerous publications. Through her writing, she hoped to accomplish and conquer a balance among politics, art, identity constructs, and love.

Her writing during this era included political poetry ("The New Pietà: For the Mothers and Children of Detroit," 1965; "What Would I Do White?" 1966; "Who Look at Me, Dedicated to My Son, Christopher," 1968; "From the Talking Back of Miss Valentine Jones: Poem # One," 1976); children's books (*Dry Victories*, 1972; *Fannie Lou Hamer*, 1972); essays (in *Esquire*, the *New York Times*, and *Partisan Review*); and reports ("Mississippi Black Home," 1970). Jordan was determined to create art and share her political views with others as if her life depended on it, even in the face of harsh criticism from mainstream publishing companies that often refused to publish her work. On this latter point, Jordan's longtime friend and professional collaborator, musician Adrienne Torf, articulated reasons why publishing companies often refused to print Jordan's writing. In an October 2005 interview, Torf commented that Jordan was always making connections among art, music, and politics that most people do not see, a point that reiterates Jordan's focus on identity politics and that made her "difficult for the literary world to market, for June would not pigeonhole; she refused to be pigeonholed." Torf continues:

> June's reputation with agents and publishers went up and down because her writings were about herself and of her life. She would not and could not limit how, what, or why she wrote. Limiting her writings meant that she was limiting herself—her life and beliefs—and such limiting would mean death for June.[24]

Rejection from publishing companies did not halt Jordan's political and poetically involved activities: she employed poetry, essay, drama, children's fiction, journalism, libretto, and performance to ask difficult questions about the role of women in political movements and the importance of raising children in their own communities. She also wrote about sexual freedom and the range of sexual choices that humans might embrace. Whatever she wrote about, marched against, or actively lived for, Jordan was not easily deterred from fighting against racism and classism—her resistance to her father's supposed violence attests to this fact. No one, including leaders of civil rights movements, could persuade her to do anything other than what she felt necessary. Jordan's involvement in political movements gave her hope that the lives of black people would be improved, in part, by demonstrating, marching, protesting, and then returning to the streets to insist on change. And fight Jordan did, by attending the rallies and writing poetry about black love, life, leaders, and movements.

Writing about civil rights movements in her essay "Declaration of an Independence I Would Just as Soon Not Have" Jordan asks:

> But where can you find serious Black spokesmen, or women, for the impoverished, hungry, state-dependent Black peoples among us who still amount to more that a third of our total population? And why does it continue to be the case that, when our ostensible leadership talks about the "liberation of the Black man" that is precisely, and only, what they mean?[25]

Jordan questions the foundation of the Black Power and Black Arts Movements in terms of the liberation, equality, and fair representation of women. Her questions, pointed directly at the leaders of these movements, speak to a universal problem with representation along racial, gender, and class lines. The Women's Movement of the 1970s is not exempt from such questions, particularly when its white female leaders take on the roles of authority figures or assume the definitive voice for black people and other unacknowledged groups. Such acts further silence and ignore the realities of large segments of the population. As an example of such unfair representation, Jordan writes about the lowly position and unmet needs of black female workers in the United States:

> Black women continue to occupy the absolutely lowest rungs of the labor force in the United States, we continue to receive the lowest pay of any group of workers, and we endure the highest rate of unemployment. If that status does not cry out for liberation, specifically as Black women, then I am hopelessly out of touch with my own pre-ordained reality.[26]

Where are the leaders who will listen to the voices and realities of the world's poor and impoverished people, particularly women? Where are the spokespersons who will rally for the rights of disenfranchised people, underpaid workers, oppressed citizens, and political refuges? Who will insist that there can be no movements without the presence and participation of black women? The absence of black women in human rights organizing was always a point of concern for Jordan. For she could not understand why major political movements did not readily acknowledge and push to the forefront the inclusion of women. Jordan was frustrated with, and unforgiving of, the fact that the multidimensional existences, struggles, and voices of women remained absent from larger conversations on human rights, equality, and love. Such points are articulated in the poem "*From* the Talking Back of Miss Valentine Jones: Poem # One" (1976):

> you (temporarily) shownup with a thing
> you say's a poem and you
> call it
> "Will the Real Miss Black America Standup?"[27]

From here, the poet goes on to protest the assumption that black women have no words when, in fact, their words—the poetry of their work and the reality of their domestic lives—are often ignored by black men, including male poets of the Black Arts Movement:

> and the very next bodacious Blackman
> call me queen
> because my life ain shit
> because (in any case) he ain been here to share it
> with me
> (dish for dish and do for do and
> dream for dream)
> I'm gone scream him out my house
> be-
> cause what I wanted was
> to braid my hair/bathe and bedeck my
> self so fully be-
> cause what I wanted was
> your love
> not pity
> be-
> cause what I wanted was
> your love
> your love[28]

Employing a crisp, feminist perspective, this poem about "talking back" demonstrates Jordan's resistance to being silenced by the very leaders of the 1960s black protest movements and the 1970s feminist movement who were supposed to represent her. Both Jordan's essay "Declaration of an Independence I Would Just as Soon Not Have" and her poem "*From* the Talking Back of Miss Valentine Jones: Poem # One" critique the role of "leader" when such a role infringes upon the voices and rights of women. For example, the "bodacious Blackman,"[29] the "you" and "your," in "*From* the Talking Back of Miss Valentine Jones: Poem # One" attempts to assume authority over and for black women, believing that his words, wisdom, and voice represent the lives and histories of black women as well. What the "bodacious Blackman" does not realize, or fails to acknowledge, are the daily "domestic routines" of black women. According to Miss Valentine, "I had to remember to write down/margarine on the list/and shoepolish and a can of/sliced pineapples in casea company."[30] The Blackman's lack of acknowledgement is a failure for Miss Valentine, especially since all she ever really "wanted was/your love/not pity."[31]

In addition to this lack of love from the "bodacious Blackman" for the working black woman, Jordan's poem points to the larger, more systemic failure by leaders of "Black" movements to deconstruct images of Blackness portrayed in popular white culture. For Jordan, a true black aesthetic could never really be actualized since some of the 1960s and 1970s political leaders did not fully take into consideration the voices and rights of black women and children. The "benign neglect" of black women at home and in political movements made Jordan—mother, artist, activist, and self-proclaimed Black Nationalist—question the validity of those movements and their leaders; Jordan had a more inclusive vision of the contributions that black women could make in political activities.

What Jordan sought, then, was a political movement representative of the widely varied experiences of women, men, and children, including black and immigrant people like her parents. This collective would revolutionize and internationalize the black protest movement in its inclusivity. Maybe Jordan's desire for such a collective was influenced by Malcolm X's recognition of the need for heightened analysis and increased commitment that could only come from an international human rights movement. Or perhaps Jordan's desire for such a collective is similar to Martin Luther King, Jr.'s call for universal love and equality through nonviolent measures. In many ways, Jordan's desire for a rich black aesthetic, inclusive of the voices and realities of black women, King's insistence on universal love, and Malcolm's call for an international collective are all rooted in a civil rights liberation movement that supports historically marginalized people by acknowledging their voices and making them visible.

Jordan critiqued the work of both Malcolm X and Martin Luther King, Jr., as well as their representative causes, as a way to interrogate her own social responsibility. This interrogation, mediating between nonviolent and violent responses, encouraged Jordan to continue to examine black leadership in relation to communality and struggles. In her timely essay "Civil Wars," Jordan discusses the lack of black leadership, King's assassination, and "the massive Black peoples' uprising of Miami, 1980." She writes,

> Again and again after the assassination of Martin Luther King, Jr., social commentators "deplored" the lack of Black leadership. But I had been thinking, maybe it's a good thing. Certainly, I couldn't see any white leadership around that left me envious. The concept of leadership itself seemed to me dangerous and tired."[32]

Such leadership, even during the 1980s, was "dangerous and tired"[33] because of the increase in violent acts directed at people of color. She wrote about the murder of Arthur McDuffie who "died because three cops beat him to death because he went through a red light and he was Black."[34] Jordan attended with her close friends, Gwendolyn Hardwick and Alexis De Veaux, "the 1979 organized, nonviolent demonstration to protest the police murder of Luis Baez,"[35] a young Brooklyn resident who was shot sixteen times. She participated in "the People's Tribunal," where artist, writer, and activist Alexis De Veaux was briefly interrupted by New York police officers as she attempted to deliver her statement about unarmed Elizabeth Magnum, one of many black women killed by police officers. It was Jordan who wrote one of the most striking lines of dedication: "This is my short list: for 1989 I dedicate myself to the memory of Lisa Steinberg [a homeless six-year-old who died of child abuse] and to the future of the Palestinian people."[36] Where is justice? Where is love? Where is leadership? Who is to be turned to for guidance? Who will stand up and lead the demonstrations, protests, and movements of resistance that once shaped black life in America? Is leadership really "dangerous and tired?"[37] Will anyone resolve to "search for relevant comrades and group initiatives to support," or are people too tired because all of the leaders are dead and gone?[38]

June Jordan's examination of black leadership and her presence at rallies and demonstrations took her in many directions. During the early 1970s, she traveled to the 36th Annual Conference of Southern Governors held in the small, white town of Gulfport, Mississippi, a town that did not have any visible black residents.[39] She attended the conference to gather information on a study she was conducting on land reform for her unpublished manual *More than Enough*. Then in 1973, Jordan, along with Inez Smith Reid, former organizer of the Black Women's Community Development Fund, began the "Afro Americans Against the Famine" campaign to raise attention and money for the millions of Africans affected by the Sahel famine. In support of this campaign, Jordan and Reid conceived of the Black Media People's gathering held at New York's formerly named Negro Ensemble Company in July 1973. According to Jordan, "it was well attended. Jesse Jackson flew in. . . . Carlos Russell moderated. . . . Roberta Flack donated a radio spot."[40] However, the support was not enough to convince lawmakers of the presence of a significant African or African American lobby. Meanwhile, Jordan simultaneously realized that Black Nationalism in this country often amounted to a concern for one's local community and not for "the continental African struggle."[41] She was dismayed with this realization because she began organizing the campaign believing in "an exclusively Black national action"[42] and she left the campaign knowing "that color is not enough to save your life. Certainly it is quite enough to kill you."[43]

Jordan also continued her contributions to the discourse on black sexuality and personal politics, topics often absent from the black liberation agenda.[44] In 1978, for example, Jordan went to the National Black Writers Conference at

Howard University in Washington, DC, where topics included conversations about feminism, lesbianism, sexuality, sexual freedom, and the black community. Jordan describes feeling powerless because "as a Black woman, as a Black feminist," she is quite often treated as such by black men and white people. Nevertheless, this powerlessness does not substitute her status as part of the majority, "because Black and Third World peoples constitute the majority of life on this planet."[45] Jordan, as part of this specific majority, has a power that others may not embrace, one based on sharp critiques of race and gender in politics. These two debatable and often highly contested terms, according to Jordan, challenge assumptions about people's abilities, roles, and rights. Jordan's power was exemplified by the body of her writing, speaking engagements, demonstrations, teaching experience, and other political and artistic activities. This was evident when Jordan attended the governors' conference in the all-white town of Gulfport, Mississippi, the academic conference on liberation and self-hidden homophobia, as well as at the Black Writers Conference in Washington, DC. These experiences not only heightened Jordan's realization of the need for universal equality but also monumentally affected her views on leadership, equality, and identities.

American politics during the 1980s also informed Jordan's views on leadership. She was convinced that the failed attempts of mobilization in underserved communities were connected to the political agenda of American Republicans and conservatives, most notably, the leadership of former President Ronald Reagan. Jordan was probably more appalled by Reagan's controversial stance on fighting for the freedom of all people affected by structures of greed, oppression, and imperialism than she was over the legacy that he was already creating for himself under the "Reagan Revolution." Jordan often wondered: What kind of a president alleges "no new taxes" in an effort to have peace and prosperity? What kind of a leader, according to Jordan, allegedly wants peace—not war, continued violence, and brutality—but insists on stockpiling nuclear weapons? Jordan's poem "Easter Comes to the East Coast: 1981," is addressed to former President Reagan and speaks of a vision of a world where diversity and egalitarianism are truly embraced. The first part of the poem reads:

Don' you worry about a thing
Mr. President and you too
Mr. Secretary of the State: Relax!
We not studying you guys:
NO NO NO NO NO!
This ain' real
Ain' nobody standing around
We not side by side
This ain' no major league rally
We not holding hands again

We not some thousand varieties of one fist!
This ain' no coalition
This ain' no spirit no muscle no body to stop the bullets
We not serious[46]

This message to the President and his cabinet represents Jordan's stance not only on civil movements during the 1980s but also on labor movements that privilege particular groups over others. In this poem, Jordan reverses aspects of history: no one is watching, no one is paying attention, no one is joining hands, there is no need to "worry about a thing,"[47] when in fact, people *are* watching and organizing, and there *is* a need to worry about the long-term implications of U.S. politics. The poem continues:

NO NO NO NO NO!
And I ain' never heard about El Salvador;
I ain' never seen the children sliced
and slaughtered at the Sumpul Riverside
And I ain' never heard about Atlanta;
I ain' never seen the children strangled in the woods . . .
NO NO NO NO NO!
This is just a fantasy.
We just kidding around

You watch![48]

For Jordan, there is no kidding around, as illustrated in the poem. The increase in violence continued to move from a national context—in this case, the United States—to an international context, and Reagan's era of power contributed to this phenomenon. Jordan protested Reagan's presidency and his insistence on using nuclear power and manufacturing more bombs.

Reagan was elected in 1980, toward the end of the long period known as the Cold War, and remained in office until 1988. During this time, power struggles dominated conversations on U.S. foreign politics. It was Reagan versus the Soviet Union over issues of communism. It was communists (the Left) versus capitalists (the Right) over nuclear power. The Soviet Union was supporting Cuba in the 1980s, while the United States was refusing to assist Cuban liberation in any way. Clearly, the threat of nuclear war still abounded, and Jordan was aware of this. In her poem "A Reagan Era Poem in Memory of Scarlet O'Hara, who said, in Gone With the Wind, something like this:" Jordan writes:

"As God is my witness, so help me God:
I'm going to live through this
And when it's over

If I have to lie, steal, cheat, or kill,
I'll never go hungry again."
The poem says:
"Amen!"[49]

On a national level, Reagan was insisting that school prayer become a require-
ment and 1980s America was experiencing a recession that was masked by foreign policies; while the United States was fighting other countries, America's
poor people continued to suffer the most because of the recession. On this latter point, Jordan admits, "I don't believe Ronald Reagan has a clue about communism any more than he knows where Managua is in relationship to
Memphis, Tennessee. . . . I am not worried about communism."[50] She continues by indicating what she is most concerned about:

> I'm worried about my country: This is where I live. And what kind of situation
> do we have here where folks can claim ultra-loyalty to these United States, and
> where average Jane and average Joe can mouth a lot of "love it or leave it"
> mumbo jumbo and then turn around and tell you majority rule is beside the
> point?[51]

Jordan—activist, poet, and fighter—did not want to lose this country to hate.
She did not want her country to succumb to foreign policies that dangerously
intervene in another country's political agenda and safety without realizing
that such interference would be met with retaliation. What Jordan wanted was
a new government, a new America, and a new foreign policy that supported
international coalition building. She wanted schools in the United States not
to feel threatened by governmental policies and mandates that do more harm
than good. Additionally, Jordan did not want a president in office who forces
children and their families to abandon their cultural and religious practices
concerning prayer, language rights, and religious observations.

In "Where Are We and Whose Country Is This, Anyway?" (1986) Jordan
remarks, "We need a new president. To save our country, we need an opposition party on the American scene."[52] For Jordan, this new president would care
about Nicaragua's Sandinistas, the people in all of Africa, and the citizens of his
or her own country—the political agenda of a democratic country that does
not engage in nuclear wars and that does not tolerate ethnic cleansing and
genocide. This message is powerfully articulated in Jordan's poem "INTIFADA
INCANTATION: POEM #8 FOR b.b.L" (1997). In part, Jordan writes:

I SAID I LOVED YOU AND I WANTED
GENOCIDE TO STOP
I SAID I LOVED YOU AND I WANTED AFFIRMATIVE
ACTION AND REACTION
I SAID I LOVED YOU AND I WANTED MUSIC
OUT THE WINDOWS

I SAID I LOVED YOU AND I WANTED
NOBODY THIRST AND NOBODY
NOBODY COLD[53]

In this chant-like song, Jordan engages in an awakening and an uprising, or an "Intifada," a word that has its roots in the first Palestinian uprising against the Israeli military rule in 1987. Jordan's uprising opposes inhumane conditions—"genocide," "thirst," and "cold"—that threaten people's livelihood. In place of such conditions, Jordan demands "action," "reaction," "music," and "love." She insists on the eradication of "boundaries" that maintain human inequality, suffering, and fear; this point reiterates her belief in a Beloved Community that is borderless and that has implications for international human rights coalitions. Jordan continues:

I SAID I LOVED YOU AND I WANTED I WANTED
JUSTICE UNDER MY NOSE
I SAID I LOVED YOU AND I WANTED
BOUNDARIES TO DISAPPEAR

I WANTED
NOBODY ROLL BACK THE TREES!
I WANTED
NOBODY TAKE AWAY DAYBREAK!
I WANTED
NOBODY FREEZE ALL THE PEOPLE ON THEIR
KNEES![54]

This poem, along with some of Jordan's other work, articulates a politics of rejection, one in which collective efforts against segregationist practices, genocide, and unfair political actions are oftentimes ignored. Jordan, however, delivered countless speeches on U.S. politics, democracy, and foreign affairs because of her disappointment with political structures. These speeches were delivered to audiences at the Library of Congress, the University of North Dakota, and at Town Hall meetings in New York City during the late 1970s and into the 1980s and 1990s. In "Waking Up in the Middle of Some American Dream," Jordan discusses democracy and human relations by referring to how one chooses to live both independently and as a participating member within various communities. This essay, demonstrative of Jordan's growth as a writer and an activist, highlights how she no longer conceptualized communities of struggle along shared racial lines; she believed such communities should be formed by a collective of visionary people who desire freedom, love, and safety for themselves and others:

We must learn how to satisfy our individual needs in the context of a heterogeneous, equally entitled, millionfold population of our peers. I am waking up in

the middle of some American dreams that have tormented most of us throughout most of our American history![55]

Throughout her life, Jordan dreamed of liberation and freedom. She examined
unjust living conditions and protested dangerous political decisions that
involved nuclear wars, the bombing of Baghdad, and the lack of U.S. support
to Nicaragua, so as not to remain "here inside the big and messy and com-
bustible haystack of these United States, and the forecast is not good."[56]
Believing that people should support worldwide efforts to mobilize, Jordan
participated in an event named after her poem "Moving Towards Home"
organized by poet-activists Sara Miles and Kathy Engel. This 1982 event, ben-
efiting UNICEF's humanitarian efforts in Lebanon, brought together various
Arab, American, and Israeli poets to talk about the harsh suffering of people in
Lebanon and "the massacre of Palestinians in the Sabra and Shatila refugee
camps in Lebanon."[57] For this occasion, Jordan read her poem "Moving
Towards Home," in which she declares:

> I was born a Black woman
> and now
> I am become a Palestinian
> against the relentless laughter of evil
> there is less and less living room
> and where are my loved ones?
>
> It is time to make our way home.[58]

Jordan is but one black woman among many others—Toni Cade Bambara,
Angela Davis, Fannie Lou Hamer, Audre Lorde, Toni Morrison, Sojourner
Truth, Alice Walker, and Phillis Wheatley—who cherished and valued human
lives. They insisted on the safe return "home" of displaced persons "without
grief without wailing aloud." The only way Jordan could return home—return
to the promise of freedom, liberty, and love imagined by and often denied to
disenfranchised people—was by publicly "talk[ing] about home."[59] Home, for
the poet, signified a sense of belonging in and to a world of justice in which
violence was not tolerated and where the imaginings of a "Beloved
Community" held within it safety, comfort, and free will. Jordan searched for
this place, this home, her entire life.

An examination of Jordan's activist work and political writing during this
period speaks volumes to her evolving beliefs and values concerning democracy, civil and political rights, and people of color throughout the world. While
she did not readily consider herself a spokeswoman for the disenfranchised,
the tired, the weak, and even the strong visionaries in the world, a critical
review of her life proves that she indeed was such a spokesperson. Momentous
are Jordan's public speaking performances and international campaigns for
justice; her protests against nuclear power, Nicaragua's Contra War, U.S.

international policies on the Israeli invasion of Lebanon, and war in El Salvador; as well as her politically influenced travels across the globe. After this period and into the 1990s she also found the energy and strength to write such significant publications as *Kissing God Goodbye: New Poems 1991–1997, I Was Looking at the Ceiling and Then Saw the Sky, Haruko/Love Poems, Naming Our Destiny: New and Selected Poems, Lyrical Campaigns: Selected Poems,* and *June Jordan's Poetry for the People: A Revolutionary Blueprint,* coedited by Lauren Muller and the Poetry for the People Collective.

In sum, the political writings and activist efforts of June Jordan, New York native, international activist, and eventual founder of Poetry for the People Collective at the University of California, Berkeley, serve as examples of the brilliance, rage, conflict, and optimism at the heart, not only of this particular black woman writer but also other political writers, artists, and activists of her time. Jordan always wrote for a clearly defined purpose, as highlighted in her statement, "I expect a distinctively Black poem to speak for me as-part-of-an-us."[60] Indeed, the poet utilized both the written and spoken word to advocate a return to the fundamental elements of human rights: civil liberties, fair treatment, education and literacy, and access to the political process. She also worked to eradicate other systems that challenge democratic order and perpetuate global injustice. Even today, Jordan's writing continues to speak for, and give voice to, the experiences of the Third World, the poor, and women everywhere. Her work, from her writing, travels, teaching, speaking performances, and life, were, and continue to be, forms of political art contributing revolutionary-based efforts to peace, prosperity, fairness, and universal equality. She was a serious artist, a revolutionary thinker, and a brave activist whose dedication to human rights can be measured, in part, by her involvement in various civil rights movements, her numerous published writings, and her commitment to political work.

Furthermore, Jordan's writing and activist work demonstrate her constant awareness of identity politics. In other words, Jordan believed her personal and political engagement with the world was heavily influenced by the art that she and other black artists produced during the time, whether in the form of essays, poetry, or librettos. Jordan's employment of figurative images and powerful words in her writing conveys messages of hope and liberation through what she often referred to as "democratic language"—language that is always political and revolutionary and that includes the realities of many voices often excluded from the mainstream discourse on human and civil rights: "our language cannot refuse to reflect the agonizing process of alienation from ourselves. If we collaborate with the powerful then our language will lose its currency as a means to tell the truth in order to change the truth."[61] Jordan's emphasis on the honesty of democratic language allowed her to self-identify as a revolutionary artist. Her writing, according to Adrienne Torf, is "about survival, about heart, and voice and where one finds power with others in the world. This can be found through honesty and truth."[62]

In a 1981 interview with Karla Hammond, Jordan shared her understanding of a revolutionary artist. She stated, "Anyone who is a serious artist is a revolutionary whether that person is a painter or a musician, etc." The poet continued with,

> That's the nature of being an artist. That's what creation is about whether we're talking about Yeats or Neruda, Garcia Lorca, Mistral, Vallejo, or Adrienne Rich. . . . Creation is revolutionary. All the artists whom I care about most in poetry, and otherwise, are political revolutionaries at work.[63]

According to Jordan, for one to identify as a revolutionary artist requires one to understand that one's work, life, and activist efforts are always political statements. Jordan herself made political statements when she traveled to Lebanon, Nicaragua, the Bahamas, Mississippi, Oregon, Israel, Palestine, and Northern Ireland. She made political statements by participating in rallies and demonstrations, and by crafting writings on the revitalization of Harlem with Buckminister Fuller, on Mississippi's proposals for land reform, and on the underrepresentation of black women in the Black Arts Movement. Clearly, she always identified herself as a revolutionary artist and activist who was unwilling to submit to inequality, violence, and benign neglect. June Jordan was devoted to protesting the systems and people that she disagreed with, both politically and personally.

FIVE

The Voice of the Children

While June Jordan was beginning a teaching career, producing scores of poetry and newspaper editorials, and participating in struggles for freedom, she was also writing important books for children and young adults. Her books *Dry Victories*, *Fannie Lou Hamer*, *New Life: New Room*, *Kimako's Story*, and *The Voice of the Children* are important multigenre and poetic resources for examinations of contemporary issues that affect and even threaten the lives of young people. What are the implications of these works in terms of social realities, language differences, and identity markers? Specifically, what are the implications of these brave books in a world where children and young adults are taught codes of standards at the neglect and disregard of their own cultural and linguistic practices? And who was Jordan becoming politically, artistically, and intellectually as she crafted these books—as she embraced the sophistication of multiple languages, including Black English, and as she left the 1960s and 1970s and entered the 1980s and 1990s? How did Jordan move from writing books for youngsters to focusing on such topics as the political agenda of the Reagan administration?

Jordan's writing career should serve unmistakably as a source of ideas and ideals for public policy, education, and the teaching of social justice. Her decision to write for children was a logical one, given her concerns with education and safety, language preservation and the politics of Black English, and children's rights. Against this backdrop, Jordan made a unique and valuable contribution to children's literature, especially to the burgeoning field of black children's literature:

> When I was a child I never wanted to grow up because it was obvious that grownups were these really unhappy people. All the time they did things they didn't want to do. They went to work. They woke up early. They pretended to like neighbors. They stayed married.[1]

June Jordan's contributions to children's and young-adult literature are worthy of examination, for they challenge readers to acknowledge the experiences of youth as valid. Her representative writings respond to the social pressures, choices, and dilemmas of young people who use language to reveal ideas about the politics of identity and the freedom of expression. Such themes have since taken center stage in the works of contemporary black children's and young-adult authors, such as Jacqueline Woodson and Angela Johnson.

The following discussion on Jordan's writing for young readers examines the aesthetics as well as the political implications and educational relevance of *The Voice of the Children* (1968), *His Own Where* (1971), *Fannie Lou Hamer* (1972), *Dry Victories* (1972), *New Life: New Room* (1975), and *Kimako's Story* (1981), as they relate to the poet's teaching and activist work.

> They are the people who have
> tried for hundreds of years
> to find their freedom.[2]

In 1968, Jordan and Terri Bush completed their young-adult text *The Voice of the Children*. This book, a collection of poetry and prose written by young people between the ages of nine and seventeen, is composed of expressions of their opinions on politics, poverty, life, and the world. The contributors, often economically disadvantaged, are students attending various New York City public schools. Jordan's work with these young people and her inclusion of their work in this volume (and also in *Soulscript*) demonstrates her ability to combine social activism and responsibility with teaching the tools of empowerment. *The Voice of the Children* brings awareness to a population whose voices and experiences are often ignored or silenced by those who hold power over them. In using the youths' workshopped writing, many of which are written in Black English, Jordan makes the point that language, in any form and at any time, is a currency of power. Language, as a currency of power, expression, love, and identity should be cherished, valued, and used to communicate differences and resolve conflict—a belief Jordan shared with the youth she worked with in New York City.

Although the writing style, sentence structure, and word choice may not be "grammatically correct" according to the rules of academic discourse, the text draws in readers with its powerful, versatile, and often pain-filled language. In the opening selection "Ghetto," fourteen-year-old Vanessa Howard writes,

"Nine out of ten times when a person hears the word 'ghetto' they think of Black people first of all. They think just about every Black child comes from a Ghetto with lots of brothers and sisters."[3] Vanessa goes on to offer what she believes is other people's understanding of the word—"Black, garbage, slum areas"—before powerfully concluding: "I think they put all Black people in a box marked 'ghetto' which leaves them having no identity. They should let Black people be seen for themselves, not as one reflection on all."[4]

This poem speaks to many personal and political issues. The young writer's employment of an unidentified "they" suggests that she is talking about a subject who is not "Black" and who has the power to relegate black people to small, isolated living spaces—"a box."[5] Likewise, the poem speaks to urgent problems that Jordan, herself, was openly battling during this period: segregation, naming, and racial mythologies that denigrated people of color. The poem's closing line, "They should let Black people be seen . . . not as one reflection on all,"[6] supports Jordan's struggle with identity, writing, activism, and love. However, just as Vanessa Howard writes in "Ghetto," the inclination of "they"—the dominant culture—is to fit you—a specifically labeled and marked "other"—into a box. Jordan, Howard, and the other writers in *The Voice of the Children* embraced the realities of their varied lives and demonstrated a commitment to honest language.

Readers can never really escape the words and ideas presented in this collection, for the young writers keep giving until the last line of the last poem. They give readers and supporters more hope, inspiration, and determination to fight for the human right to have their voices heard. These poems invite readers to enter into a world where differences are embraced, languages are cherished, and injustices are absent. The world imagined by Jordan and the young authors is in juxtaposition to the actual world in which these same youths lived during the 1960s and 1970s. On the one hand, there were groups campaigning for social, political, and civil rights. On the other, there were those who supported the maintenance of the status quo—a system of intolerable inequalities—which included the threat of nuclear war and underfunded public schools, especially in minority communities. Wherever the divisions lie, *The Voice of the Children* contributes to a public discussion on rights, politics, and the state of the world. Each piece presents feelings of bitterness and resentment at the marginalization of inner-city youth in society; highly developed analyses of the way in which the world is constructed are alive on every page.

According to Jordan,

The Voice of the Children has given poetry readings on WBAI, Channel 31, Channel 13, Channel 7, and at Hunter College, Queens College, and St. Marks in the Bowery. These poets and writers have been published in *The Village Voice*, *McCall's*, *UHURU*, *The New York Times*, *The Now Voices*, *HERE I AM*, *SOULSCRIPT*, and the list is very long.[7]

Jordan writes about the collection's namesake, "Voice of the Children" [8]—a group that she cofounded with Terri Bush and the director (1967–1970)—in her closing line: "Who really matter are these young people: these new lives: original, furious, gentle, broken, lyrical, strong, and summoning."[9] Unfortunately, the work with the youth came to an abrupt halt because public funds to support the program were cut. On this latter point, Bush, one of the teachers in the program, responded, "The children were really doing very well and showed real writing talent. . . . But it became difficult to go on without the proper staff and support."[10]

It can be assumed that *The Voice of the Children*—the group and the book—motivated Jordan to do even more work with youth as a teacher and research assistant, especially as she came increasingly to notice that the politics of movements, including the Civil Rights Movement, and legislation in this country ignore the rights of children. At a 1978 conference for America's Child Welfare League, Jordan presented a narrative-based position paper on the neglected, abused, and forgotten children in the world, from "the desolate fixity of the Puerto Rican teenagers who sat on my stoop, on 20th Street in Manhattan, trying to make babies to the sound of plastic radios . . . [to] the torn-up gut quandaries of my son, a Black man at Harvard University."[11] It should be noted that Jordan never fully reconciled sending her son to Harvard University, given her mixed feelings about Ivy League universities, her own involvement with them, and her political disposition concerning the education of students of color in America. In a moving keynote address entitled "Old Stories: New Lives," the poet tells of why young people will not grow to adopt the common adult way of thinking and behaving and will not allow our failures and heartaches to become theirs: "In the name of motherhood and fatherhood and education and good manners, we threaten and suffocate and bind and ensnare and bribe and trick children into wholesale emulation of our ways."[12] Once they are "tricked," they eventually grow into older people who either believe that they are hated "and that nobody really liked [them],"[13] or struggle with their identities in relation to other people.

The position paper she presented at the America's Child Welfare League conference and the publication of *The Voice of the Children* are benchmarks of Jordan's development as a teacher, writer, activist, and intellectual. Her primary stand was a concern for the welfare, protection, and education of all children, affirming that youths are "legitimate human beings"[14] whose voices must be heard. Adrienne Torf articulates this message best when she insists that Jordan had faith in young people's abilities to collaboratively instigate social and political change that can greatly impact all of humanity.[15] E. Ethelbert Miller echoes this sentiment as well, by informing me that on the rare occasion of meeting the poet's son, June Jordan and Christopher David Meyer appeared to be as close as a mother and son could be.[16] Clearly, Jordan's dedication to children stems, in great measure, from her relationship with her son, her own childhood upbringing—one scarred by possible abuse, name calling, and family and school-based fights—as well as her early experiences with love, and her youthful experiments with sex.[17] Her dedication to young people, and thus her drive to return *home* by examining her own multifaceted identities, signifies Jordan's desire to reclaim life and living spaces for all people, including the youngest of us. This message is expressed in her poems "Moving Towards Home," "Home: January 29, 1984," and "Calling on All Silent Minorities," works that are crucial to one's understanding of the poet's social activism, freedom fights, and children's and young-adult writings.

> Sheep-eye Sheep eye
> where yo' little lamb?
> Way down in the valley. . .[18]

In her 1972 biography titled *Fannie Lou Hamer*, written for children of all ages, Jordan recounts Mrs. Hamer's life by addressing disparities between rich and poor, black and white, and boss and employee. As mentioned in a previous chapter, the biography demonstrates that racism and hunger should be challenged by ordinary, loving, conscious visionaries, such as Mrs. Hamer, who are willing to organize and work for social change, even under the threat of death.

Throughout the book, Mrs. Hamer's voice is portrayed in rhythmical Black English Vernacular, which does not diminish Mrs. Hamer's experiences. Rather, it makes available a language of belonging, protest, and love used by Civil Rights activists in the Mississippi Delta and other black communities during the 1960s and 1970s. The loving portrayal of Mrs. Hamer's Black English Vernacular represents her humanity and tolerance, as captured in the activist's belief, "Ain' no such a thing as I can hate anybody and hope to see God's face."[19]

It is significant to note that Jordan celebrates Mrs. Hamer's intelligence, courage, and ability to affect positive social and political change because of the invaluable influence she had on the poet's life. The book's portrayal of the activist as a heroine is, nevertheless, out of the ordinary. Traditionally, young people are made to identify heroes as academics, athletes, and political leaders who are, for the most part, male. Mrs. Hamer is a woman who had few educational opportunities: "Her family was so poor, Fannie Lou soon had to help out, full-time. She had to leave school, at the end of the sixth grade."[20] She learned how to create her own opportunities by taking advantage of the limited resources at her disposal: "As a teenager, she would go around to her friends, and she would say, 'Now what you think? Black people work so hard, and we ain' got nothin' to show for it. . . . You know one thing: that ain' hardly right.'"[21] Mrs. Hamer's activist efforts were greatly impacted by the systematic denial of civil rights and equal opportunities for black people in America. At the same time, she continued to develop a powerful, steadfast voice cultivated from her childhood encounters: "When she was thirteen, a white man had poisoned and killed her family's favorite cow, Della. . . . Fannie Lou never forgot the murder of her cow. Right then and there, she decided that, whatever it would take to overcome this white hatred, she would do that thing."[22]

Mrs. Fannie Lou Hamer fought in every imaginable way to secure civil rights—mainly voting allowances—for Southern black people. Her fights inspired Jordan to quite literally follow in her footsteps: Jordan's indomitable spirit led her to Mississippi and other places in the American South on many occasions. Later, the poet traveled to, and wrote about, the Middle East, Bosnia, Nicaragua, Northern Ireland, Cuba, and other politically devastated places with committed revolutionaries. Jordan believed that all forms of injustice are connected and, therefore, all such forms of injustice should be eradicated: "The difference between South Africa and rape," Jordan once stated, "and my mother trying to change my face and my father wanting me to be a boy was not an important difference to me."[23] She believed wholeheartedly that all such sufferings are violations of the human spirit and the right to live a safe, threat-free life everywhere and at all times.

Jordan's values, connected to her mentor and mother figure, Mrs. Fannie Lou Hamer, defined for her the significance of international protests and organization, and the necessity of international campaigns to rescue all people, especially children, from abuse, poverty, and hunger. The children's biography of Mrs. Fannie Lou Hamer serves as a testament to Jordan's admiration of the activist and her commitment to the struggle.

In a *New York Times* review titled "Can't hate anybody and see God's face," Pulitzer Prize-winning author Alice Walker[24] writes of Jordan's biography of Mrs. Fannie Lou Hamer: "Yes, this book is short and slight," begins Walker, "and the illustrations are pale and soulless, unlike their subject or the vivid, vigorous language of the text. But happiness is the first full-length book about so great a woman as Mrs. Fannie Lou. Read on, children."[25] If Jordan always had her way, then all children would be reading books that affirmed the beauty of their identities—a point reaffirmed by Jordan's travels throughout the Mississippi Delta in the 1960s and 1970s, and eventually to Nicaragua in the 1980s.

Jordan's admiration of Mrs. Hamer stayed with her long after the activist had died. In her poem "Mrs. Fannie Lou Hamer: In Memoriam," Jordan opens with the following:

You used to say, "June?
Honey when you come down here you
supposed to stay with me. Where
else?"
Meanin home
against the beer the shotguns and the
point of view of whitemen don'
never see Black anybodies without

some violent itch start up.
                        The ones who
said, "No Nigga's Votin in This Town . . .
Lessen it be feet first to the booth"
Then jailed you
beat you brutal
bloody/battered/beat
you blue beyond the feeling
of the terrible

And failed to stop you.[26]

Jordan ends the poem with "of love," which both honors Mrs. Hamer's undying commitment to black life in Mississippi and the entire South, and immortalizes this important heroine who was obviously a role model, mother figure, and mentor to Jordan. In Mrs. Hamer's political likeness, Jordan continued to teach, write, fight, travel, and love. The poet's various other writings attest to her commitment to honoring the struggle of past heroines, such as Fannie Lou Hamer and Phillis Wheatley, by acknowledging the power of young people.

Her text *Dry Victories* (1972) is a perfect example of Jordan's pursuit to continue Mrs. Hamer's work. It begins as a conversation between two young black boys Jerome and Kenny, about misunderstood elements of U.S. history during and after the Civil War and Reconstruction. The conversation, written in the form of an interview and in preparation for a performance that the boys are planning at a local community center, establishes strong parallels between those earlier periods and the political events of the 1960s and 1970s. Images invite comparison between the Civil War and the Vietnam War, and between the lives of black people in the 1870s and the 1970s. Young Jerome and Kenny reflect on how people lived over one hundred years before. They also discuss revisionist history, facts, and events excluded from their formal public-school education. While this conversation occurs between the boys, Jordan employs various illustrations—a copy of the Declaration of Independence, images of war, depictions of the lives of sharecroppers, and pictures of burial sites—to prove to readers that not much has changed over the course of a century. This is the overall message of *Dry Victories*. In the "Note to the Reader" at the beginning of the book, Jordan writes the following brief message:

> "We" is poor and tired of poverty, Black and white, right here, in America. "We" is poor and bored by piece a papers don't hardly mean nothing at all. "We" is poor and want to change the paper into land and liberty and like that, no delay. We hope you dig the pictures and get into the truth behind them terrible things you need to know. And, if you don't know, right away, what these pictures mean, then check them out.[27]

Although the book was written over thirty years ago, the images are so well captured and placed in the book that a present day reader can readily understand the points Jerome and Kenny make about social and political struggle:

> Jerome: What you think the parents and them other folks will do? After they hear all this?
> Kenny: Hard to say, brother. But maybe they do something. Be about time. About time to do something.[28]

Writer Janet Harris, in her *New York Times* review of *Dry Victories*, writes, "I could dig knowing Kenny and Jerome. They're a couple of black teenagers having a rap about a show they want to put on at the Center." Harris continues: "It's called 'Dry Victories,' and that means, as Jerome explains, '*nothing-like-victory*' be taking place, ever, during Reconstruction days or in them other days, the days of Civil Rights."[29] Harris writes that throughout the entire book, from the boys' conversations to the various images, Jordan rightfully captures many historic events, such as slavery and emancipation, and evokes human emotions, namely anger and bitterness. Though the end of the book is ambiguous, Harris believes that *Dry Victories* is an example of a call to social action and responsibility. Like all of Jordan's books for young readers, *Dry Victories* rejects the argument that children of color from low socioeconomic backgrounds and urban communities are a part of a deficit model, that they are intellectually and emotionally inferior to their white counterparts, and that their perspectives are unimportant and undeveloped. In this rejection, Jordan reaffirms both the rights and the privileges of young people, including those of her own son. Published in 1975, Jordan's children's book *New Life: New Room* focuses on familial love by emphasizing the elements of compromise and collective responsibility between siblings as they prepare their home and lives for the addition of a new baby: "On top of Momma getting so big and so sleepy, the apartment was beginning to be small." Jordan continues by turning attention to the young characters in the book: "Rudy [ten-year-old], Tyrone [nine-year-old], and Linda [six-year-old] were not ready for a small house. But they had to get ready because, if they didn't, one night, the new baby would come home."[30] The story is told through the eyes of a young girl, Sister Linda, whose family lives in a two-bedroom apartment. Since her mother is about to have a baby, Linda must give up her space on the living room sofa and share a room with her two older brothers.

The story centers, in part, on Linda's efforts to work with her brothers to determine how they will make the transition to sharing the small space of the room, from organizing the beds to decorating and deciding which toys to keep so that everyone is satisfied: "Linda couldn't understand. No matter who told her, again and again, she couldn't understand why she had to give up her place."[31] In time, Linda and her brothers come to understand the importance of sharing space and making room for the new baby, and they eagerly celebrate the change: "And they [Linda, Tyrone, and Rudy] were off, painting, bumping, spilling, dabbing, dripping, poking, streaming, splashing, red and yellow and blue over the glass [the window]."[32] Jordan asserts that the situation presented in *New Life: New Room* is a common one for many children, especially in New York City—large in population and building size, but small in living space.

This children's book represents another of Jordan's attempts to showcase the ability of young people to take on responsibility and to collaborate on important decisions. Around the time that Jordan wrote this book, she was working on other pursuits, leading writing workshops and teaching college-level courses. She was also writing plays. *In the Spirit of Sojourner* was produced at the Public Theatre in New York City in the late 1970s; the documentary *The Issue* was performed in the 1980s and *For The Arrow That Flies by Day* had a staged reading at the Shakespeare Festival in New York City in the early 1980s. With musician Adrienne Torf, Jordan completed *Freedom Now Suite* in the early 1980s as well as *The Break* and *Bang, Bang Uber Alles* in the mid 1980s. These collaborations are discussed in greater detail in a later chapter. *Kimako's Story*, published in 1981, is a short book inspired by and dedicated to "Rebecca Walker Leventhal [Alice Walker's daughter] and to Little Valerie on West 20th Street in Manhattan, New York."[33] *Kimako's Story* is a stream of consciousness tale told from the perspective of a seven-year-old girl who lives in Harlem, New York. It opens, "My name is Kimako. I am seven going on eight. This is the best way I always like to sit./On the bottom step of the stoop and in front of my mother I can see everything and everybody."[34] Through Kimako's descriptions of her daily activities—having her hair braided, playing in the park, walking Bucks, her friend's dog (not surprisingly the name of young June Jordan's dog), or interacting with people in the neighborhood—readers gain insight into how one young, curious, black girl conceptualizes her world in a large metropolitan city. The inclusion of pictures, poetry, puzzles, and maps enhances the narrative style and illustrates Kimako's actions. Readers connect to Kimako easily because of the vivid language Jordan employs to describe Kimako's surroundings:

> The park was full of trees and bushes and dogs and men who wore the same shirt and the same pants, and no socks, day after day, while they played checkers on the concrete tables or they passed around brown paper bags of wine and whiskey. That was one end of the park.[35]

Readers also hear the seriousness and concern in Kimako's voice upon discovering a sleeping man in the park:

> One morning, on Bucks's first walk for the day, it was raining hard. We went over to the park to look at everything, and do you know what we found? Inside the concrete monkey jungle there was a regular man, a real man, squeezed up into one of the holes! The man was fast asleep. He must have been there all night long. Bucks and I stood there for a minute, to see if he would snore or wake up, but he didn't, so we left him alone.[36]

At the story's end, Kimako reluctantly returns Bucks to his seventeen-year-old owner, Bobby, who has just returned from a wedding ceremony in Puerto Rico. In a voice of hope and care, Kimako says,

> I never stopped loving Bucks. And I never forgot the way the two of us did every-thing, or what we did. And this is my plan. When my mother asks me what do I want for my birthday, which is coming up in August (I'm a Leo), I am going to tell her I want a little Bucks.[37]

With Bucks, Kimako felt protected as she ventured throughout her neighbor-hood; she never felt lonely when her mother went to work, leaving Kimako and her younger brother Charlie alone in the house.

In this short story, set in the time span of one week, Jordan captures, through words and poetry, pictures and memories, the curiosities of the cen-tral character, Kimako. She also demonstrates a need for the experiences of young people to be affirmed, or recognized. This point is confirmed by Jordan's friends, poets Bob Holman, Suheir Hammad, and E. Ethelbert Miller, and well articulated by Adrienne Torf in her declaration that "Jordan had faith in young people to do what is right."[38] Torf's sentiment echoes loudly in all of Jordan's writings for and about youths. As with her own work, Jordan always wanted to protect young people from censorship and exclusionary measures that dis-miss their experiences as insignificant; *Kimako's Story* serves as one example of such an effort, an effort toward justice.

One can assume that Kimako represents a young June Jordan based on obvi-ous similarities: As a child, Jordan lived with her parents in Harlem, New York and owned a dog named Bucks, and many years later, she owned a dog named Amigo. Jordan, like Kimako, was preoccupied with exploring communal rela-tionships and admiring the architectural designs of public spaces, including parks and museums. Another connection can be made with the assumption that the title character in *Kimako's Story* (1981) is named after one of Jordan's friends, Kimako Baraka, sister of the Newark, New Jersey poet, political activist, and teacher, Amiri Baraka. Kimako Baraka's and June Jordan's personal connec-tion with one another occurred in New York City during the late 1970s and early 1980s. Shortly after Kimako Baraka—an out lesbian, Broadway dancer, actress, and political activist—was killed in Manhattan Plaza in 1984, [39] Jordan wrote the poem "3 for Kimako," published in her 1985 collection *Living Room: New Poems*. The short, two-line poem thus reads, "Kimako Baraka/1936–1984."[40]

Whether Jordan was writing about aspects of her own life, dedicating the story to one of her friends, or a combination of the two, it is wise to conclude that *Kimako's Story* is a continuation of Jordan's journeys and explorations of various sociopolitical issues in America. Through Kimako's voice and the youthful, experienced voices of her other characters, Jordan confronts press-ing political and social issues such as homelessness, overcrowded urban living spaces, segregation, inequality, and the responsibilities of adolescence. Her writing does not exclusively adopt an audience of young people, but includes

June Jordan sits on a horse-drawn produce cart near 7th Avenue and 152nd Street in Harlem, New York, date unknown. Courtesy of Valerie Orridge.

parents, teachers, and leaders who claim an investment in the rights of children as well. One can connect the poet's children's and young-adult writings to the prevalent socioeconomic conditions of underfunded schools in "urban" communities and of schooling for children of color during the 1960s and 1970s. In her essay "Problems of Language in a Democratic State," Jordan recalls her initial entrance into the teaching profession. She writes:

> Back in the 60s, popular wisdom had it that the only American boys and girls who could neither read nor write were Black. This was a function of the poverty of culture or vice versa: I forgot which. But anyway, Black children had something wrong with them. They couldn't talk right. They couldn't see straight. They never heard a word you said to them. . . . And another thing, their parents were no good or they were alcoholics or illiterate or, anyhow, uninterested, inept, and rotten role models.[41]

Black children such as Kimako (*Kimako's Story*); little Fannie Lou Hamer (*Fannie Lou Hamer*); Rudy, Tyrone, and Linda (*New Life: New Room*); or Jerome and Kenny (*Dry Victories*) represent the voices of countless children living in black communities. They also represent the shared realities of communities and families that honor experiential forms of learning such as exploring one's own neighborhood, interacting with neighbors, and speaking Black English. They also depict forms of black culture, black aesthetics, and modes of survival that are often unaccounted for or undocumented in popular narratives of success, literacy, and belonging. In her children's books, Jordan sought to create a forum of lively discourse that would forever combat racist notions of black life and childhood. This point represented the poet's personal and political devotion to social change.

As a teacher and then as a writer of children's and young-adult literature, Jordan noticed the rich varieties of language and literacy activities that were brought into classrooms by these same young people: "Their language, their style, their sense of humor, their ideas of smart, their music, their need for a valid history and a valid literature—history and literature that included their faces and their voices."[42] Simultaneously, Jordan paid attention to the need for black children, and all children of color, to have "serious teachers who would tell them, 'C'mon, I see you. Let me give you a hand,'—all of this was pretty well ridiculed and rejected, or denied to them."[43] Her writing, teaching, philosophy of life, and love for children led her in the direction of collaborative social activism with people committed to political and educational change. Such people included poets and writers Sara Miles, Jan Levi Heller, E. Ethelbert Miller, Marilyn Hacker, Adrienne Rich, Alexis DeVeaux, Jodi Braxton, Ruth Forman; musician Adrienne Torf; political commentator Matthew Rothschild; and numerous students in the Poetry for the People Collective at the University of California, Berkeley. However, there were some people who believed that Jordan was beginning to shift her focus more toward politics at the expense of her art form.

On asking Julius Lester, author, educator, and former friend of Jordan, about any aspect of Jordan's political involvement following the vibrant decade of the 1960s, he explains: "I think June and I were moving in separate directions, she more toward political involvement. . . . I think I had been more involved in the sixties in the civil rights movement, black power movement, and anti-war movement, a time when June was raising a son, etc."[44] Lester did support Jordan's literary pursuits during this time, especially upon her acceptance of the Prix de Rome prize in the 1970s and with the publication of her 1971 collection *Some Changes*. However, Jordan and Lester's relationship came to an end in the mid 1970s with Lester's critical review of one of the poet's books. The review, commissioned under the editorial direction of John Leonard for the *New York Times Book Review*, was never published; nevertheless, Jordan, according to Lester, held a grudge. Lester continues:

> When I wrote the review of June's book, which cost us our friendship, our lives had moved in perhaps opposite directions. She was passionately involved politically; I was a single parent trying to live the ideals of humanism and non-violence I had learned in the sixties and integrate them into the life of an 8 year old boy who liked to play hockey because "I like to hit people," as he gleefully explained to me. . . . One way was not superior to the other. I saw them as different paths toward the same end, namely the transformation of society into one in which the overriding value was the lives of people rather than profit.[45]

Jordan's thinking, as Lester explains, was moving in more political directions. Her work with various activists, artists, and students in New York City and eventually in other places, such as California, and her manifesto of rage and hope, are the things that helped to create her political agenda.

The visionary power of her children's and young-adult literature are indicative of June Jordan's quest for justice. Her writing career—as evident by the publication of *The Voice of the Children*, *Fannie Lou Hamer*, *New Life: New Room*, *Dry Victories*, *Kimako's Story*, *Civil Wars*, and particularly her memoir, *Soldier: A Poet's Childhood*—represents a dedication to make words work, to rally and call forth the spirit of a people invested in love and freedom, and to respond to injustice wherever it is found.

These particular children's and young-adult books by June Jordan outline the multiple sites of injustice that she sought to critique, establishing a link among ethos, pathos, and logos in writing for and about youth. Such sites include her childhood home; her writing classrooms and poetry workshops through Teachers & Writers Collaborative and Poetry for the People Collective; her visits to Nicaragua, Israel, Palestine, Lebanon, and Northern Ireland; the locations of the East Los Angeles riots; and the spaces of rape and all forms of hatred. Furthermore, for Jordan, this link oftentimes places revolutionary writers—especially black women writers and thinkers, such as Angela Davis, Audre Lorde, Alice Walker, and Sojourner Truth—within the confines of a revolution for freedom of expression. This point is well developed in Jordan's poem "Independence Day in the U.S.A.":

> But I am living inside the outcome
> of the only legitimate revolution
> in human history
> and the operator will not place my call to Cuba
> the mailman will not carry my letters to Managua
> the State Department will not okay my visa
> for a short-wave conversation
> and you do not speak English
>
> and I can dig it[46]

Once "inside the outcome," Jordan advocates that people write about that place and script narratives of progressive emancipation. These are the things she taught to her students in the group "The Voices of the Children," in her books for young people, and in her work for universal justice.

Given the sociopolitical conditions in society that attempted (and still attempt) to categorize black children as inferior to their white counterparts and efforts by nonprogressive educators to invalidate the languages of non-white students,[47] Jordan, during the years 1968–1971, accepted an active role as writer for children and young adults. Jordan believed, as do contemporary black educators Geneva Smitherman, Lisa Delpit, and James Rickford,[48] that in classrooms across America students are often taught to abandon their cultural and linguistic practices, to keep the "nonstandard" ways of living separate from how "real" people talk, think, and function in the public sphere. Yet black, Puerto Rican, and Asian kids, for example, have traditions that cherish varied and complex learning mediums—the languages that are spoken, the code switching that is heard, the music that is listened to, and the stories that are passed down from one generation to another. Such traditions, and their accompanying practices, can impact positively how children and young adults are taught in schools and come to participate in multiple discourse communities throughout society. Jordan articulates these points in essays collected in *On Call: Political Essays* (1985), *Affirmative Acts: Political Essays* (1998), and *Some of Us Did Not Die: New and Selected Essays of June Jordan* (2002); and in children and young-adult writings, such as *The Voice of the Children* (1968), *His Own Where* (1971), and *Dry Victories* (1972). The poet's articulation of such points reiterates, in one way, the necessity for human beings to learn how to coexist among other human beings, a sentiment expressed by Latoya Hardman, a New York City high-school teacher who values and teaches many of Jordan's writings: "To teach Jordan," according to Hardman, "is to examine her writings and life in relation to historical experiences of people during various time periods, . . . a lesson that has important implications for education and language instruction, and that can be gained from studying her literary contributions."[49]

Jordan's writing can be used to teach students and adults how to read texts by reading experiences. In some way, all of the poet's books, especially the ones for youth, highlight the value of song, resistance, optimism, education, cooperation, humor, love, and the power of critical thinking for survival in light of the historical fact that in American cities, especially "in Mississippi, Black people could be killed for thinking out loud."[50] Furthermore, Jordan's books for and about young people support her belief that it is okay for people to "be really different." This message was presented in her 1971 award-winning young-adult novel *His Own Where*, which is the first known young-adult novel in this country written exclusively in Black English.[51] *His Own Where* is a love story of political protest in which Jordan creatively establishes connections between language—Black English—and space—the urban redesign of Brooklyn's Bedford-Stuyvesant neighborhood—through the central characters, fourteen-year-old Angela Figeroa and sixteen-year-old Buddy Rivers. In her essay "Thinking About My Poetry (1977)," Jordan informs readers that the characters of Figeroa and Rivers are "based upon two 'regulars' of our workshop [Voices of the Children], and, of course, upon my own, personal life as a child growing up in Bedford-Stuyvesant."[52] Jordan's ability to do what critic Violet J. Harris (1990) refers to as "captur[ing] the orality of Black vernacular English without resorting to inaccurate dialect"[53] is experienced on every page of the text. In her authentic use of Black English—suggestive of the black literary tradition of orality, aurality, and signifying—Jordan demonstrates how young Buddy Rivers, with guidance from his father and after the abrupt departure of his mother, takes an interest in the design of safe space: "Buddy father clean the house down to the linoleum. Remove the moldings, . . . teach him, Buddy, how to calculate essentials how to calculate one table and two chairs. . . . House be like a workshop where men live creating how they live."[54]

The collaboration between Buddy and his father comes to an end when a car accident injures the father; nevertheless, Buddy does not falter in his commitment to safe space. He plants a community garden, repairs his home, paints the sidewalk in his Brooklyn neighborhood, and protects Angela, his girlfriend, from her parents' physical assaults and from being sent away to a strict home for young girls. At school, Buddy argues for the distribution of condoms and coeducational classes on sex for the students. Additionally, he reflects on the inadequate, unsafe city planning and street layout of public space that is to blame for his father's injuries:

> Call it accidental but to him, to Buddy, was no accident. Things set up like that. You cross the street you taking chances. Odds against you. Knock his father down, down from the sidewalk stop, down from the curb, down bleeding bad, ribs crushed. The lungs be puncture, and his father living slow inside a tent.[55]

Woven throughout the plot and narrative of this story are significant points articulated by Jordan in a number of her writings: the necessity of safe, unrestrictive public spaces; and the value of Black English. Jordan worked to make it possible for people to come together and talk with one another without the threat of spatial boundaries. For example, she wanted to lift buildings off street level so people could walk from river to river to engage in spontaneous interactive occasions. This point is reflected strongly in her collaborations with Buckminster Fuller. Together, they sought to remove the grid meant to dictate where people were forced to walk. *His Own Where*, according to Adrienne Torf, is an example of "a text that questioned space and spatial designs of where one could and could not walk and where cars could and could not park. Both Jordan's work with architect Fuller and her completion of the novel *His Own Where*, call for the creation of people's power and determination to improve living conditions."[56]

Jordan's second message, that Black English is a vital language and communicative form in that it allows users to confront and make sense of a world full of abandonment, violence, social inequality, and unsafe, restrictive street layout is clearly presented throughout *His Own Where*. The poet's words insist, "You be really different from the rest, the resting other ones."[57] Jordan uses this novel to enter into conversations on the victimization of children, children's bodies, and childhood; the value of cultural practices of black children; and the diverse language features and heritages of people of color in America. Such points are cleverly expressed in her 1970 edited collection *Soulscript: Afro-American Poetry*.[58]

Thematically connected to *His Own Where*, *Soulscript: Afro-American Poetry*, and her other children's and young-adult books is her work "Poem About My Rights." Here Jordan writes,

the point being that I can't do what I want
to do with my own body because I am the wrong

sex the wrong age the wrong skin and . . .
who in the hell set things up
like this[59]

Who insists on inequalities, violence, rape, imposed silence, and political isolation? Certainly not young people; therefore, Jordan committed herself to
writing for an audience of youths and to encouraging them to become writers
who will affirm cultural practices and campaign for the rights of other children
and young adults. Jordan was committed to these goals throughout her lifetime, probably because of the struggles of her parents and the violence she
experienced as a daughter and a woman "alone in the streets." The years
1968–1975, marked by the publication of her children's and young-adult
books (with the exception of *Kimako's Story*, published in 1981), served as a
time for Jordan to interrogate her concern for the welfare of young people,
the lyricism and brutality of her own childhood, her political responsibilities as
a black writer, and her participation in the Civil Rights Movement. Such interests further defined the poet's activities from the 1980s until her death in 2002.

Jordan's teaching experiences in the 1980s and the publication of her article "Nobody Mean More to Me Than You and the Future Life of Willie Jordan"
(1985) are intricately connected to her children's and young-adult writing of
the 1970s. During the 1980s, the poet was teaching literature courses at the
State University of New York at Stony Brook and writing essays and poems on
Black English, political protest, racism, and violence. Addressing all of these
concerns, "Nobody Mean More to Me" draws attention to the connections
among language, voice, power, and identity in its argument that black children
and members of black communities utilize Black English as a system of communication. According to Jordan,

> Black English is not exactly a linguistic buffalo, but we should understand its sta-
> tus as an endangered species, as a perishing, irreplaceable system of community
> intelligence, or we should expect its extinction, and, along with that, the extin-
> guishing of much that constitutes our own proud, and singular identity.[60]

Black English—which Jordan writes of in "Nobody Mean More to Me" and she
employs in *His Own Where, Soulscript, Fannie Lou Hamer, New Life: New Room*,
and other writings—signifies belonging, ways of knowing, freedom, citizenship, and language rights of black people. In the beginning of the essay, Jordan
discusses her course at Stony Brook, entitled "In Search of the Invisible Black
Woman," and her students' reactions to the language of Alice Walker's character, Celie, in *The Color Purple*. As the class discussed the novel, many of the
black students expressed their discomfort with Celie's language, specifically its
sound and structure. Instead of ignoring her students' reactions, Jordan facili-
tated an activity of translation that soon led to the class developing guidelines
for using Black English. This example illustrates Jordan's commitment to pre-
serving the cultural practices of people in both classrooms and communities.[61]

Her books on children's rights, her classroom teaching, and her championing for universal equality are all hallmarks of her activist agenda.

As argued throughout this volume, Jordan's books, essays, poems, keynote addresses, and reports are connected to major political events of the time. The publication of *His Own Where*, and eventually her essay "Nobody Mean More to Me," occurred at the outset of heightened attention toward the structure and functionality of neighborhoods in American cities and increasing levels of diversity in public-school classrooms. Similarly, Jordan's political essays collected in *Civil Wars* (1981) are signs of her political growth toward, and progressive vision of, an international and feminist agenda. Her involvement, activism, and writing were no longer limited to the politics of Black Nationalism in U.S. cities. She was now more concerned with addressing the politics of struggle among black Americans and people in so-called "Third World" countries, a term, as I mention in the first chapter, that denotes nations colonized by other nations and that are typically considered underdeveloped, nonindustrialized, and poor. For Jordan, such countries include, Palestine, South Africa, and Lebanon as well as the region of Central America. The subjects of and audiences for her work had grown from being exclusively black Americans in urban and rural black communities to a universal audience willing to resist imperialism, discrimination, war, and systemic violence. This became Jordan's way of embracing Martin Luther King, Jr.'s ideal of the beloved community and Malcolm X's call for an international rights movement; the poet openly joined with a community of conscious, serious artists and activists.

During this transformative period, Jordan demonstrated her commitment to fighting for the welfare of marginalized people by contemplating possible definitions of peace. For example, as a child she thought that she could encourage the government to intervene in the violent actions of her father, Granville, against her mother, Mildred. She called the government—political representatives, anyone with official power and authority—only to be ignored; no help or return phone call arrived. As an adult, Jordan soon realized that to fight this kind of abuse, and to get one step closer to peace, required solidarity among people from all parts of the world—from South Africa and Palestine to Cuba and the United States.

In 1989, Jordan crafted the poem "War and Memory" and dedicated it to creative writer, Jane Creighton, now an associate professor of English at the downtown campus of the University of Houston. The poem establishes connections between familial violence, such as the kind experienced in her childhood home, and systemic violence, such as global wars, the murderous deaths of millions of poor people, and racial domination. Jordan writes:

Daddy at the stove or sink. Large
knife nearby or artfully
suspended by his clean hand handsome
even in its menace

> slamming the silverware drawer
> open and shut/the spoons
> suddenly loud as the yelling
> at my mother[62]

Later in the same poem, she continues:

> I'd match him fast
> for madness
> lineage in wild display
> age six . . .
> I would race about for weaponry
> another chair a knife
> a flowered glass
> the radio
> "You stop it, Daddy! Stop it!"[63]

As a six-year-old child, young June Jordan quickly realized that she needed to take the power of physical violence away from her father and to break the silence imposed on her mother. She used her own weapons to defend her mother and herself from the "bully." Near the poem's conclusion (although there is never really an ending to any of Jordan's poems) she asserts, "Peace never meant a thing to me," before declaring,

> And from the freedom days
> that blazed outside my mind
> I fell in love
> I fell in love with Black men and White
> men Black
> women White women
> and I
> dared myself to say The Palestinians
> and I
> worried about unilateral words like Lesbian or Nationalist
> and I
> tried to speak Spanish when I travelled to Managua . . .
> and I wrote everything I knew how to write against apartheid[64]

All of these actions taken by June Jordan confirm her resistance to the humiliation and degradation of humanity. In committing to an anti-imperialist, international movement of resistance, she revisited her familial past, including the realities of a violent father with loving tendencies. Her writings, from her children's and young-adult books—including *Fannie Lou Hamer* and *Kimako's Story*—to her political articles in *The Progressive*—including "The Big-Time

Coward" and "Eyewitness in Lebanon" (reprinted in Jordan's *Affirmative Acts*)—all represent responses to inequalities of some kind: inattention to black activism, public neglect of the rights of youth, or the failure of U.S. foreign policy to avoid international warfare. The poet's responses to these issues, and the activist efforts that followed, always found themselves in her classroom. In the 1980s at the State University of New York at Stony Brook, she led teach-ins on apartheid and South Africa. In the 1990s at the University of California, Berkeley, she founded Poetry for the People, where she worked with young writers in poetry workshops and encouraged them to share their work at public readings.

Around the same time as the founding of Poetry for the People, Jordan spearheaded teach-ins on the Persian Gulf War. In the "Introduction" to *June Jordan's Poetry for the People: A Revolutionary Blueprint*, she writes:

> Towards the end of the previous semester I had conceived, organized, and directed a campus-wide "Teach-in" on the Persian Gulf War. Faculty colleagues of many disciplines, and student activists of several ideologies, and of every color and ethnicity and sexual persuasion fused their energies to create a very powerful day that was decently documented by local television, radio and press. Ours was, I might add, proudly, the first such "Teach-in" in the U.S.A.[65]

Finally, Jordan "had become part of an academic community where you could love school because school did not have to be something apart from, or in denial of, your own life and the multifarious new lives of your heterogeneous students!"[66] She could finally connect her art, her teaching, and her activism, and they all served political purposes. She learned how to examine and reexamine her childhood in New York City in order to uncover the reasons for her protests and resistances. All the while, she learned, with the support and admiration of her students, colleagues, and other activists, how to battle physical and global war with war—the kind of war that reflects the experiences of disenfranchised people. This latter lesson is also captured in *June Jordan's Poetry for the People*. In particular, the previously anthologized section in the blueprint entitled "Poetry for the People in a Time of War," a collection of writings by Jordan and her students, interrogates warfare from various vantage points: familial relationships, feminist perspectives, women and war, women and poverty, and women and body politics. In the poem "What I Mean," student-poet Leslie Shown writes:

> I mean who do I really think might hear me
> shout across three thousand miles of telephone line
> that there's nothin
> an Iraqi soldier might do to a Kuwaiti woman
> that an American soldier wouldn't do to an Iraqi woman[67]

Then in "To the Queers in Desert Storm," Vu qui Trac writes:

As I look for you
in the madmen's wet dreams
I never see the Hollywood casualties
the Pentagon would-be stars
Just hopeful upstarts
in the aisle waiting
to play heroes
to pay cultural dues
to die for bad art.[68]

Both Shown and Trac's poems reveal depictions of war. The first poem is rooted in dangerous politics, policies, ignored protests, and the failure of public morality: women living with no public protection from rape, brutality, or ongoing war. The second poem addresses fabricated news stories, capitalist perceptions, and glamorizations of war and fighting that forget the real casualties of violence and dismiss the horrors of the victimization of homosexuals in movies and the public sphere. Such ideas are further captured in "Case in Point," "Bosnia Bosnia," "The Bombing of Baghdad," "Apologies to All the People in Lebanon," "Rape Is Not a Poem," and "A Poem about Vieques, Puerto Rico," poems by Jordan that are collected in her various collections.

As Jordan embraced an anti-imperialist, international, and feminist agenda, her identity shifted from a black woman writer in New York City to a writer and activist educator in Berkeley, California. She was becoming a strong advocate for children, young adults, and women. In a 1990 *Essence Magazine* interview with writers and activists June Jordan and Angela Davis, conducted by columnist Cheryll Greene, Jordan elaborates on the need for women to create networks of solidarity, insisting that such networks can bring to the forefront issues that affect and threaten all women:

> Well, if you put together, for starters, Native American, Latina and African American women in this country, . . . I think we would be able to bring about the kinds of drastic changes that we need—much more . . . quickly than otherwise. And these issues . . . also have their reverberations among impoverished Asian women. And then there are the poor white women.[69]

Jordan wanted active alliances built in order to affect positive social change, be it peaceful or radical, for women, children, and communities of people tormented by violence. In 1987, she participated in a Washington, D.C.-based reading series for the Washington Project on the Arts exhibit *War and Memory: In the Aftermath of Vietnam*. At this event she read her poem "War and Memory," making difficult parallels between the violence in her Brooklyn household and neighborhood to the violence of the Vietnam War and the Jewish Holocaust. In the 1990s, she continued to lead and participate in teach-ins, demonstrations, and rallies. In early 2000, she joined Alice Walker, Angela Davis, and other activists to protest the death warrant and possible execution of political activist and journalist, Mumia Abu-Jamal, who was convicted of the 1982 murder of Pennsylvania police officer, Daniel Faulkner. (Abu-Jamal still asserts his innocence today.)

In 2001, Jordan participated in a reading to benefit the Boston Women's Fund for Breast Cancer. Throughout her life, she remained an active writer, even if, at times, it came at the sacrifice of her son, family, and intimate relationships. In her final days, she committed herself to completing her last book *Some of Us Did Not Die: New and Selected Essays of June Jordan*, which was released three months after her death. During her lifetime, Jordan read her poetry at the Studio Museum of Harlem, the Library of Congress, the United Nations, the U.S. Congress, the Guggenheim Museum, the Folger Shakespeare Library, Stanford University, the University of Iowa, and on Pacifica Radio and National Public Radio.

On September 22, 2002, members of the Black Caucus of the National Writers Union (NWU), the Seven Principles Institute Network (SPIN), and The Jazz Ministry Church in Manhattan sponsored "Remember June in September II: A Tribute to June Jordan" at Saint Peter's church. In attendance were NWU founding member Sarah Wright; poets and writers E. Ethelbert Miller, Amina Baraka, Amiri Baraka, Louis-Reyes Rivera, and Aka Weekes; and pianist Richard Cummings, along with a host of more than two hundred supporters. In the spring of 2004, a coalition of University-Five College groups in Massachusetts collaborated to honor Jordan's legacy by sponsoring "A Revolutionary Convening: The 2004 June Jordan Conference." Then, on October 6, 2005, the Poetry Society of America along with Cave Canem, Copper Canyon Press, and the MFA Program in Creative Writing at Hunter College in New York City sponsored "A Celebration of the Life and Work of June Jordan" in honor of the publication of *Directed by Desire: The Collected Poems of June Jordan*. Participating in this event were writers Cornelius Eady, Joy Harjo, Bob Holman, Yusef Komunyakaa, Jan Heller Levi, Donna Masini, Sara Miles, Honor Moore, and Adrienne Rich; as well as former Poetry for the People director Junichi Semitsu; author, Air America radio host, and close friend of Jordan, Laura Flanders; and Cave Canem fellow Shelagh Patterson. Additional tributes to recognize the publication of Jordan's collected poems are scheduled in New York City and in San Francisco, California.

Jordan's life was anything but ordinary, and her quest for a "Beloved Community" without national borders was admirable. Throughout her lifetime, she stood against police brutality and the murders of countless black and Puerto Rican youths, especially in New York City. She supported the Palestinian struggle, the Sandinistas in Nicaragua, and the fight against South African apartheid. Her poetry, such as "Moving Towards Home," "Lebanon, Lebanon," and "Apology to the People of Lebanon," represents Jordan's commitment to internationalizing coalitions to fight for freedom and justice, and to publicize the interconnectedness of local struggle to international struggle.

She sought freedom, love, justice, and equality for people, for herself, even if, as she admits, "Peace never meant a thing" to her.[70]

Years after Jordan began to write books for children and young adults and after she began to write an increasing amount of poetry in response to the social and political conditions of life in America, she became disheartened with media portrayals of nationhood, especially in the United States. In particular, she believed that both the media and the government promote visions of nationhood, nationalism, identity, and citizenship that exclude nonwhite peoples, including youth, from integrating fully into the mainstream. Such beliefs are clearly articulated in her essay collections *Civil Wars: Observations from the Front Lines of America* (1981), *Technical Difficulties: African American Notes on the State of the Union* (1992/1994), *Affirmative Acts: Political Essays* (1998), and *Some of Us Did Not Die* (2002). These writings establish parallels in the media's treatment of black people between the 1960s and the 1990s. In her essay "Black History as Myth," Jordan writes of how the media purposefully ignore the organizing efforts of communities of color. She writes, "At the end of the 1960s, American mass media rolled the cameras away from Black life and the quantity of print on the subject became too small to read."[71] Before mentioning the book *Black Macho and the Myth of the Superwoman* by Michelle Wallace in *Civil Wars*, Jordan insists, "the number of books published by and about Black people has been negligible since the beginning of this decade."[72]

One reason for such negligence is the portrayal of beauty and belonging that has become prevalent in popular culture and media circuits: "White Western authorities on beauty and honor and courage and historical accomplishment have denied and denigrated whatever and whoever does not fit their white Western imagery."[73] For example, many of the young people throughout the New York City boroughs with whom Jordan worked, did not fit into this imagery. She realized this early on, and she decided to take action against such images by mentoring and working with the talents of young people while affirming the beauty within them. In the late 1960s, she collaborated with educator, Terri Bush, and students in New York City. In the 1990s, Jordan worked with Lauren Muller and university students in California. In this way, she showed young people how words and emotions—their poetry—can work to combat racist and classist politics that govern mass media, state-based operations, and unfair educational practices.

In addition to Jordan's ongoing questioning of imposed standards and politics, she critiqued supposed ideals of liberty, democracy, and freedom as they help to define American leadership. For example, in her essay "America in Confrontation with Democracy," Jordan writes about activist Jesse Jackson's 1988 pursuit of the Democratic Presidential nomination: "Certainly, the phenomenon of a Black man bidding for the most powerful office in the world has raised, irreversibly, the expectations of Americans who . . . never even dreamed about accurate, or responsive, political representation."[74] After traveling to London in the late 1980s and realizing the lack of attention given to Jackson's campaign by international media, Jordan came back to New York City and tried to convince black media groups and leaders that Jackson "really had a shot at the title" and that "white Americans were listening to him."[75] Unfortunately, Jordan's efforts were short lived. Media moguls, white and black alike, censored Jesse Jackson just as public support for his candidacy dramatically increased.[76] Black media outlets did not have adequate resources to challenge the dominant media's rejection of Jackson's political vision, which included farmers, auto workers, working-class men and women, gays and lesbians, children and young adults, the Palestinian people, AIDS victims, and other people considered disfranchised. Further, Jordan believed that the censoring of Jackson via mass media reiterated "racist habits or attitudes in America" that did not decline during the Reagan administration despite popular belief to the contrary.[77]

During his presidential candidacy in 1988, Jesse Jackson beat Michael Dukakis to win the popular vote in the state of Michigan, but Jackson still did not become the Democratic nominee. He never reached the Oval Office; he was never inaugurated as president of the "free world." Nevertheless, according to Jordan, his

> Radiant temerity in the face of negligible funding, press censorship, and attack has elicited the respect, and restored the activist self-respect, of a new American majority: a multiracial populist coalition of citizens intent upon the *humane* expansion of their citizen entitlements.[78]

Jackson did not become the president, but for Jordan he "transformed the nature and the substance of acceptable political discourse in America."[79] Jordan learned a lot from Jackson's campaign concerning politics. She was learning even more "about American censorship."[80]

Jordan's opposition to "white Western imagery" and her dedication to Jackson's presidential campaign point to her own level of resistance to censorship.[81] A few years before Jackson's bid for the presidency, South End Press published Jordan's essay collection *On Call: Political Essays*. In the book's "Introduction" the poet discusses, among other things, how editors of publishing companies "whitelisted" her because of her political stance on issues affecting U.S. foreign relations with the Middle East and Nicaragua. She writes, "These editors hide behind 'many of us' who 'have problems' with me. Apparently, there is some magisterial and unnameable 'we' who decided—in the cowardly passive voice—what 'is publishable' or not." Jordan continues, "I need to know who is this 'we,' exactly? And what are 'the problems?'"[82] Jordan did not appreciate being censored; she refused to compromise her values and the direction she wanted her writing to follow.

As previously suggested, Jordan's uncensored language of democracy and freedom implies a continual need to fight against acts of silence and degradation. Throughout *On Call: Political Essays* the poet documents firsthand encounters with the dangers of being different (the media can censor you) and with the consequences of concealing those differences (silencing one's beliefs, values, and identities; accepting injustices; not fighting back). Her affirmations of freedom and justice and her refusal to be silenced took her to many places: London, Nicaragua, Israel, Palestine, and Lebanon. On many missions, she opposed racism, sexism, and violence in the United States and campaigned for human rights at home by conducting teach-ins, attending rallies and poetry readings, sitting in emergency rooms with police brutality victims , and organizing for and supporting Jesse Jackson's presidential campaign.

It is no coincidence that several years after the publication of *On Call: Political Essays* (1985), Jordan wrote the essay "Do You Do Well to Be Angry" (2001), in which she discusses the destruction of "the world we thought we knew" and poses the question in relation to the aftermath of the September 11th attacks in 2001: "And how shall we rebuild?"[83] How are we, the people living in this world, going to work together to create a new world that will not tolerate hate and will not promote hatred and oppression? For Jordan, such a world can only come to fruition through populist coalitions that are multifaceted: multiracial, multireligious, multilingual, and multicultural. She believed in "breaking the law:" when the law is wrong and unjust, "when the law produces and enjoins manifest and undue injury to a people, when the law punishes one people and privileges another, it is our moral obligation to break the law!"[84] One could say that Jordan broke the law by marrying a young white man in the 1950s at the onset of her involvement in American politics and civil rights movements, or by publicly admitting, years later, that she was a bisexual who was not afraid to love beautiful women as well as men. One could also assume that the poet—in concert with organizer Kathy Engel, poets Sara Miles, Jane Creighton, and others—broke the law by participating in a 1982 UNICEF benefit *for* humanitarian relief and *against* violence in Lebanon.

Clearly, Jordan's obsession with how violence, persecution, and censorship control the actions of some people further reiterates her belief in "breaking the law" by muddying how people are labeled and categorized. In her essay "Hunting for Jews?" Jordan admits, "I am a walking ground zero because I am, obviously, not white," before ending with, "I'm saying, 'Are you hunting for Jews? You're looking for me.'"[85] This controversial passage signifies how Jordan began to reimagine the very boundaries that exist between and among people, and which often prevent coalitions from being formed across religious, ethnic, and racial lines. Through her language—her open, uncensored, and provocative language—Jordan joins with people whose lives are in danger, whether Jewish, Palestinian, gay and lesbian, black, poor, or working class. She insists that we all confront the darkness of categorization to search for truth and justice through language. Her determination to cross ethnic and religious lines in order to collaborate with Palestinians and Jewish people attests to this ideal. Such a search can lead to rebuilding a free and democratic world.

In "Declaration of an Independence I Would Just as Soon Not Have" (1976), Jordan takes up the issue of truth and language solidifying the pathway of unity by writing:

> Suppose the hunger and the famine afflicting some 800 million lives on earth is a fact that leaves you nauseous, jumpy, and chronically enraged. No matter how intense your wrath may be, no matter how personally knowledgeable you may be about the cause and the conceivable remedies for this monstrous and unnecessary curse upon innocent human beings, you, by yourself, can do damned little, if anything, to destroy these facts of abject experience. But what can you join? Where can you sign up, sign in?[86]

Jordan's question, "where can you sign up?" illustrates her belief in a democracy that includes all people and supports the efforts of these people to acquire their identities, histories, and rights. Reason, democracy, and justice should be restored if the people are to ever have a chance to reclaim their lives, a point presented in her poem "Moving Towards Home" (1982). In this poem, the poet declares:

> I was born a Black woman
> and now
> I am become a Palestinian
> against the relentless laughter of evil
> there is less and less living room
> and where are my loved ones?
>
> It is time to make our way home.[87]

To understand the dynamics of June Jordan as poet and essayist, black woman and mother, teacher and author of children's and young-adult literature, local and international advocate for justice is to understand her life in relation to politics and education. She was a political writer, a revolutionary artist, and a respected educator who valued the voices and experiences of people working toward justice, love, equality, and democracy. Her resistance to violence in all forms is the cornerstone of her legacy—one that draws on the "Beloved Community" of socially committed activists and artists from every part of the world. Jordan always returned to her classrooms to advocate this message. In the following chapter, I visit this message of empowerment by examining June Jordan's Poetry for the People Collective at the University of California, Berkeley, and her focus on teaching students that "what [they] have to say is not only valid but necessary."[88]

SIX

Affirmative Acts: Political Essays

I n "Travelin' Shoes (for June Jordan)," poet Ruth Forman recalls how
Jordan challenged her Poetry for the People students at the University of
California, Berkeley to move beyond printed words in order to critique the
languages of their own lives in relation to larger narratives of belonging and
ownership. Forman begins:

> June,
> I remember your blues words, pieces of a blues collective, from our first
> poetry reading.
> The one that came from us around the table in 102 Barrows with our poetry
> guidelines and you sitting at the end challenging us but with laughter, always
> with laughter. Was it 102 Barrows? Whatever room it was, in the middle of all
> that theory and ivory tower, we noticed something real going on. Something
> magical. . . . We have power in learning what we have to say is not only valid but
> necessary. . . . You push us to locate our voices despite a language that teaches us
> distance from our own homes. And we can celebrate each other in this process
> for now our words know exactly their meaning, their place in context of this
> world, and we are a different people and we are not alone.[1]

As articulated in the selected passages from Forman's published letter, June
Jordan's teaching appointment in the Department of African American Studies
at Berkeley, and her sentiments concerning the role of the poet and the importance of quality, creative, and inclusive forms of education, are factors that
influenced her writing and activism from the 1990s until her death in 2002.

Some of Jordan's representative publications during this time include *Technical Difficulties: African American Notes on the State of the Union* (1992); *Haruko/Love Poetry* (1993); *I Was Looking at the Ceiling and Then I Saw the Sky* (1995); *Kissing God Goodbye* (1997); *Affirmative Acts: Political Essays* (1998); *Solider: A Poet's Childhood* (2000); and, posthumously, *Some of Us Did Not Die: New and Selected Essays of June Jordan* (2003) and *Directed by Desire: The Collected Poems of June Jordan* (2005). Her many writings and teaching appointments, especially "around the table in 102 Barrows"[2] at Berkeley, demonstrate her commitment to using words and working with people to change the world.

During her tenure at Berkeley, Jordan was an active participant in student-organized readings and she spoke at many political protests and academic conferences. She developed the Poetry for the People Collective, organized a teach-in on the Persian Gulf War, and accepted an invitation from Matthew Rothchild, editor of *The Progressive*, to be a regular contributor to the magazine. And it was at Berkeley where she confronted her breast cancer while continuing to teach, write, and work for social justice.

This chapter examines Jordan's professional and political involvements during this time by paying close attention to how the poet's life and writings were greatly influenced by associations with personal friends, academic colleagues, and students, particularly the students in her Poetry for the People program.[3] It begins with a detailed description of the pedagogical practices of the Poetry for the People collective and moves into an examination of Jordan's stance on affirmation action, bilingual education, and the racialization of poverty. The chapter concludes with a discussion of the June Jordan School for Equity in San Francisco, California, the poet's writing assignments for *The Progressive*, and her position on rape and the politics of sexuality.

Poetry for the People (P4P), founded by June Jordan at the University of California, Berkeley in 1991, is a student-centered poetry workshop/program that addresses writing, language, literacy development, and social activism. Designed to help bring about democratic education both on the university campus and in the surrounding community, the program provides students with knowledge and practice in writing poetry as a tool of expression. Additionally, the program is designed to help historically underrepresented populations of students, participants, and citizens develop poetry skills and produce writings and performances that promote genuine awareness of their surroundings. On one level, P4P is invested in making poetry accessible to everyone, not just academics of a dominant culture: the P4P course description explains that "all students, regardless of academic discipline or status (Freshmen to Graduate) are eligible for enrollment."[4] On another level, P4P is committed to providing everyone, particularly those who feel silenced and ignored, with empowering ways to use poetry as an expressive tool. Students investigate their roles in social, political, and educational spheres; develop spaces where their opinions and voices can be heard; and "reach towards the development of literacy in today's world literature of poetry."[5] Poetry for the People is not concerned with producing writing for publishers, academics, and various mainstream discourse communities;[6] instead, P4P is focused on the validation and empowerment of people in communities as they learn how to use poetry and language to enact change in society.

P4P began as a course with approximately twenty students when Jordan was a professor in the African American Studies Department at Berkeley.[7] In 1995, the P4P class had "sixty to seventy students" who met for three hours one day a week;[8] in January 1998, there were approximately one hundred and seventy-five students. At the inception of the program, Jordan established "ground rules" to foster an inclusive classroom community that promoted values of social justice in education and an activist pedagogy. Jordan's initial rules for a respectful classroom include the following:

> 1. "The People" shall not be defined as a group excluding or derogating anyone on the basis of race, ethnicity, language, sexual preference, class, or age. 2. "The People" shall consciously undertake to respect and to encourage each other to feel safe enough to attempt the building of a community of trust in which all may try to be truthful and deeply serious in the messages they craft for the world to contemplate. 3. Poetry for the People rests upon a belief that the art of telling the truth is a necessary and a healthy way to create powerful, and positive, connections among people who, otherwise, remain (unknown and unaware) strangers. The goal is not to kill connections but, rather, to create and to deepen them among truly different men and women.[9]

In addition to maintaining an inclusive learning environment, members build a classroom community of tolerance and respect, while refusing to devalue various types of experience, literacy, and knowledge that have academic value. The poetry in the classroom comes from a variety of sources with particular emphasis placed on those poets who are not a part of the traditional academic canon, but rather poets whose work reflects the diversity of students at Berkeley and in the Bay Area.[10] Students push the act of writing beyond the simple structuring of words on paper to engage in the processes of critical thinking, collaborating, writing, and performing. At the end of every semester, student poets perform and publish a collection of their work. Students also have an opportunity to become student-teacher poets (STP) who instruct future groups of P4P students and lead poetry-writing programs in local high schools.

The P4P curriculum and program have achieved much success at the University of California, Berkeley and in the surrounding communities of outreach. In California, for example, the program works with Dublin Women's Prison, Berkeley High School, Mission Cultural Center, and Yerba Buena Center for the Arts. There is also growing national interest in programs similar to P4P: Youth Speaks—based in San Francisco, with affiliate programs in New York City and Seattle, and expanding to other cities—is a spoken-word poetry and creative-writing program that encourages young people to write and perform their work and get involved within local communities. While it appears as though many programs have been founded with similar goals and under the direction of P4P alumni and student-teacher poets, the extent to which these programs are running and following Jordan's pedagogical practices is somewhat unclear.[11]

What is clear, however, is that interest in P4P and in the literary contributions of Jordan did not diminish when the poet died: P4P continues to thrive as a successful educational program at UC Berkeley, and a Senior Seminar class on June Jordan was offered by Berkeley's English Department shortly after the poet's death.[12] Additionally, there are many poets who studied with P4P who are pushing boundaries and demonstrating the influence such a program can have. Former P4P student Michael Datcher is author of *My Brother's Keeper* and *Raising Fences: A Black Man's Love Story*, editor of the poetry collection *Black Love*, and coeditor of *Tough Love: Cultural Criticism & Familial Observations on the Life and Death of Tupac Shakur*. Other P4P alums include Ruth Forman, author of the poetry collections *We Are the Young Magicians* and *Renaissance*, and Samiya Bashir, the 1994 Poet Laureate of the University of California system.

Jordan's efforts at establishing P4P in California, a conservative state with liberal tendencies, speak to her devotion to expand the public's understanding of higher education. In "Finding the Haystack in the Needle or, The Whole World of America and the Challenge of Higher Education," the poet asserts the following position:

> The challenge of higher education in the whole world of America is this: to lift the standards of the teachers and of the required core curriculum so that we who would teach can look into the eyes of those who would learn from us without shame and without the perversions of ignorance disguised as Noble Mystery.[13]

In many of her related writings, Jordan compares higher education to "finding a needle in the haystack," in which a tiny portion of the population is rewarded for educational performance based on class privilege: material and economic resources, wealth, status, and power. So as not to engage in this privileging of the wealthy majority over the nonwealthy minority, the program pairs critical and sophisticated instruction in poetry writing with political empowerment in the greater urban communities of the San Francisco Bay Area. For Jordan, this pairing is fundamental in extending the ideals of higher education into literacy activities, life experiences, and effective service-learning initiatives. It is also fundamental to the democratization of language, the changing of political structures, and the achievement of real civil rights.

The latter point is articulated in Jordan's essay "For the Sake of People's Poetry: Walt Whitman and the Rest of Us," in which she conceptualizes the value of poetry as a means of creatively urgent expression inherently connected to an understanding of American-based democratic systems. She writes that, at times, she feels like "a stranger trying to figure out the system of the language that excludes her name and all of the names of all of her people. It is this last that leads me to the poet Walt Whitman."[14] She is drawn to Whitman, the father of American poetry—"What in the hell happened to him? Wasn't he a white man?"[15]—because of the moral issues present in his work. She is drawn to Whitman, a poet she describes as her "equal" and "colleague," because he and other New World poets[16] "insistently devise legitimate varieties of cultural nationalism."[17] Of Whitman, Jordan remarks,

> It so happens that Walt Whitman is the one white father who share the systematic disadvantages of his heterogeneous offspring trapped inside a closet. . . . But I didn't know about Walt Whitman. Yes, I had heard about this bohemian, this homosexual, even. . . . Not only was Whitman not required reading, he was, on the contrary, presented as a rather hairy buffoon suffering from a childish proclivity for exercise and open air.[18]

June Jordan's writings on Walt Whitman confirm, at least for the poet and her students, that poetry has the power to critique class privilege, racism, sexism, and homophobia by employing inclusive and democratic language. Or as Whitman writes, "I do not trouble my spirit to vindicate/itself or to be understood,/I see that the elementary laws never apologize."[19] These spiritual laws signify a continual search for the truth and justice of humanity; Whitman's search is marked by his experience as a nurse during the Civil War and then as a poet documenting concerns over race, sexuality, and discrimination after the war. His work became a symbol of a young America.

Jordan follows Whitman's tradition of writing poetry that connects politics with passion and attempts to make sense of a strange country supposedly based on democratic principles of justice. Many of her poems repeat key words and phrases, are written in free verse, and are about sociopolitical matters that affect groups of people. Additionally, Jordan's erotic poetry follows the tradition of Whitman's erotic poems in its honest confessions of love, passion, and sexual desire. Her teaching and community work, particularly as related to P4P, offers a radical commentary on the significance of Whitman's work. In the "Introduction" to *The Portable Walt Whitman*, editor Mark Van Doren writes, "The life he [Whitman] praises is still to be lived; or it can be imagined as existing now if details are not scrutinized." Van Doren continues by articulating Whitman's position on living as connected to education and citizenship:

> He asserts it with all his might, dismissing as he does so the feeble thing which passes for education in seminaries and colleges. Such an education enervates and tames the citizen. Whitman would release that same citizen, whoever he is, into a larger world where education would go under its own power, with no one but America for schoolmistress. . . . Let there be no more heroes; or rather, let every individual be a hero, let the average man become divine.[20]

Whitman's insistence that every human is a "hero" is reiterated in Jordan's claim that poetry, in belonging to the people, should employ democratic language that addresses human conditions. With her participation in the literary tradition of Whitman, Jordan claims language as a currency of power that tells the truth and demonstrates the heroic nature of "every individual" brave enough to document experiential learnings within the world. Such points are indicative of Jordan's democratic vision for P4P, a collective based on community involvement, communicative interactions, and mutual exchanges through poetry writing.

Jordan's reflections on Whitman also confirm the need for P4P to include less frequently studied poets in its curriculum in ways that require student poets to read, write about, and make contact with published New World poets.[21] This confirmation presents itself even more vividly in Jordan's belief in a shared struggle that she, like Whitman, is a part of—one that "tell[s] the truth about this history of so much land and so much blood, of so much that should be sacred and so much that has been desecrated and annihilated boastfully."[22] Through her work with students in P4P, Jordan made conscious efforts to unveil this truth of injustice, public effort at silencing groups of people, and contempt by searching for available languages that would account for multiple truths and justices in the world.

As she searched for available language and as she challenged her students to make use of their prior knowledge and experience, Jordan introduced them to a wide range of poets, poetry, innovative structures, and literary techniques for writing. P4P's community involvement and outreach efforts extended into schools, community centers, churches, jails, and prisons, offering a model for the artist as activist. The involvement of P4P in surrounding communities is exemplary of Jordan's platform for developing democratic forms of education and effective, meaningful teaching. As a teacher, Jordan recalls her early dislike of "compulsory education" because of its failure to connect to her personal and familial experiences, and gendered and raced identities: "When I was going to school, too much of the time I found myself an alien body force-fed stories and facts about people entirely unrelated to me, or my family."[23] Jordan's sentiments here are reminiscent of those expressed by Brazilian educationalist Paulo Freire in *Pedagogy of the Oppressed* regarding the "culture of silence" experienced by countless people and perpetuated by educational systems.[24] Jordan was a part of this "culture of silence" and confirms that the lessons learned and tasks performed in school ignored her familial history:

> The regular demands upon me only required my acquiescence to a program of instruction predetermined without regard for my particular history, or future. I was made to learn about "the powerful": those who won wars or conquered territory or whose odd ideas about poetry and love prevailed inside some distant country where neither my parents nor myself would find welcome.[25]

Always the outsider, June Millicent Jordan was forever searching for "welcome," beginning with her educational experience at PS 26 elementary school and other New York City public schools as a child, and then later at Milwood High School, Northfield School for Girls, Barnard College, and the University of

Chicago as a young adult. Year after year, her curiosity increased with regard to the homogeneity of the literary canon. Year after year, she noticed an absence of works by nonwhite artists in her required educational curriculum. Instead of turning away from schooling, however, she vented her frustration with the one-sided American educational system by writing poetry, reading canonical *and* noncanonical works, and committing herself to a life of social activism and teaching. Writer George Orwell's "The Politics of the English Language" (1946) and architect W. R. Buckminster Fuller's *Operating Manual for Spaceship Earth* (1969) were significant texts in Jordan's contemplations about education, language, and the fate of humanity. The latter text influenced Jordan's way of thinking as well as her political and intellectual developments. With this in mind, P4P represents Jordan's conscious effort to confront the dilemmas of educational and political systems that ignore multiple human realities and conditions and perpetuate the status quo. Her P4P effort consciously revises "compulsory education" and its operational methods by placing students in active, participatory roles alongside their teachers, and by redefining the relationship between the classroom and the community.

Yet P4P did not completely reject traditional educational methods. Jordan wholeheartedly believed that people should know the history that has occurred before them, and how they are placed within that history, if they are to organize for systemic changes in the present. She believed that a lot can be learned from studying canonical works, literary histories, poetic forms (Orwell, Shelley, and Whitman, for example), and from inviting into academic spaces the experiences of students who are taught to critique such works as they contribute to knowledge construction, expressive forms of communication, and new ideas. The poet hoped that such lessons would open new possibilities: "As a teacher I was learning how not to hate school: how to overcome the fixed, predetermined, graveyard nature of so much of formal education: come and be buried here among these other (allegedly) honorable dead."[26]

As a teacher, particularly at UC Berkeley, Jordan demanded that her classrooms and pedagogical practices be student centered. In the "Introduction" to *June Jordan's Poetry for the People*, she writes about how she "revise[d] and devise[d] a reading list and a method of handling diverse writings" for *overwhelmingly* heterogeneous students in her African American Freshman Composition course.[27] In her Women's Studies course "The Politics of Childhood," she discovered a group of "White . . . young women packed together in an expectant, rabble-rousing spirit." In her Contemporary Women's Poetry and African American Poetry courses, she taught "James Weldon Johnson or Adrienne Rich" alongside writings by her very own students.[28] In her teaching experiences with diverse student populations at Berkeley, Jordan demonstrated an invested interest in students' lives and work. This interest manifested itself in the organization of P4P courses along multiple literary, linguistic, social, geopolitical, and cultural traditions. Likewise, Jordan's interest in her students showed itself in the public poetry readings of both students and published poets, radio broadcasts, media appearances, and publications of student work, all of which augmented the student learning experience. Of such practices, she writes eloquently: "This outward and inward attunement seems to me a most reasonable basis for the political begin- ning of a beloved community: a democratic state in which the people can trust the names they have invented for themselves and for each other." On the lat- ter point of trusting names, Jordan continues, "It is this trustworthy use of words that poetry requires, and inspires. It is this highest ideal of trustworthy intersection among differing peoples that poetry can realize: POETRY FOR THE PEOPLE!"[29]

A pattern emerged in June Jordan's teaching life—from her days with Teachers & Writers Collaborative (1967) and at open admissions City College (1967) to her time at the University of California, Berkeley (1989–2001)— especially against the backdrop of the demise of both affirmative action and bilingual education in California. In her essay "Finding the Haystack in the Needle or, The Whole World of America and the Challenge of Higher Education," Jordan offers the following sentiments on education, following her poetry reading to a diverse student audience at Los Angeles Community College:

> And for those of us stranded inside the conundrum of teaching English to a fully entitled American population that is neither English nor, increasingly, born to the language of those who set the standards of power in our country, perhaps we can try to teach what we are learning, now, with so much pain . . . but timorous hope: If you want to talk with somebody you have to arrive at the same language . . . talking the same language cannot and must not mean "my language and not yours" or "your language and not mine." It means finding a way to understand, not to change or to eclipse or to obliterate.[30]

Jordan had learned that the college was not equipped with "a nurse or health faculty," "psychological counseling," or "doors on the bathroom stalls." In fact, most composition courses at Los Angeles Community College were over- crowded, with approximately 30 students per class and 150 total students for each composition instructor in a semester.[31] Even in this underfunded educa- tional environment, Jordan's belief that people must locate ways to communi- cate experiences still prevailed, as conversing with others requires a genuine commitment to negotiating what one knows with what one needs to know through the currency of language. It is this intellectual exchange that opens the possibilities for creating equity in education, understanding the lives of others, and implementing quality resources for students in invigorating learn- ing environments. Jordan left that reading at the community college motivated to continue the fight for justice and the quest for truth.

Unfortunately, Jordan's belief in diversifying languages and her vision of having an array of experiences present in the schools did not prevail in the political arena. When Californians voted against affirmative action in 1996 through the passage of Proposition 209, also known as the "California Civil

Rights Initiative," affirmative action was officially deemed illegal in California schools. At Berkeley, where Jordan had been a popular professor for over a decade, affirmative action could no longer be used in admissions decisions—a move that questioned former President Lyndon B. Johnson's statement: "We seek not just freedom but opportunity, . . . not just equality as a right and a theory, but equality as a fact and as a result."[32] Affirmative action was no longer viewed as a welcome tool for equaling the educational playing field as it was purported to be in the 1978 Baake Case. In this case, the Supreme Court voted in favor of Justice Lewis Franklin Powell, Jr.'s argument that affirmative action is a justifiable necessity that has educational benefits for dynamic, diverse, and intellectual collegiate experiences. Nevertheless, recent arguments from the political Right against affirmative action included the belief that affirmative action had outlived its useful life as a policy that addresses a national history of discrimination and inequality, as in the Baake Case. Some even called affirmative action "reverse discrimination."

Against this backdrop of reactionary mainstream politics, Jordan campaigned with others for the continued existence of affirmative action in the University of California system. In her many essays, particularly "An Angry Black Woman on the Subject of an Angry White Man" and "Affirmative Acts: Language, Information, and Power," she countered the conservatives' assertions with political analysis and arguments of her own. Jordan's essay "An Angry Black Woman" is "Dedicated to the Negro U. C. Regent, Ward Connerly, who gave more than $100,000 to the campaign of Governor Pete Wilson and who led the U. C. Regent attack on Affirmative Action, 1995."[33] Jordan cites American slavery as a primary example of brutality, economic exploitation, and greed. She writes,

> We didn't always need affirmative action
> when we broke this crazy land into farms
> when we planted and harvested the crops
> when we dug into the earth for water
> when we carried that water into the big house and
> bedrooms[34]

Affirmative action, Jordan argues, was not always needed when black people were valued primarily as property, the legal subordinates of those who used black bodies to create and maintain wealth and dominance:

> when we fed and clothed other people's children with the
>   food we cooked and served to
> other people's children wearing the garments that we fitted . . .
> when we bleached and pressed linens purchased by the dollar
>   blood profits from our
> daily forced laborings[35]

Obviously, "the dollar/blood profits" refer to unpaid labor, calling into question just how such human labor and debt would be repaid, if at all. Affirmative action, argues Jordan, is not enough: "we did not need affirmative action. No! We needed overthrow/and a holy fire to purify/the air./And so we finally got freedom on a piece of paper."[36] The proposition that makes affirmative action illegal in a state such as California is too much. One does not forget about the Ku Klux Klan, violence, and discrimination. Affirmative action, for Jordan, is indeed needed in order for people to have

> . . . a way into
>   the big house
> besides the back door. We needed a chance at the classroom
>   and the jobs and open
> housing
> in okay neighborhoods[37]

Jordan argues that affirmative action is still necessary in America, and specifically in California, because the past is not the past; racism and violence, discriminatory practices and unfair representation, are present-day realities that must not be ignored in mainstream narratives of belonging and assimilatory strategies:

> But (three decades later) and come to find out
> we never got invited to the party
> we never got included in "the people"
> we never got no kind of affirmative action worth
> more than the spit in the wind[38]

While affirmative action was initially deemed illegal in California and could no longer be used in admissions decisions, "faculty Senates of the University of California system and all nine chancellors and the official University of California student organizations voted in 1996 to retain and improve and expand affirmative action policies."[39] For Jordan and many others, affirmative action is still essential if the rights of people of color are to be supported within the public sphere. Jordan, "an angry black woman," writes on the subject of "the angry white man" who claims affirmative action puts him at a disadvantage because it denies him equal opportunity and protection under the law and affords historically underrepresented people educational and political progress. On this latter point, the poet acknowledges historical contradictions as pertains to colonization and emancipation by complicating the relationship between slavery as exploitative and freedom as a continual struggle for human rights:

And so we finally got freedom on a piece of paper.
But for two hundred years in this crazy land the law and the
    bullets behind the law
continued to affirm
the gospel of God-given white supremacy[40]
...the law affirmed the gospel of God-given white
    supremacy God-given male
white supremacy.

Jordan's use of the phrase "God-given male/white supremacy" asserts her belief that national identity in America is associated with the markers "white" and "male." Such an association points to the need to have policies, such as affirmative action and even quality bilingual education programs, that do more than privilege "the angry white man," "The Face of America," or "the law-abiding American citizen" at the expense of more inclusive representations of American identity along the lines of race, ethnicity, class, gender, and sexuality.[41] Given the proliferation of narratives about American citizenship, national identity, and media-generated images of success, affirmative action, according to Jordan, is needed more than ever today.[42] In her essay "In the Land of White Supremacy," Jordan discusses this latter point: "Hence, affirmative action, for example, is a federal government policy. Hence, the viciously orchestrated attack on 'affirmative' for the sake of 'angry white men' who, statistics inform us, continue to occupy 95 percent of all senior management positions."[43]

The poet's arguments on affirmative action, race, and inequality from the essays "An Angry Black Woman on the Subject of an Angry White Man" and "In the Land of White Supremacy" connect well to her arguments in favor of bilingual education. In her essay "Affirmative Acts: Language, Information, and Power," she spells out the consequences of an insufficient national dialogue on race and the general public's resulting lack of, and otherwise incorrect, information about affirmative action issues as related to the education of students of color, and specifically the significance of bilingual education programs. On the subject of bilingual education, Jordan notes that in 1967 the then-governor of California, Ronald Reagan, "repealed the state's ninety-five-year-old English-only mandate," proving that students could benefit from school instruction in their native language.[44] Nevertheless, bilingual education came under attack in California in the mid 1990s with Proposition 227, or the "Anti-Bilingual Education Initiative in California." This initiative sought to prevent use of languages other than English in California-based classrooms, end programs in bilingual education, and advance approaches in which learners would be immersed in English-only instruction, with consideration of extenuating circumstances for use of one's first language. According to a news

report published in the *San Francisco Chronicle*, dated June 3, 1998, propo-
nents of Proposition 227 were victorious against bilingual education programs
in the state of California; opponents to the proposition, including the state
superintendent, candidates for governor, various other politicians and educators, vowed to file suit.[45]

Filing suit against this new proposition was not enough for Jordan, who
took immediate action by forming and joining coalitions and organizing public protests; however, "creative support, of the California Teachers Association
and the California School Board Association" was still being sought.[46] She
could not believe that such a proposition was endorsed and supported by a
majority of the voting public in California. By this time, she was a battle-
scarred veteran of human rights movements and America's culture wars. In the
late 1960s, she had participated in the massive student and faculty uprising at
City College in New York in support of the college's open admissions policy. In
the early 1970s, she had weathered a public outcry from parents over the publication of her young-adult novel *His Own Where*, because she wrote it exclusively in Black English. Later, in the early to mid-1980s, she had experienced
the dismay of her own college-level students over Alice Walker's use of Black
English in *The Color Purple*. However, these same students came to acknowledge and respect Black English as a language, which they unknowingly
incorporated in terms of speech acts and in the appearance of written discursive structures.

In the 1990s, Jordan was again in the frontlines of protest. This time she
took part in the activities supporting the continuance of affirmative action in
California, but it was not enough; she wanted to witness and participate in protests that supported bilingual education in California as well. She wanted to
highlight the research of "Virginia Collier and Wayne Thomas at George
Mason University" that followed "42,000 students tracked over thirteen years"
and found that "*those who receive solid native language instruction eventually do
better in English than those who don't.*"[47] Jordan wanted to fight against this limiting proposition, one that she believed threatened the diversity of students
entering academic institutions with native languages other than English. In
one way, this proposition sought to racialize immigration through education:

> Calculated racialization of poverty, inequality, immigration, and education colors
> these realities so that too many of us begin to perceive these issues as strictly
> equivalent to this or that race/this or that language/this or that ethnic heritage
> when, actually, the issue is how will we . . . devise a democratic, and peaceable,
> means to go on, or not! And actually the question underlying all of that is about
> principles of equality, principles of justice, principles of democratic entitlement.[48]

Jordan's argument connects well to her position on the validity of language, as
articulated in later essays.

In "Bilingual Education and Home Language," Jordan presses the need for
multiple languages in the education of linguistically diverse students. She

poses the provocative questions: "What is the best teaching method to adopt for children with different levels of fluency in one or more languages? How shall we best hope to enable all of our children to become competitively fluent in English?"[49] She answers these questions by turning to bilingual education as a successful method to teach academic-based knowledge and critical skills to students. Acknowledging the changing demographics of communities and classrooms, Jordan asserts that English is no longer *the* language—and it has not been for quite a long time—that defines the American public: "Fewer and fewer American children enter compulsory public schools equipped with English-language fluency."[50] The issue of bilingual education remains a hot topic in California, and Jordan's position on inviting multiple languages into the classroom attests to the value of a democracy that legitimizes the diversities of its students, or in her own words: "When will a legitimately American language, a language including Nebraska, Harlem, New Mexico, Oregon, Puerto Rico, Alabama and working-class life and freeways and Pac-Man become the language studied and written and glorified in the classroom?"[51]

Jordan's work in California—from her university teaching position to her founding of the P4P collective—is related, in many ways, to such programs as the Teachers & Writers Collaborative (New York City) and the Writers-in-the-Schools program (Houston, Texas). Also, one can assume that Jordan used the California Poetry in the Schools program (CPITS), initially funded by the National Endowment for the Arts and the California Arts Council, as a model for P4P. CPITS, having begun as the Pegasus Project at San Francisco State University in 1964, placed local poets in classrooms throughout the Bay Area to read and teach the elements of poetry writing to youths.[52] One of the overarching goals of CPITS, as with the Teachers & Writers Collaborative (T&W) and the Writers-in-the-Schools (WITS) program, is to encourage student experimentation with writing as a means of expression, creativity, and exploration through words.

Through her work with T&W in the 1960s, Jordan gained invaluable experience conducting poetry workshops for, and participating in, community-outreach initiatives with young black and Puerto Rican students. T&W, founded by local writers, artists, and educators in New York City in 1967, is a nonprofit organization that conducts various literacy programs, writing workshops, poetry readings and performances, after-school events, and literary seminars for students and teachers in school sites and in its Center for Imaginative Writing located at 5 Union Square West in Manhattan. In addition to June Jordan, participating T&W poets have included Muriel Rukeyser, Kenneth Koch, Anne Sexton, Ron Padgett, and Phillip Lopate. As mentioned in an earlier chapter, Jordan was encouraged to participate in T&W from the organization's inception in the late 1960s.

In 1983, Phillip Lopate of the University of Houston and Marvin Hoffman, former T&W director, founded WITS in Houston, Texas. On founding the program, Lopate and Hoffman sought innovative methods to introduce students in the primary and secondary grade levels to the teaching of writing. Today, WITS continues to place creative writers, playwrights, poets, novelists, dramatists, and community writers in public-school classrooms to work with students to enhance reading and writing skills through the use of contemporary poetry, literature, art, music, and museum visits. According to Lopate and Hoffman, creative writing and critical thinking allow students to understand themselves in ways that shape their experiences with words and their interactions with others.[53]

In many ways, T&W, WITS, and CPITS are initiatives that utilize creative media to teach students poetry, to help them shape their critical capacities, and to conceptualize how education can be democratic in practice and method. The three initiatives also respond to Jordan's questions: "What is the best teaching method to adopt for children with different levels of fluency in one or more languages? How shall we best hope to enable all of our children to become competitively fluent in English?"[54] T&W, WITS, and CPITS encourage students to take "control of the language of your life" and to "build a revolution in which speaking and listening to somebody becomes the first and last purpose to every social encounter."[55] They motivate teachers and poets to use what the students bring into classrooms—various languages, personal experiences, and literacy activities—as knowledge is co-constructed and perspectives are challenged. Together, T&W, WITS, CPITS, and P4P embrace the power of people's languages in "a beloved community [where] these young American men and women devise their individual trajectories into non-violent, but verifiable, power."[56] To devise "individual trajectories," for Jordan, is to collaborate with people in schools and in the surrounding communities as well as to interrogate who one is in relation to others and their struggles. This point was well advanced by Walt Whitman during and immediately following the Civil War, and articulated by Jordan in a poem included in the 1995 text *June Jordan's Poetry for the People: A Revolutionary Blueprint*:

I ain't goin nowhere unless you come with me
I say I ain't goin nowhere lessen you come with me
I ain't about to be some leaf that lose its tree
So take my hand see how I'm reachin out for you
Hey here's my hand see now I'm reachin out for you
We got a whole lot more than only one of us can do[57]

An examination of Jordan's involvement in P4P and T&W, and the connections her work made to other groups such as CPITS and WITS, demonstrates her commitment to democratic forms of education for students who come to understand the beauty and power of language in written and oral forms.

Jordan's commitment to literacy, freedom, student apprenticeships in the community and to social equality have been recognized by the San Francisco Unified School District's Board of Education, which passed a proposal in 2004 to rename a local public high school The June Jordan School for Equity (JJSE) as a way to honor Jordan's many contributions. Students attending the school spent the first year (2003) researching the life and work of Jordan and voted to name the school after the poet. The official naming ceremony was held at the school on Thursday, August 26, 2004.[58] Adrienne Torf recounts the following about the school:

> The school was built on the small school model. There were three teachers who realized that kids were dropping out of school because no one was paying attention to them. They worked to get this school opened through the California Board of Education. They supported democratic exchanges through student work and explorations to determine for whom the school would be named after, and that's how the school was named in honor of June Jordan.[59]

According to the school's official Web site, the JJSE's primary mission is the academic preparation of students who are able to "give voice to their dreams and grow into healthy, productive adults." The school seeks to do this by "guiding young people to discover and explore their passions, to grow into independent, reflective thinkers, and to build connected, socially just communities, both inside and outside of the school."[60]

The parent organization of the JJSE, the Small Schools for Equity, collaborates with local students, parents, and educational institutions, including San Francisco State University and California State University. It seeks to sustain Jordan's legacy by fostering democratic relationships among educators, students, and parents. Jordan's teaching at UC Berkeley, her creation of P4P, and the naming of the JJSE reiterate her devotion to education and to the politics of humanity. The latter point is echoed in her work with *The Progressive*.

Sometime after Jordan moved to California and began her work with P4P, she was invited by Matthew Rothschild to write a regular column for *The Progressive*. The magazine, based in Madison, Wisconsin, serves as "a journalistic voice for peace and social justice at home and abroad [by] opppos[ing] militarism, the concentration of power in corporate hands, the disenfranchisement of the citizenry, poverty, and prejudice in all its guises." *The Progressive* is a public forum that produces a political magazine and a radio show; it also directs a media project aimed at distributing op-ed pieces "in large and small newspapers around the country. *The Progressive Media Project* has also hosted more than 40 skills-building op-ed writing clinics from foundation grantees, nonprofit organizations, activists and community groups."[61] Contributors to the political magazine have included social critics, political leaders, and literary thinkers such as Jane Addams, James Baldwin, Noam Chomsky, Martin Luther King, Jr., Carl Sandburg, and Edward Said. Jordan joined the list of contributors and became a regular columnist with the publication of her February 1989 essay "Finding the Way Home." Her final column, published in the magazine in November 2001, is entitled, "Do You Do Well To Be Angry?"

Other essays written by Jordan for *The Progressive* include "The Invisible People: An Unsolicited Report on Black Rage" (2001, March), "The Hunters and the Hunted," originally titled, "Hunting for Jews?" (1999, October), "A Letter to Maria" (2000, October), "Requiem for the Champ" (1992, February), "Can I Get a Witness" (1991, December), "A New Politics of Sexuality" (1991, July), "The Big-Time Coward (1991, April), "On War and War and War and . . ." (1991, February), "Diversity or Death" (1990, June), "Unrecorded Agonies" (1989, December), and "Where is the Rage?" (1989, October).

The poet wrote many more essays for the magazine, some of which were published, while others were rejected: the latter included essays on Palestine, Lebanon, Islam, Bosnia, U.S.-based racism, state violence, genocide of the Jews, refugees, political commitments, Anita Hill, and Rodney King, among other topics. Many of her *Progressive* works are reprinted in her essay collections *Technical Difficulties: African American Notes on the State of the Union* (1992), *Affirmative Acts: Political Essays* (1998), and *Some of Us Did Not Die: New and Selected Essays* (2002). In all of her writing, Jordan articulates the point that she is "always hoping to do better than to collaborate with whatever or whomever it is that means me no good."[62] Her *Progressive* magazine work, essay and poetry collections, children's and young-adult literature, keynote addresses, recorded interviews, teaching appointments, and the creation of P4P represent her conscious decision to use language to fight against the enemies and to devise "methods of resistance against tyranny of any kind."[63]

While she wrote political essays for the magazine, Jordan continued to produce essays against war, ethnic cleansing, and genocide. Fully aligning herself with the struggles of the Palestinian people in the 1980s with the reading of her poem "Moving Towards Home" (eventually translated into Arabic) only heightened her commitment to historically underrepresented people throughout the world. Jordan strongly supported the fights against rape; breast cancer; South African apartheid; the Gulf War; the Bombing of Baghdad; U.S. policies supporting the Taliban; the violence perpetuated against the Sandinistas of Nicaragua and against gays and lesbians; and every other conceivable hatred and real oppression in the world. The poet was elated by the 1992 election of Bill Clinton; however, her elation quickly disappeared with Clinton's silence at the realities of rape: "And here are more than 20,000 mostly Muslim women systematically suffering gang rape around the clock in the former Yugoslavia. And here is nobody powerful in this country, from President Clinton up or down, opening his—or her—mouth."[64] Jordan was also angry with American leadership for ignoring the evil of ethnic cleansing throughout the world: "And I do not and I will not forgive the elected leadership of my country for its inertia and its silence and, therefore, its complicity with the evil of so-called ethnic cleansing."[65] After the Rodney King trial, Jordan expressed dismay over the freeing of the police officers accused of beating King almost to unconsciousness (see Jordan's essay "The Truth of Rodney King").

On the Anita Hill–Clarence Thomas hearings, Jordan expressed her anger over how the U.S. Senate Judiciary Committee interrogated Hill, practically accusing her of lying about sexual harassment charges against Thomas (see Jordan's essay "Can I Get a Witness?"). She expressed more anger about these hearings because of "those brothers who disappeared when a black woman rose up to tell the truth."[66] After the September 11th attacks in 2001, Jordan indicated the need for Americans, in collaboration with the rest of the world, to put forth efforts of equality, justice, and democracy in fighting against hatred.[67] On every political topic deemed important, she wrote as if she would never write again. She poured her anger, love, and fear into her well-researched essays, poems, and speeches. The poet employed an available language of democracy to reach and to move the masses into action. Language, for Jordan, always has been the common currency of communication and activism.

Jordan was determined to be honest with her language and tell the truth, even when it hurt. In 1986, she wrote about when she was raped, the first time by a white man who had "overpowered the supposed protection of my privacy, he had violated the boundaries of my single self. He had acted as though nothing mattered so much as his certainly brute impulse."[68] During that period of her life, Jordan was working on her art and living single-handedly in a "rented, pseudo-Walden Pond" home on Long Island.[69] After being raped, she realized that there is no true human autonomy, and that one's safety, happiness, and democratic right to exist can be jeopardized at any time. Instead of adopting a passive voice that claims rape ("I was raped"), Jordan quickly learned the value of using an active voice ("He raped me"), in order to reclaim power. She writes, "For rape to occur, somebody real has to rape somebody else, equally real. Rape presupposes a rapist and his victim. The victim must learn to make language tell her own truth: He raped me."[70] She reiterates her belief that honest language must tell the stories of the people—those who continue to be disenfranchised, abused, silenced, and raped by political systems.

In 1996, ten years after the first rape, Jordan writes about a second rape, this time by a black man who, allegedly, was a local political leader. While Jordan does not identify the person by name, she does write that "he was, in fact, head of the local NAACP./And I'd met him at a bar when a community/(I thought) of my friends from a writers'/colony went out."[71] Given Jordan's burgeoning commitment to freedom of expression, civil liberties, and the liberation of people, particularly in black communities, it is ironic that a black political leader raped her. His act of human degradation intensified Jordan's anger toward systems of violence and the catalysts behind such acts, particularly as these things transgress racial boundaries and loyalties. Jordan continues the poem by writing the following:

He had introduced himself to us and to me . . .
he'd invited all of us to his house . . .
when I arrived, I discovered
my community had disappeared . . .

> I said good night and started toward
> the door,
> and that's when this friendly, head of the
> local NAACP Black man
> raped me.[72]

Jordan draws parallels between the first and the second rape in order to comparatively describe them as "violent domination," violations of "boundaries," and sodomizing acts—physical acts that Jordan does not admit to ever having prosecuted.[73] Instead of remaining a victim, she turned to language and the act of writing to establish larger parallels between rape and state violence. To do this, the poet posits a relationship of violence between the powerful—the state—and the powerless—women, children, and people of color.[74]

In "Notes Toward a Model of Resistance," she observes that "According to the New York Times of November 17, 1996 . . . Marine Corps drill instructors still led training runs with chants like: 'One, two, three, four. Every day we pray for war. Five, six, seven, eight. Rape. Kill. Mutilate.'"[75] Here, Jordan highlights how the safety and protection of women are under fire: how the military and "the powerful" encourage such chanting and attitudes toward women and the act of rape as if these things are justifiably normal. "Notes Toward a Model of Resistance" discusses rape, victims and perpetuators, as a way to make a larger point about national protection in the form of U.S. citizenship and political asylum for women seeking safety from gender-based persecution. Jordan writes, "I don't think you can ever completely/'recover' from rape;" yet serious efforts at protecting girls and women from rape and other "universal threats" must be made by conscious citizens and governmental bodies, including military units.[76] Jordan believed that rape is a reality that deserves international attention, and in the late 1980s she publicized the crime by writing several poems on the subject, such as "Rape is Not a Poem." Here, she declares,

> And considering your contempt
> And considering my hatred consequent to that
> And considering the history
> that leads us to this dismal place where (your arm
> raised
> and my eyes
> lowered)
> there is nothing left but the drippings
> of power[77]

In her poem "Case in Point," Jordan writes more explicitly about the experience of rape:

> Today is 2 weeks after the fact
> of that man straddling

his knees either side of my chest
his hairy arm and powerful left hand
forcing my arms and my hands over my head[78]

Around the same time, she wrote the poem "Moving Towards Home" for the 1982 humanitarian relief benefit in Lebanon. In the poem, Jordan offers yet another, albeit different, perspective on rape:

Nor do I wish to speak about the nurse again and
again raped
before they murdered her on the hospital floor . . .
because I do not wish to speak about unspeakable events
that must follow from those who dare
"to purify" a people
those who dare
"to exterminate" a people[79]

This poem highlights one of Jordan's biggest challenges: to make the unspeakable speakable, something she does by talking about how the nurse was raped by a tyrannical regime even as she, ironically, tried to heal sick and wounded patients. With this poem, Jordan gives voice to what the unspeakable—rape and murder—has done and how she has to use her available language in order to get closer to the process of becoming free. This would allow her to join with other people in an attempt to move toward home by muddying racial and religious categories: "I was born a Black woman/and now/I am become a Palestinian."[80]

Jordan's poems make known her connection to a Beloved Community rooted in political action and concern. Simultaneously, her poems stress the point that people who have been raped, tormented, or brutalized must not passively accept the names and labels given to them. This latter idea is seen in her assertion that "I was raped" should become "he raped me" and "he is a rapist." Jordan's writings on rape and state violence are attached to her works on the violence of war and the abuse of power, as exemplified in her poem "War and Memory" and her essays "South Africa: Bringing it All Back Home" and "The Big-Time Coward." Taken together, such works encourage giving voice to voicelessness and publicly mobilizing against acts of sexual abuse, political persecution, and state-sanctioned violence. For Jordan, rape, ethnic cleansing, and genocide are intolerable acts linked by intentional and inexcusable violence.

The poet's examination of rape occurred through various critical lenses, including feminist, internationalist, and anti-imperialist perspectives. She even analyzed the platform of the "Women in Black" in Jerusalem, a coalition of Palestinian and Jewish Israeli women who joined together in 1988 to fight systematic forms of violence.[81]

In the same spirit, she examined the efforts for peace and justice by Jewish Americans seeking to stop Israel's occupation of Palestinian territories. All such examinations for Jordan reiterate that rape is a symptom of a universal dilemma in which human and civil rights are too often threatened by national policies and political structures used to reinforce the status quo at any cost. On this latter point and in relation to her own rapes, Jordan reveals the following to writer-journalist Jill Nelson in a 1994 interview for *Quarterly Black Review of Books*:

> I have been raped myself, twice. I happen to think rape is one of the most heinous things that can happen to anyone. But there's a victimization of people that is systematic. . . . The media do not want to deal with that, they want to ignore the causative context that determines our lives, sometimes for great unhappiness and tragedy.[82]

Jordan clearly noted that the media avoid certain issues, including racism, patriarchy, diversity, sexism, and sexuality, and she refused to remain quiet. She was convinced that with language one could expose the dangers of silence pervasive in various factions of society; her decision to talk and write about being raped reveals a larger commitment to universal justice. This idea, in many ways, is connected to writer R. D. Laing's assertion on the nature of human experience. In *Politics of Experience*, which was one of Jordan's favorite texts, Laing writes, "for the experience *of the other* is not evident to me, as it is not and never can be an experience of mine." Laing continues, "I cannot avoid trying to understand your experience, because although I do not experience your experience, which is invisible to me . . . yet I experience you as *experiencing*."[83] Jordan sought to understand other people's experiences by "experiencing" how people are connected to the larger trajectory of humanity, an idea that surfaced in her open declarations, via writings, interviews, and poetry readings, of her own bisexuality.

During her interview with Jill Nelson, Jordan was asked about her writings on bisexuality. She responded: "I'm not going to make a choice, I'm not going to say I'm this or I'm not that. I'm gonna say I'm bisexual, which means moment by moment." Elaborating on her point of not making a choice, Jordan articulates her devotion to freedom and how "sexuality is perhaps the last place we have to go with freedom, and maybe that's why we're getting there so slowly." The slow progress of talking about sexuality and freedom attests to a longtime American resistance to talking about an identity that does not include the threat of violence or the ability to talk about identity without fear of violent retribution for doing so.[84] From the 1960s on, especially after her divorce from Michael Meyer, Jordan spoke frequently about sexuality. In one of her popular essays, she describes a time in the 1960s when she met and became intimate lovers with a beautiful black woman from Mississippi. In a different essay, she describes a time when she met a black male activist who confessed that he was longing to make love with her, even while he was rallying black parents in New Jersey into political action, though Jordan believed he instead should have been focused on his activist agenda.

Jordan loved both women and men and did not need anyone's approval about whom she could intimately interact with, care for, and love. Her identification with sexual freedom meant that she could fully embrace the various realities of her life without accepting a single, linear group identity of "black," "woman," "bisexual," or "activist." In "A Politics of Sexuality," Jordan confesses, "I am Black and I am female and I am a mother and I am bisexual and I am a nationalist and I am an internationalist. And I mean to be fully and freely all that I am."[85]

She made conscious attempts to be "all that I am" by joining forces with different movements for justice and by admonishing people who refused to support other efforts at attaining freedom championed by different groups. In particular, she refused to join any movement or organization that publicized their oppressions while ignoring the oppressions of others in society. She initially criticized the gay and lesbian rights movement in America for its self-centeredness, believing that the fight for the rights of gays and lesbians can never be "won without coalition support from Americans who are *not gay* and *not lesbian* and *not bisexual*."[86] It is not enough for a movement to campaign exclusively for their own rights at the neglect of those who are denied the same civil liberties. It should be noted that Jordan also criticized the Women's Movement in America for its narrow visions and its exclusion of nonwhite women from a variety of socioeconomic backgrounds. Jordan's concern with movements that separated their particular oppressions from other oppressions rested in her belief that human life is sacred, and that all people are entitled to freedom, justice, equality, and sexual liberation without punishment.

In many ways, Jordan's focus on sexuality is a focus, however incomplete, on issues of gender and power relationships and the larger human condition:

> When I say sexuality, I mean gender: I mean male subjugation of human beings because they are females. When I say sexuality, I mean heterosexual institution-alization of rights and privileges denied to homosexual men and women. When I say sexuality I mean gay or lesbian contempt for bisexual modes of human relationship.
>
> The Politics of Sexuality therefore subsumes all of the different ways in which some of us seek to dictate to others of us what we should do, what we should desire, what we should dream about, and how we should behave ourselves, generally.[87]

The "politics of sexuality" undermines relationships among all sexual beings by encouraging men to suppress women and disregard children. To ignore the importance of women's rights and gay and lesbian rights, according to Jordan, is to disband the coalitions that fight for all forms of human and racial equality, political freedom, and universal justice—points discussed earlier in this text. Jordan made the choice not to live as a singly labeled human being as defined by other people's standards; she did not want to be shadowed by labels that did not, and could not, represent the fullness of who she was and what she believed. She did not like "either/or" distinctions and tried not to use them herself; her affirmation of her own bisexuality demonstrated her quest to live and love not only with "a multicultural, multi-ethnic, multiracial world view,"[88] but a sexually liberated one as well.

In 1980, Beacon Press published Jordan's collection of poetry *Passion: New Poems, 1977–1980*. The collection includes many different theme-based poems, including "Case in Point" ("there is no silence peculiar/to the female"),[89] "Rape is Not a Poem" ("I let him into the house to say hello"),[90] "A Short Note to My Very Critical and Well-Beloved Friends and Comrades" ("Then they said I was too confusing altogether . . . /They said . . . /Are you straight/or are you gay"),[91] and "Poem About My Rights" ("I have been raped/be-/cause I have been the wrong the wrong sex the wrong age/the wrong").[92] From being raped to being a sexual human in love with countless women and men, Jordan writes of how some see her and others similar to her as "wrong." Yet this way of seeing does not limit how Jordan sees herself in relation to acts of peace, protection, and the right to be in love, which is similar to the Whitmanesque model of being a soldier and bearer of words that indicate truth about the human condition. Meanwhile, Jordan's actions and accompanying poems in *Passion: New Poems, 1977–1980* are natural outcomes of the way her father, Granville, taught her literature and raised her to be his "son."

In 1994, Serpent's Tail publishers released *Haruko/Love Poems: New and Selected Love Poems*, a collection of poetry written about Jordan's female friend and lover, "Haruko," between 1991 and 1992. The collection is "dedicated to love"[93] and includes a "Foreword" by poet Adrienne Rich. In the opening of the "Foreword," Rich begins, "WHAT IS THIS thing called love, in the poems of June Jordan, artist, teacher, social critic, visionary of human solidarity?"[94] This thing that Jordan writes of and willingly experiences—this love—can be partially described as her freedom to experience a serious connection with her lover. On a larger scale, this love relates to the rights of people to love and be loved by whomever shares a mutual attraction. Jordan's *Haruko* poems, always political and, in this case, written in a delicate and tender voice of affection, make reference to both the joys and rejections, excitements and humiliations of love: "Then how should I/subsist/without the benediction of our bodies/intertwined/or why"[95] or "I will love who loves me/I will love as much as I am loved/I will hate who hates me . . . /I will make myself a passionate and eager lover/in response to passionate and eager love."[96] While she provocatively admits a reciprocal relationship of loving and being loved in the latter poem, Jordan never really offers an answer to how and why she should subsist. Instead, *Haruko/Love Poems* looks back to include love poems selected by writers Adrienne Rich and Sara Miles from Jordan's other collections dated 1970–1991.

In a 1994 interview with writer Peter Erickson, Jordan answers the question "Do you see the *Haruko* poems as a new development in your work?" by saying: "Yeah, because that's a whole series of poems that document the trajectory of a love affair with one person as against a miscellany of poems about miscellaneous people."[97] The poems in *Haruko* have a "transcultural or cross-cultural identity"[98] that display an urgency for human interaction, understanding and acceptance, and the human ability to "call things right or wrong"[99] when they are unjust, harmful, or inhumane. Jordan's love poems express her sexual freedom as connected to love and politics, and as directly related to her other freedoms: the right to be herself, black and female, woman, activist, bisexual, writer, lover, intellectual, mother, friend, warrior, supporter of Palestinian rights, advocate against ethnic cleansing, rape, and genocide. From her poetry collections *Haruko/Love Poems*, *Living Room*, *Kissing God Goodbye*, and *Things That I Do in the Dark* to her essay collections *Affirmative Acts: Political Essays*, *Technical Difficulties*, *Moving Towards Home*, *On Call*, and *Civil Wars* to her Poetry for the People blueprint to her children and young-adult novels to everything she created and participated in: June Jordan combined the power of political action with revolutionary art and love to advocate a concept of universal justice in a beloved community. Her actions, both as a writer and an activist, are as important today as they were when she emerged as an artist, thinker, and educator in New York City during the 1960s.

SEVEN

Kissing God Goodbye

"Woe is me. I could start fighting instead./But no, I am the victim. I am already dead."[1]

One of June Jordan's intimate friends and literary companions, E. Ethelbert Miller, describes Jordan as "one of the most important writers to come through the last several years. She was someone who had a broad and inclusive vision that many did not quite understand."[2] In one way, Miller's sentiments relate to the scores of political essays, articles, poems, and young-adult literature written by Jordan in the last thirty-seven years. In another way, his assertions speak to Jordan's vision of family, community, and politics that was always at the center of her work. One cannot deny that Jordan's early writing was greatly influenced by the lessons afforded by her West Indian parents—a father who taught Jordan how to experience the beauty of literature and a mother who taught her biblical stories and childhood rhymes. The poet's approach to familial encounters and struggles extended into her myriad love relationships as indicated by her numerous love poems and letters, most of which are published and the rest of which are housed in library collections, including the Givens Collection of African American Literature at the University of Minnesota[3] and The Arthur and Elizabeth Schlesinger Library on the History of Women in America at the Radcliffe Institute for Advanced Study at Harvard University.

Jordan's inclusive vision, often in the tradition of Walt Whitman as well as Langston Hughes and others, allowed her to discuss matters about which people were—and are—often silent: bisexuality, love, rape, police brutality, the Gulf War, the Bombing of Baghdad, and Propositions 207 and 227 in California. For Miller, this intellectual versatility of topics makes Jordan an important writer, one who should be remembered. He states: "We cannot find another African American women writer with as many books of essays on a wide variety of topics . . . who can write about Whitman and Wheatley . . . other than June Jordan. She wrote about everything that mattered."[4]

In her later years, particularly from the period between 1992 and 2002, Jordan would take up the task of writing "about everything that mattered"[5] to her by turning attention toward her battle with breast cancer. In a 1994 interview with writer Peter Erickson, Jordan openly admitted her emotionally draining experience fighting breast cancer and her involvement with breast cancer awareness campaigns: "I'm going to do a benefit for the Women's Resource Center here in Berkeley, and for that event I will write something that I hope I can present without breaking down."[6] June Jordan, having exhibited strength and passion throughout her tumultuous life, remained strong during her ten-year battle against breast cancer.

It is this strength and the poet's undying commitment to literary and political matters that I discuss in this closing chapter. If Miller is correct in his description of Jordan as a dedicated writer "on a wide variety of topics," then an examination of the things most important to her—in the midst of a life altering battle with cancer—deserves recognition. I open this chapter by first presenting a narrative description of Jordan's travails upon discovering her cancer, the measures that she underwent, and the end of her life, honored by memorial ceremonies and published editorials that announced her death. Then, I discuss the body of work she produced during her final years, supporting my long-standing claim that Jordan was a warrior who refused to be defeated or silenced, even by illness, and perhaps not even by death itself. Because of her resolve to fight against systemic injustices, including breast cancer, her literary and political contributions continue to affect multitudes. For this reason, I end by offering sentiments expressed by the poet in published writings that echo her belief in "the good fight" for human rights. June Jordan's life and work must be remembered, honored, studied, and critiqued.

In California in early 1992, June Jordan's doctor and friend, Dr. Allen Steinbach, informed her that she had breast cancer. Only a few years earlier, the poet was considering breast implants, thinking that they would make her "more desirable, or irresistible, or, anyway, secure, in what was a consummately crazed and volatile love affair."[7] Her potential surgeon required a mammogram before any work could be done. A mammogram would determine the healthiness of her breasts; it would be the final and most important step to take before surgery. Instead, this mammogram led to the discovery of her breast cancer and the necessity of a partial mastectomy. Having survived so much already, Jordan became a survivor once again:

> And so I became one of the millions of American women who must redefine courage and who must redefine the meaning of heroic friendship if we will survive./And my son and my lover and my friends gathered around like Dare Devils daring themselves and their devotion and their walking of my dog and their changing of the dressing. . . . And it was not easy. And it was not brief. And it is not over.[8]

Every year the reported number of breast cancer cases increases for American women, and as Jordan writes, the amount of money allocated for research on breast cancer—for early detection and the dissemination of information to the general public—decreases. Every hour of every day to every month of every year, the number of women dying of breast cancer increases substantially. While awareness of breast cancer has increased, there is still no public outcry for major, longitudinal studies of breast cancer and for finding a cure. Nevertheless, Jordan admitted that she was "happy beyond belief" when she joined with others who were searching for ways "to end the disease of breast cancer and the disease of race hatred and the disease of misogyny."[9]

Upon the discovery of her cancer, Jordan phoned her cousin, Valerie Orridge, to tell her the news: "And when June called me hysterical that she had breast cancer, I started having panic attacks. . . . I said, June, you are going to have to come back to New York."[10] Orridge, still a practicing nurse and health-care educator, wanted Jordan to move back to the City and into her Harlem home; that way, Orridge would be able "to take [Jordan] to Sloan-Kettering"[11] for treatment. Jordan refused, declaring that she would seek help from the University of California and would rely on the scholarship of friends Alice Walker and Angela Davis, "who were doing some research about the treatment, the best treatment for breast cancer."[12] Despite the pleas from her cousin to return to New York, Jordan decided to remain among her friends and colleagues in California; she soon underwent a biopsy at Alta Bates Hospital.

After the biopsy, Dr. Steinbach informed Jordan that the location of the cancer was her right breast. Before this, Jordan did not know much about breast cancer. After being diagnosed by Dr. Steinbach, she actively pursued research to determine its causes, effects, and known treatments—anything and everything that she could learn about breast cancer, she did. Her research led her to dismal statistics: from "Every year there are 183,000 cases of breast cancer reported" to "According to the San Francisco's Department of Health, 6 women die from breast cancer every hour, 144 women die from breast cancer every day" to "25 *percent of all the women diagnosed* with breast cancer in any given year *will die within five years*."[13]

Jordan attempted to make sense of her diagnosis. She gathered statistics and continued her research, all the while baffled that there was seemingly no mass movement in this country to fight breast cancer. Her life had changed forever.

In her 1996 *Keynote for the Mayor's Summit on Breast Cancer, San Francisco, California*, Jordan delivered her speech "Besting a Worst Case Scenario." In it, she recounts being told that she had cancer. Even more painfully, she writes, "So when I received the written report of the biopsy performed on my right breast from the hospital I noticed that the malignancy had been attributed to my left breast./And I thought that was a major, unpardonable mistake. And I still think so."[14]

Soon thereafter, a partial mastectomy was performed to remove the malignancy and the lymph nodes, and to determine whether or not there was cancer elsewhere in her body.[15] But Jordan did not confront breast cancer alone—she had the support of a community of loving colleagues and friends, including:

> The Women's Cancer Resource Center of Berkeley and the National Black Women's Health Network and Dr. Craig Henderson and Dr. Susan Love and Dr. Denise Rogers and Christopher and Angela and Adrienne and Dianne and Stephanie and Martha and Haruko and Amy and Sara and Pratibha and Lauren and Roberta and Camille and my colleagues and students at school and the neighbors next door and Amigo, the Airedale who lives with me.[16]

They all worked together to encourage Jordan to fight the disease, and to live to tell about it. She took on this charge and lived for a decade after being diagnosed with cancer, telling others about her struggles and rallying for increased governmental funding of breast cancer research. She committed herself to winning the battle and reclaiming her life. In "Besting a Worst Case Scenario," Jordan writes the following:

> Prior to the mastectomy procedure, which my next oncologist urged me to agree to, I was told that if I had the procedure I would have an 80 percent chance of surviving more than five years. A mastectomy would secure those 80 percent odds in my favor.[17]

However, the procedure did not secure Jordan's 80 percent chance of survival. In fact, Jordan writes that after the surgery was completed, her high-profile San Francisco surgeon reduced her probability of survival for five years from 80 percent to 40 percent, citing that "the mastectomy procedure had discovered that the malignancy had spread into the lymph nodes and there was, now, no way to track, . . . to locate, let alone eliminate, the dread interior dissemination of the disease."[18]

June Jordan's "worst-case scenario" was staring her in the face: her chances of survival had substantially decreased after the mastectomy procedure; her surgeon had not told the nursing staff to periodically "empty the drain he had installed in the wound site;"[19] and this same surgeon had gone on vacation. All this time, as Jordan lay in a hospital bed, "no one was checking the drain and letting out the blood, [and] the tissue of the wound site became perilously thin and unable to generate new cells."[20] No one could make a decision about what to do, and the surgeon was still on vacation. Some of Jordan's friends came to her assistance, and a decision was made to attend to the wound, but there was little that was dignified about this process. Later, Jordan informs readers about the tremendous amount of support given to her during this extremely difficult time:

> And I felt overwhelmed by the exhaustive, seamlessly graceful, and indispensable caretaking. . . . How could I possibly have survived any of the ordeal of this fight, and how could I possibly hope to heal, and defeat this cancer, without the unstinting love given to me?[21]

In her essays "Root Canal to the Future of Women," "Ruth and Naomi, David and Jonathan: One Love," "A Good Fight," "Besting a Worst Case Scenario," and in several poems, the poet writes about her breast cancer and indicates that "the prognosis is very bad, but I'm very well."[22] Jordan tells of the physical and emotional pain that resulted from her surgeries, medical procedures that Orridge describes as terribly "botched-up."[23] Jordan then explains how she could not use her right arm for months after the unchecked drain was left in the wound site. Unable to write, Jordan questioned whether or not she "would again ever be able to use and to move my right/arm/my right/hand/it was not clear for months if I would write again."[24] Nevertheless, she did write again, penning such important works as *Affirmative Acts: Political Essays, Soldier: A Poet's Childhood, Haruko/Love Poems, Kissing God Goodbye, I Was Looking at the Ceiling and Then I Saw the Sky* (a published libretto), and *Some of Us Did Not Die: New and Selected Essays of June Jordan.*

The collection *Directed by Desire: The Collected Poems of June Jordan* was released from Copper Canyon Press in September 2005, three years after the poet's death. The 649-page volume includes a most powerful poem about the physical scar left on Jordan's body as a result of surgery. In the poem "To Be Continued:" the poet writes, "The partial mastectomy took a long time to execute/And left a huge raggedy scar/Healing from that partial mastectomy took even longer."[25] Later in the same poem, Jordan openly admits:

> A wound fifty times more implacable and more intractable
> Than the psychological chasm produced by the healing process
> That was twice as enormously damaging as the surgery
> Which left a huge raggedy scar
>
> And so I go
> on[26]

But neither breast cancer nor the reality of "a raggedy scar"[27] can take Jordan away from the people. She lives among us all. Her literary, educational, and political gifts, her commitment to justice, her courage to love, and her attempts to defeat cancer should be honored and cherished.

Additionally, her struggle to survive breast cancer is demonstrative of her challenge to speak the unspeakable so as to "move towards home" and to arrive closer to a life of safety and freedom. This latter point is explored in detail in her "Poem at the End of the Third Year." In part, Jordan writes:

> How we began
> a galaxy apart/me
> driving on this street
> to reach the hospital to take
> away one breast
> or more
> than that[28]

Jordan's battle with breast cancer and the ensuing pain, immobility, and physical and emotional scars relate to her other life struggles concerning family, love, violence, war, and demands for quality educational opportunities for students of color. Such connections are important for Jordan to make and pronounce because they reiterate one of her most important beliefs: while not all struggles are one in the same, their interconnectedness is manifested in the need for people to collaborate against all forms of injustices, a collaboration that, for the poet, signifies a deeper understanding of life and the universal laws that govern both life and death. Jordan does not shy away from confronting the dilemmas of life—abuse, injustice, and death—nor does she shy away from addressing the quandaries of political struggle—censorship, abandonment, and death. She highlights these points in her work with students in Poetry for the People Collective, in her life-altering travels to Nicaragua and Lebanon, and in her final battle with breast cancer. Jordan was, according to Miller, a "visionary writer"[29] whose works have significant implications for everyone concerned with the welfare of humanity, a concern that is as important in the poet's death as it was in her life, which ended on June 14, 2002.

June Jordan's last breath of air occurred on a calm June day in her home on Carlotta Avenue in Berkeley, California at the age of 65. As her fight with breast cancer came to a gradual end, Jordan was surrounded by close friends and loved ones. Poet Sara Miles describes Jordan's intimate departure as a "coming back." In "Directed by Desire," her personal tribute to Jordan, Miles writes of the poet's life commitment to always return to the people who mattered the most to her:

> She came back to people—as June lay dying, she was surrounded and cared for by many she'd sworn, at one point or another, never to speak to again. She remained faithful to the idea that love—heated, passionate, brave—is what gives spirit and sustenance to all politics. She stayed true to the messiness and contradictions of desire. Mostly, she remained open to one of love's greatest blessings—surprise—and to the possibility that always, somewhere, there is more.[30]

During the years leading up to her death, after the mastectomy procedures and months of being practically immobile, Jordan was determined to "come back" by adopting a rigorous exercise and diet regimen. Also, she was committed to fully enjoying the things that personally mattered to her, including walking in her garden in the early mornings, looking at "the ninety-seven-year-old willow tree and the jasmine blooming aromatic and the honeysuckle bulging into the air and Amigo [her dog] gulping at a bumblebee and a stray bluebird lifting in flight above the roof."[31] Although she often experienced excruciating physical pain, the poet was committed to making use of the energy she did have so as to continue her activist work and prepare for her final days. Before her death, she appointed Junichi Semitsu as director of Poetry for the People Collective at Berkeley, an appointment that received the support of the Poetry for the People students, staff, and the university governing board.

Jordan also began outlining her final requests for her memorial "on a series of Post-It notes, attached seemingly at random to the inside of a file folder containing her UC benefits information."[32] In "For June's Memorial Celebration, 15 September 2002," Adrienne Torf writes about some of Jordan's requests, most of which pertained to musical selections to be played at her memorial service:

The first: (undated)

> Music for my memorial, please:
> Gladys Knight
> Isley Brothers
> Donny Hathaway
> ("Song for You / "For All We Know")
> Jr. Walker![33]

Torf continues by providing additional instructions that were handwritten by Jordan on several different dates:

The second, stuck to the first: dated 10/31/99

> I'd really really love
> to have Me'Shell
> jam "Take Me Higher"
> with her whole band

Then the third, on delicate light blue note paper, in a matching envelope, from January 29, 2000:

> Dearest ABBT Bongo:
> If there's a funeral or memorial service

for me, after I check out, please please
play "The Rock Will Wear Away" and "Find A
Way" + "Brooklyn From the Roof" for me.
And ask Bernice to sing "Amazing Grace"
and Sweet Honey to sing "In the Upper Room"
+ The 1st Bach's Unaccompanied—for cello +
his Suite #2 in D Major—you know the one I love
Otherwise much happy happy Doo Wah[34]

Torf adds that the poet wanted the popular musical group Sweet Honey in the Rock to perform "Sometimes I Feel Like a Motherless Child" by Carol Maillard and Junichi Semitisu to perform "Amazing Grace" on his accordion.[35] Many of Jordan's requests were honored, and her days of mourning turned into a powerful day of celebratory gatherings and a "grand send-off"[36] in California that honored the life, legacy, and political commitments of the poet.

On September 15, 2002, nearly three months after the poet's death and private cremation,[37] Jordan's family and friends, in conjunction with the Department of African American Studies at Berkeley, held an on-campus memorial service in her honor. Some of Jordan's family members, friends, and colleagues in attendance at the service included Christopher David Meyer, Valerie Orridge and her son, artists Cornelius Eady, Sara Miles, Janice Mirikitani, Vicki Randle, Bernice Johnson Reagon, Adrienne Rich, Adrienne Torf, many of the Poetry for the People students, and Robert Berdahl, Chancellor of Berkeley. Authors Toni Morrison and Alice Walker appeared via videotape.[38] Prior to this event, Thulani Davis, a Barnard College alumna, former Barnard College English professor, and friend of Jordan, wrote about the need for Brooklyn residents and community activists to create a memorial for Jordan in their neighborhood. In the article "June Jordan, 1936–2002," which appeared in the July 2, 2002 edition of *The Village Voice*, Davis insists, "In a borough that has landmarks for the writers Thomas Wolfe, W.H. Auden, and Henry Miller, to name just three, there ought to be a street in the Bed-Stuy called June Jordan Place, and maybe a plaque reading, 'A Poet and Soldier for Humanity Was Born Here.'"[39]

Although June Jordan has physically departed this earth, she lives on through the legacy of the work she accomplished while here. From her "running buddies" friendship with New York based writer Alexis De Veaux, to her relationship with the language of Whitman, Neruda, and Kipling,[40] Jordan's death represents more than the passing of sixty-five years of human breath. It signifies political statements on life, sacrifice, struggle, and devotion to social change that have implications for how humans will continue to search for universal love amid assaults to the human spirit. Even as she battled cancer and prepared for her final days, Jordan remained committed to justice—as is evident with how she continued to produce important writings from 1992 to 2002. A brief examination of the literary accomplishments of the poet at that time is significant because it reveals her larger, selfless devotion to humanity during a personal battle against death.

As discussed throughout this book, June Jordan's political and creative interests spanned from New York City to the Bahamas, and from the Middle East to California and Lebanon, among other places, and took the forms of poetry, essay, and drama. The poet's work did not diminish as a result of her cancer diagnosis; instead, Jordan increased her number of writing assignments. This is significant because it proves Jordan's refusal to be defeated and give into death without a "good fight," a point that has long-lasting political consequences for generations of activists. In the following section, I discuss the literary pursuits that the poet marveled in and fulfilled during her breast cancer battle in order to demonstrate how she remained focused on living and writing.

June Jordan was known for collaborative work with other world-class artists. She worked with Peter Sellars and John Adams on the opera *I Was Looking at the Ceiling and Then I Saw the Sky*, with Adrienne Torf on the musical compilation *June Jordan and Adrienne Torf: COLLABORATION*, and with various other artists who included her poetry in musical projects. Jordan was involved with documentary projects such as *Bang Bang Uber Alles* in the 1980s and *A Place of Rage* in the 1990s. In framing this discussion it is vital to note the poet's early reflections on the work of Angolian political leader Agostinho Neto and writings on the universal education of women, ideas that helped shape the work Jordan produced during her final ten years of life. This discussion highlights the effects of Jordan's creative work on her dedication to a political life undefeated by cancer. Even with death looming before her, the poet stood steadfast, immovable, and relentlessly devoted to her craft—points befitting of analysis.

In 1995, composer John Adams and director Peter Sellars asked Jordan to write the libretto for *I Was Looking at the Ceiling and Then I Saw the Sky*, described as "a contemporary romance carried by seven young men and women living on the West Coast of the United States in the nineties. For them, it's earthquake/romance."[41] She agreed and eventually gave birth to the speech of all seven Los Angeles-based characters dealing with the effects of race and love at the outset of the 1994 Los Angeles Northridge earthquake. (The opera derives its name from the quotation of a survivor of the earthquake cited in an article in the *Los Angeles Times*.) The main characters are Dewain, a black man described as a "reformed gang leader" who is the opera's lead role; Mike, a white police officer, who arrests Dewain for stealing liquor from a convenience store; and Tiffany, a white reporter, who documents the heated confrontation on tape. Shortly after the incident, an earthquake strikes the city, causing various insights, and emotional and physical injuries to Dewain, Mike, and Tiffany. The audience also glimpses the lives of lovers, Leila, a counselor, and David, a preacher, and various others. They are all connected by their confrontations with life and love; their commitments to themselves, their communities, and their country; and the struggles they share with other people. The music that accompanies the performance combines the sounds of gospel, doo-wop, blues, and R&B, allowing the piece to appeal to a nontraditional opera audience. *I Was Looking at the Ceiling and Then I Saw the Sky* premiered in May 1995 at the Zellerbach Playhouse in Berkeley, California and went on to the Festival de Theatre des Ameriques in Montreal, the Edinburgh Festival in Scotland, and other locations. Clearly, Jordan's work as a librettist highlighted her creative talents with words, realities, artistic collaborations, and romance.

Jordan began writing about Lebanon as early as the 1980s and, in the 1990s, her attention to the country increased. Some of the poet's representative writings include the poems "Apologies to All the People in Lebanon," "The Cedar Trees of Lebanon," and "Lebanon Lebanon," and the essays "Eyewitness in Lebanon" and "Life After Lebanon." In the latter essay, Jordan writes about the feelings that circulated after Israel invaded Lebanon:

> The complicity of Americans through tax monies that supported the invasion, the slaughter of Lebanese peoples, the decimation and rout of the Palestinian peoples, the awesome determination by whitemen, in this country, to silence or to discredit American dissent, the vicious wielding about of the term anti-Semitic whenever anyone protested the interminable carnage executed and precipitated by that invasion, left me extremely embittered, shocked, and wondering about life after Lebanon: What would that be like?[42]

The poet's feelings of disillusionment and resentment motivated her to increase her activist writing in the form of poems and essays. Particularly during the final fifteen years of her life, Jordan reexamined the political landscape of America, taking note of the journeys of many—from the decision of Jesse Jackson to try "to become President of our country" to the organizing efforts of the many "Jewish women who never quit from sending out flyers and making phone calls" to the strong women advocating civil rights and peace in Lebanon and elsewhere.[43] In 1996, many years after Jordan penned the aforementioned sentiments and pondered the Israeli invasion of Lebanon, she traveled to Lebanon to document how the region was devastated by militarism. Concerning her travels to the country, Jordan documents the following:

this massacre
I photograph
the withered aftermath
the oozing consequence
the swollen stump
the burned out cranial configuration
of a 6 year old
recovering
from abrupt incineration
of her dress her hair

her plastic daisy bracelet singed
into a 3rd degree
tattoo
    do I exaggerate?[44]

Then, in 1999, Jordan increased her creative writing on the war in Kosovo and the ensuing efforts to rebuild that country. Some of the poems include "April 7, 1999," "April 9, 1999, for Ethelbert," and "April 10, 1999." These poems, among others, are recorded in her collaborative project with musician Torf, entitled *June Jordan and Adrienne Torf: COLLABORATION, Selected Works, 1983–2000*. The compilation includes selections on South Africa (*Every Night, Winnie Mandela* and *Song for Soweto*), Nicaragua (*Dance: Nicaragua*), and the experience of living in a hurtful, pain-filled world (*One of Them Is You*). Jordan's poetic creativity accompanying Torf's compositional and instrumental talents creates a music of urgency, immediacy, and rage that forces an audience to search for the reasons to love and live as well as the reasons to fight and protest—indicative of the collaborative relationship between the poet and the musician. As Torf writes,

> We were of different races, different generations, different backgrounds. Yet the collaboration flourished, rooted in our shared desires as artists and our shared responses to political events in America and in other countries. Each of us classically trained, we shunned ivory-tower isolation: the sounds and rhythms of the city were our lifeblood.[45]

The opening selection on Jordan and Torf's *COLLABORATION* "Freedom Suite Now: Part 1," speaks well to their "shared responses to political events."[46] It is comprised of a powerful rhythmic sound infused with the soft, yet forceful voice of Jordan: "this is Selma, Lord," "this is Birmingham, Lord," "this is Albany, Georgia, Lord, Lord," and "this is Mississippi Mud and I am marching through."[47] As the force of the musical vibrations increases, so does the poet's "marching through" in ways reminiscent of the 1960s civil rights protests. Jordan and Torf demonstrate a conscious effort to "march through" defining national and international political events through poetry, performance, and activism. *COLLABORATION* serves as one of Jordan's and Torf's political statements; they prove that by collaborating with vocalists and instrumentalists they can work toward the eradication of injustice through art. In 2001, Jordan and Torf performed for the final time in front of an audience of supportive listeners in Boston, Massachusetts. In 2003, just a year after the poet's death, *COLLABORATION* was released on CD.

While *COLLABORATION* is Jordan's final recording, it was not the only one. In 1977, musician and composer Leonard Bernstein created a duo with Langston Hughes' poem "I, Too, Sing America" and Jordan's poem "Okay 'Negroes,'" and included them as the first in a series of other duets and songs on his album *Songfest*. Other duets include "Trio: To My Dear and Loving

Husband" by Anne Bradstreet and "Duet: Storyette H. M." by Gertrude Stein. Jordan's poem "Okay 'Negroes'" reads:

Okay "Negroes"
American Negroes
looking for milk
crying out loud
in the nursery of freedomland:
the rides are rough.
Tell me where you got that image
of a male white mammy.
God is vague and he don't take no sides.
You think clean fingernails crossed legs a smile
shined shoes
a crucifix around your neck
good manners
no more noise
you think who's gonna give you something?
Come a little closer.
Where you from?[48]

One can hear the music in this poem, from the lines that question the "image" of righteousness in relation to a "white mammy," "a crucifix," and "no more noise," to the line that protests, "Where you from?" One can feel the seriousness and urgency that jumps from this poem's inquisitive tone—"crying out loud," "God is vague," "who's gonna give you something?" It is no surprise that Bernstein, much like other composers and performers, such as Roy Brown, Stanley Walden, and Bernice Reagon Johnson, founder of Sweet Honey in the Rock, could feel the music in Jordan's poetry and therefore decided to set many of her writings to music. The poet's words, let alone her reading of them, are sophisticated in their lyricism and musicality. Paired with Hughes' poem "I, Too, Sing America," Jordan's sentiments contribute to a resistence movement, by black artists, grown out of hisorical rejection.

Jordan's creativity and popularity are further marked by the inclusion of some of her poems on Sweet Honey in the Rock's musical recording . . . *Twenty-Five*, . . . released by Rykodisc in 1998. The lyrics from the CD's first selection, "We Are the Ones," are from Jordan's "Poem in Honor of South African Women;" the music is provided by Jordan's close friend and colleague, Bernice Johnson Reagon. In 1989, Flying Fish records released Sweet Honey in the Rock's CD *Breaths*, on which Jordan contributed lyrics to the third track, "Oughta Be a Woman." Included before the lyrics to this song in the CD's jacket is Reagon's message: "I talked to June about my mama and she sent me these words on thin blue paper. I think she just about got it right." The tenth track,

"Alla That's All Right, But," is from Jordan's poem of the same title, published in her collection *Passion: New Poems, 1977–1980.* In part, the poem reads,

> I been scheming about my people I been scheming about sex
> I been dreaming about Africa and nightmaring Oedipus the Rex
> But what I need is quite specific
> terrifying rough stuff and terrific[49]

Jordan was always "scheming about my people" in ways that called for a revolution of minds, bodies, and action. Given that she was a classically trained pianist who studied the art form as a child in New York City before receiving professional training during her young-adult years, it is no wonder that so many people took a serious interest in setting her poetry to music—her writing always embodied elements of lyrical sophistication. In her home in Berkeley, California sat "a well-worn volume of Beethoven Sonatas perched on the music stand of her piano." On this point, Torf continues, "If you ever surprised her with a visit, you may have heard her playing one of those Sonatas, those most beautiful hands moving comfortably across the keys, pausing only to flip the page."[50] The poet's love for music was phenomenal, and the recognition that this love received was remarkable; it ranged from artists performing Jordan's words against the backdrop of music to the inclusion of her work on musical compilations, as was the case with the 2000 release of *Our Souls Have Grown Deep Like The Rivers: Black Poets Read Their Works* by Rhino Records.

This particular CD is a striking compilation of more than seventy spoken-word poems. Set against the vibrancy of the Harlem Renaissance, the Civil Rights Movement, and hip-hop culture, it contains works by poets and writers Al Young, Amiri Baraka, Langston Hughes, W.E.B. Du Bois, E. Ethelbert Miller, Gil Scott-Heron, Lucille Clifton, Sonia Sanchez, Wole Soyinka, and many others. Jordan reads her very popular poem "In Memoriam: Martin Luther King, Jr."

Then, on *Cookie: The Anthropological Mixtape* by Me'Shell NdegéOcello, released in 2002 by Maverick Records, Jordan once again reads "In Memoriam: Martin Luther King, Jr." The poet's voice is clear, crisp, and tender, and her words are as powerful as the memory of King's activist work:

> we share an afternoon of mourning
> in between no next predictable
> except for wild reversal hearse rehearsal
> bleach the blacklong lunging
> ritual of fright insanity and more
> deplorable abortion
> more and
> more[51]

In 1992, the French Institute Alliance released a two-disc recording titled *The Academy of American Poets: Marilyn Hacker and June Jordan* with "Introductions" by Jordan's friend, the poet Jan Heller Levi. The recording features readings by the two extraordinary artists and longtime friends, Hacker and Jordan, on topics ranging from love and sex to politics and human rights. Jordan reads some of her most powerful poems, including "Case in Point," "A Poem About Intelligence for My Brothers and Sisters," "*From* The Talking Back of Miss Valentine Jones: Poem # one," and "Poem About My Rights." As discussed in previous chapters, the widely anthologized "Poem About My Rights" asserts Jordan's frustration with racial discrimination by establishing obvious connections between personal aspects of human life and political struggles that require human defiance—a statement that the poet articulated even more clearly in writings published during her last years. The poem insists,

> I am the history of rape
> I am the history of the rejection of who I am
> I am the history of the terrorized incarceration of
> my self
> I am the history of battery assault and limitless
> armies against whatever I want to do with my mind[52]

The poetic manner in which Jordan talks about her identities can be connected to the stories of her childhood in New York City as detailed in her memoir *Soldier: A Poet's Childhood,* a book so popular that it was released as an audiobook by Recorded Books in 2001 (read by actress/performer Robin Miles).

Jordan's involvement with various music projects can be traced to her early experience with theater and film work in addition to her own musical talent on the piano. In the mid-1980s, she wrote the libretto and lyrics for *Bang Bang Uber Alles*, a full-length opera created by Jordan and Torf. Joseph Papp, founder of the Public Theater in New York City, and Leonard Bernstein, American music composer and conductor, encouraged Jordan and Torf to extend their early collaborative work into a fully developed story, and the result became *Bang Bang Uber Alles*. In a 1985 interview published in *HOT WIRE: A Journal of Women's Music and Culture*, Jordan and Torf explain their thinking behind the piece. On the meaning of the work's title, Jordan says, "It refers to the violence hanging over, hovering above and penetrating into all of our lives." She continues by stating, "'Uber Alles' is part of a phrase made infamous by Adolph Hitler at his mammoth over rallies. 'Uber alles' means 'over all' or everywhere. Hence, 'Bang Bang Uber Alles.'"[53]

The opera involves a group of young, multiracial actors, singers, and dancers who come together on stage to express contempt for the Ku Klux Klan. In her "Alternative Commencement Address at Dartmouth College, June 14, 1987," Jordan describes the intentions of the opera in detail, citing the various questions that it explores: "Can importantly different people—Black and white and gay and straight and romantically rivalrous and Latino and Jewish and poor and Ivy League somehow coalesce, despite their differences, and then, together, confront a common enemy?"[54] The cast members and director demonstrate how people from different backgrounds and experiences can unite to respond to the hatred, violence, and elitist mindset of the KKK. Torf informs me of aspects of the political landscape in America when she, Jordan, and the cast members committed themselves to stage the production. In 1984 in Concord, California—a town in the San Francisco Bay Area—"a beautiful, young, black, gay student artist was found hanging from a tree near the BART subway station, and it was rumored that the KKK was seen in the area." Torf continues by remarking that around the same time "Jesse Jackson was running for President and Ronald Reagon was dismantling federal programs meant to help 'poor' and 'underserved' people; Reagan was also invading Grenada." In 1985, according to Torf, there were "no obvious connections being made in New York City with Reagan's war policies, Jackson's presidential campaign, and the fact that the state of Connecticut was home to many KKKs."[55] A public response of outrage was needed; Torf and Jordan took up the challenge of producing one.

In 1985, *Bang Bang Uber Alles* premiered off-Broadway, funded by the Women's Project at the American Place Theater. On June 14, 1986, it was produced at Seven Stages Theater in Atlanta, Georgia. During the third performance of *Bang Bang Uber Alles* in Atlanta, the KKK threatened to disrupt it. Jordan writes of the KKK-initiated activity, which had been the first of its kind in Atlanta in thirty years: "In full Klan regalia, ranging from black satin robes and headdress to Marine combat outfits to white silk sheets, several carloads of Klansmen got out of their cars and began their attempt to shut down *Bang Bang Uber Alles*."[56] Disputing rallies broke out between members of the KKK on one side and cast members of the documentary and residents from the local neighborhood on the other. According to Torf, "Cast members and the band faced the KKK outside of the theater"[57] before returning inside to perform the documentary that night and all of the other nights of its five-week scheduled run. *Bang Bang Uber Alles* went on to receive glowing reviews.

Then in 1991, Jordan participated in the 52-minute documentary *A Place of Rage*, with Angela Davis and Alice Walker. The documentary, by British filmmaker and one of Jordan's good friends, Pratibha Parmer, offers insight into the role of black female activists, including Septima Clark, Fannie Lou Hamer, and Rosa Parks, in the context of monumental rights movements in the United States such as the Black Power, feminist, civil rights, and 1970s gay and lesbian rights movements. The film opens with an image of the Brooklyn Bridge and then moves into vivid flashes of black people within New York City neighborhoods before turning to a confident Jordan sitting in front of the camera. She begins by discussing the organizing efforts of countless black people who were determined to change biased institutions and policies. She comments, "They changed because we made them change."

The film supports this statement, as Angela Davis and Alice Walker highlight black people's experiences with unconstitutional housing laws, unemployment, segregated schooling, and inadequate governmental representation. Jordan stresses the importance of coalition building during the 1960s, a time in which she felt a part of a national community of black people living in communities such as Watts, California; Birmingham, Alabama; Harlem, New York; and Jackson, Mississippi. She describes such a community as "a stunning concept" for a people who had "suffered a common set of restrictions in a hostile white country." The realization that "we could do something about it, and we did" spurred all three activists—Jordan, Davis, and Walker—to commit their lives to social activism, political protests, engaged teaching, and radical self-expression in creative art forms.[58]

In 2003, a dozen years after Jordan's work with Parmer on *A Place of Rage*, director Peter Sellars, whom Jordan had collaborated with on the 1995 opera *I Was Looking At The Ceiling and Then I Saw The Sky*, created a powerful political translation of Antonin Artaud's text *For an End to the Judgment of God*, and paired it with Jordan's epic poem "Kissing God Goodbye." In this staged performance, delivered as a mock U.S. Department of War press conference, a male performer assumes the dramatic role of a Pentagon official who offers a briefing on the government's progress on the war on terrorism, particularly in Afghanistan. The play uses Artaud's "radio play" as its main text. In response to Artaud's words is Jordan's lengthy poem, which, in part, reads:

> The emperor of poverty
> The czar of suffering
> The wizard of disease
> The joker of morality
> The pioneer of slavery . . .
> That's the guy?
> You mean to tell me on the 12th day or the 13th
> that the Lord
> which is to say some wiseass
> got more muscle than he
> reasonably
> can control or figure out/some
> accidental hard disc
> thunderbolt/some
> big mouth
> woman-hating/super
> heterosexist heterosexual
> kind of a guy guy
> he decided who could live and who would die?[59]

Together, *For an End to the Judgment of God* and "Kissing God Goodbye" offer startling commentary on the possibility that a redefined twenty-first century could embody "passion," "clarity," and "love," without the control of "the emperor of poverty" or "the czar of suffering."[60] In fact, this new twenty-first century could represent a time of freedom and equality for its courageous people who come to resist the "big mouth/woman-hating/super/heterosexist heterosexual."[61] Similar points that advocate social justice and political resistance are articulated in many other poems and essays by Jordan. Additionally, the poet's lifelong opposition to systemic control and unjust political struggles, as alluded to in the poem, are rooted in her early protests against colonialism. Her support of Agostinho Neto, the first president of the People's Republic of Angola, in the mid-1970s attests to this fact, for Jordan attempted to bring attention to the poetry, political work, and health-care advocacy efforts of Neto.

While the poet's focus on Neto's work seems far-fetched given the geographic distances that existed between the two, Jordan's commitment to social change and her resistance to colonialism through poetic and political endeavors warrant this connection. In her essay "Angola: Victory and Promise," Jordan writes of Angola, a place that she describes as "nine times larger than New York State, or three times the size of California, with a population of approximately six million."[62] This wealthy African nation has a history of resistance to colonialism and Portuguese rule. Past efforts to rebuild and reconstruct Angola's political and economic persecutions have "led . . . to the appointment of Angolan women to some of the highest governmental responsibilities . . . which became a critical aspect of the revolution when Angolan women shouldered their rifles and went to war, side by side with Angolan men."[63] Agostinho Neto, having been imprisoned, exiled, and threatened by Portuguese officials, became head of the revolution in Angola and "Honorary President of the MPLA [Popular Movement for the Liberation of Angola] directly following his 1960 imprisonment."[64] Neto, according to Jordan, is an unrelenting political poet determined to secure the freedom of the people, especially women, in Angola. Like Jordan, he did not separate his poetry from his politics and his revolutionary fights for freedom against colonialism and, like Jordan, Neto valued the voices and participation of women in the politics of nation building.

Jordan shares with Neto a political commitment to poetry. She believed poetry is an act of political activism that allows truths to be told even when they appear too difficult to confront. Jordan used poetry to speak the truth about children's rights, black women and health-care issues, poverty, segregation, rape, cancer, homophobia, foreign policy, violence, apartheid, sexism, and war. She fearlessly exposed her own vulnerabilities through writing, believing that such exposure could motivate others in their search for strength. A moving example of this practice can be found in her essay "Many Rivers to Cross," which documents the poet's trials with unemployment, divorce, single parenting, her mother's death, her absence from her mother's funeral, and her personal promise "never to be late again."[65]

Even in death, Jordan belongs to the people and to the universal fight for human freedom: her life and work exemplify the voice of a woman unmoved by censorship. In the 1980s, the *New York Times* refused to ever again print Jordan's work; her New York City publisher vowed to let her books go out of print; and one of her literary agents removed her from the client list, mainly due to her increasing focus on Palestine. Nevertheless, Jordan continued to write, publish, and speak out no matter the consequences. During a rally in California against the first Gulf War, Jordan proposed that the U.S. government reallocate some of the $56 billion dollars used to fund the war to pay for public resources in Oakland, California. For one billion dollars a day across a span of seven days, the government could pay for educational facilities, highly equipped and staffed health clinics, hospitals, drug rehabilitation centers, and affordable housing. She repeated such sentiments during a public rally in California held shortly after the September 11th, 2001 terrorist attacks.

This unconventional feminist writer—a woman who rejects traditional feminist theory and practice—not only protested the Gulf War but proposed ways to rebuild a country devastated by the September 11th attacks, while simultaneously rejecting all U.S. social, economic, and political policies that disrupt people's civil rights. Through an antiwar, antihate, antihomophobic stance, Jordan insisted on creating and sustaining a Beloved Community that holds at its center the civil liberties, freedoms, and the true voices of the people.

Jordan's commitment extended to a focus on the universal endangerment of women. Whether she was writing about the adventures of the fictional young Kimako in the children's story *Kimako's Story* or dedicating poetry to the memory of the real-life woman, Kimako Baraka, in the poem "3 for Kimako," Jordan always found a way to bridge divisions between the realities of girls and women. Whether she was reflecting on her New York City childhood in *Soldier: A Poet's Childhood* or documenting painful episodes from the life of young Valerie—"See Valerie afraid," "Valerie does not play," "Nobody really likes Valerie," or "Valerie thinks . . . her mother may strangle her"—Jordan insisted on the safety and unconditional love of young women.[66]

This insistence on physical protection is linked to Jordan's demand for quality educational resources and instruction for women and girls, a message her own cousin, Valerie Orridge, believes in.[67] In the "Introduction" to *Some of Us Did Not Die: New and Selected Essays of June Jordan*, the poet asserts a voice of concern and offers a critique of the educational opportunities afforded to females. Jordan writes,

> Education is denied to most female human beings on the planet. And even if you disregard the significance of that for girls and women, you just might, nevertheless, begin to care about the documented correlations between illiterate female populations and the impoverishments, the barbaric hardship of every

society maintaining and/or imposing such an unequal, such a literally suffocat-
ing status quo.[68]

Jordan advocated fighting against the "status quo"[69] because she believed that
the relationship between universal illiteracy and poverty is reflected in the
public's understanding that the roles of girls and women are determined by
societies' political structures, which are oftentimes dominated by traditional
gender and class standards. Jordan called for ongoing resistance to patriarchal
systems by insisting on female-led coalitions and campaigns. In 1993, the poet
advanced this point well in her essay "I Am Seeking an Attitude," in which she
provides statistics on the women affected by rape, ethnic cleansing, genocidal
war, and a violence of silence. Then, in 1996, Jordan argued for increased
attention to violence perpetuated against women in the essay "A Model of
Resistance." Jordan condemned rape and violence of all forms. Furthermore,
she found female illiteracy and poverty inhumane and intolerable in any society. She believed that the formation and livelihood of a community depends on
the integration of women into every aspect of society, from education to government and beyond.

The written word, as represented in Jordan's volumes of poetry and essays,
published speeches, recordings, and interview transcripts, attests to the need
for more coalitions—a fact that lives on even after her death. Jordan's writing
will live beyond us all, reaching generations of people in countless countries
who, like her, seek to change the world through activism and poetry. Having
been translated into different languages, including Japanese, Arabic, French,
Spanish, German, and Swedish, and having traveled around the globe from
Nicaragua to Palestine, Jordan's poetry jumps off of the page that is intended
to contain it. Her words confront readers and either captivate their hearts or
upset their political views. The poet did not merely state, "I oppose colonialism in South Africa," "I stand against the war in Vietnam and all other wars
that kill thousands upon thousands of people," or "I detest racism and homophobia." She campaigned against these things, often at the risk of losing her
job, her relationships with friends and lovers, and always at the expense of her
own inner being.

June Jordan, our "people's poet" and the world's "universal poet," died on
June 14, 2002, but her memory, her legacy, and her writing are still with us.
Readers should turn to her poems and essays when they need to be encouraged to fight "the good fight" in support of the Beloved Community, when they
need to be encouraged to write and speak out, or when they need direction.
Jordan was, as she called herself, a "dissident poet."[70] As discussed earlier, the
poet discovered ways to establish connections between local and international
issues. Jordan's body of work signifies her ongoing effort to be knowledgeable
about every aspect of humanity, however impossible an undertaking it may
have been—from understanding that injustice is rampant throughout the
world, to embracing a lifelong fight for freedom, and to calling herself a
Palestinian. Whatever and whomever she was writing about, she drew attention

This art piece was a part of the June Jordan Collaborative Community Project by Brett Cook-Dizney. It measures 8 feet by 18 feet and is made of spray enamel, acrylic on wood, as well as other miscellaneous submissions. It was a nonpermissional public work, displayed at 127th Street and St. Nicholas Avenue in Harlem, New York, from July 2002 to January 2003. By permission of Brett Cook-Dizney.

to the emotional, physical, and political spaces required for the survival of marginalized peoples everywhere. Her commitment to people in the United States, Nicaragua, Lebanon, South Africa, Israel, Bosnia, and to the People, in general, can be seen in her explorations of multicultural and multiracial identities, feminist politics, Third-World activism, power movements, and human persecutions.

Needless to say, Jordan's dedication to humanity and to freedom has had positive, revolutionary effects on politics and civil rights and the individual lives of women, children, and men who are often categorized as disenfranchised:

This is the promise
I am making it here on the road
of my country

I am raising my knife
to carve out the heart
of no shame

The very next move is not mine[71]

Artist Mascha Oehlmann created this large, outdoor mural of June Jordan, which graces the side of the Bedford-Stuyvesant Restoration Plaza Building, located at 1360 Fulton Street in Brooklyn, New York. It measures 23 feet by 12 feet and was unveiled on March 10, 2005, during the launch of the "Heart and Soul of Bedford-Stuyvesant" media campaign honoring Brooklyn icons. Photograph taken by Valerie Kinloch.

There are no holidays that honor Jordan, no annual gatherings of activists across the world to celebrate her life on the day of her birth, and no documented call to travel to Palestine and join forces with its people, as she did in the 1980s. There are few bookstores that carry more than one copy of her books at any one time, and yet she is one of the most published black American writers of all time, even in death.

There is now a physical monument, however temporary, to the life and work of June Jordan. Residents and community activists in Brooklyn honored this cultural warrior in March 2005 with the unveiling of a life-sized mural of the poet, which hangs from the Restoration Plaza Building located at 1360 Fulton Street in the poet's former Bedford-Stuyvesant neighborhood. Let us remember June Jordan and honor her because:

Some of Us Did Not Die
We're Still Here
I Guess It Was Our Destiny To Live
So Let's get on with it![72]

The poet never failed to "get on with it"[73] when it came to her many literary pursuits. She published twenty-eight books of poetry, fiction, and essays, and contributed political writings to *The Nation*, the *New York Times*, *The Progressive*, and the *Harvard Educational Review*. Beginning with *Who Look At Me* (1969), *Soulscript: Afro-American Poetry* (1970), *Some Changes* (1971), and

New Days: Poems of Exile and Return (1973), Jordan articulated her belief in the sanctity of human life by using writing to capture those intersections where politics and personal struggle coexist to fight against unlawful behavior. This latter point is evident in Jordan's children's and young-adult books *His Own Where* (1971) and *Dry Victories* (1972); in her plays *In the Spirit of Sojourner Truth*, produced at the Public Theatre in New York City (1979), and *For the Arrow That Flies by Day*, which received a staged reading at the Shakespeare Festival in New York City (1981); and in the poet's musical collaborations with Torf, Reagon, and Adams. Indeed, the poet's accomplishments were plentiful, even in her final days.

Jordan accumulated numerous awards for her writing and humanitarian work, though these cannot fully testify to the amount of time, energy, and dedication she devoted to her craft. During the last ten years of her life, Jordan received the PEN Center USA West Freedom to Write Award (1991), the Ground Breakers–Dream Makers Award from the San Francisco Women's Foundation (1994), The American Institute of Architecture Award for a joint proposal for the African Burial Ground Project in New York City, the Lila Wallace Writers Award from *Reader's Digest* (1995), and the Critics Award and Herald Angel Award at the Edinburgh Arts Festival for *I Was Looking at the Ceiling and Then I Saw the Sky* (1995). In 1998, the poet received a Lifetime Achievement Award from the National Black Writers' Conference and was presented with the Students' Choice Louise Patterson African American Award for outstanding black faculty at the University of California, Berkeley. Just before her death, Jordan was honored with the Poets & Writers *Writer for Writers'* Award (2002) and with the Women Who Dared Award from the National Black Women's Health Project. I would be remiss not to mention that Jordan's face has even appeared on a postage stamp in Uganda.

The poet's contributions to literature, education, politics, and activism are phenomenal. Jordan's essays and poems tell many stories that indicate her perpetual search for universal freedom, love, and equality as they connect to a politics of inclusion for marginalized people. Amazingly, the poet continued this search even as she battled breast cancer during her last ten years, an act of heroism that redefines human strength, endurance, and political commitment. For these reasons, June Millicent Jordan (1936–2002) must be remembered, read, and her work studied. Without a doubt, her sentiments from *Things That I Do in the Dark* should be taken to heart as we continue the "good fight," always in love with the promise of a better day:

These poems
they are things that I do
in the dark
reaching for you
whoever you are
and
are you ready?[74]

Notes

INTRODUCTION

1. June Jordan, *Soldier: A Poet's Childhood* (New York: Basic Civitas Books, 2000), 260.

SOLDIER: A POET'S CHILDHOOD

1. Jordan, *Civil Wars: Observations from the Front Lines of America* (New York: Touchstone, 1981), xx.

2. Sara Miles, "Directed by Desire," in *Still Seeking an Attitude: Critical Reflections on the Work of June Jordan*, eds. Valerie Kinloch and Margret Grebowicz, 265 (Lanham, MD: Lexington Books, 2004).

3. Ibid., 265.

4. Jordan, *Soldier*, 25.

5. Robert A. Hill and Barbara Bair, eds., *Marcus Garvey: Life and Lessons*, repr. ed. (California: University of California Press, 1987), 184.

6. Ibid., 184–185.

7. James Weldon Johnson, *The Autobiography of an Ex-Coloured Man* (New York & London: Alfred A. Knopf, 1927). Johnson first published this book anonymously in 1912.

8. Ralph Ellison, *Invisible Man* (New York: Vintage Books, 1972), 560.

9. Ibid.

10. June Jordan, *Things That I Do in the Dark: Selected Poems* (New York: Random House, 1977), 20.

11. Jordan, *Soldier*, 4. See also Jordan's essay "For My American Family" in June Jordan, *Some of Us Did Not Die: New and Selected Essays of June Jordan* (New York: Basic Civitas Books, 2002), 141.

12. Valerie Orridge, interview by author, December 14, 2005.

13. Ibid.

14. Ibid. Orridge informs me that her grandmother, Mrs. Marie Taylor, was "livid" that her youngest daughter went away to school only to return pregnant: "After my mother went to Hunter and she met my father, she became pregnant. And my grand-mother was livid—'after having come from Jamaica and so poor . . . working and strug-gling to give you a better life . . . you [Lynne] come home pregnant.' . . . And so she married my father. My father was a very good man; he was a kind man . . . a gentle-man." Orridge goes on to tell me, "After three or four years of that [marriage], she [Lynne] left him." Lynne then retreated, temporarily, to the Jordan's household to ask Mildred to care for young Valerie.

15. Orridge, interview by author.

16. Jordan, *Soldier*, 15.

17. Jordan, *Soldier*, 135, original spacing.

18. Jordan, *Soldier*, 136.

19. Jordan, *Soldier*, 136–137.

20. Emphasis added.

21. Audre Lorde, *Zami, Sister Outsider, Undersong* (New York: Quality Paperback Book Club, 1982), 41.

22. June Jordan, *Kissing God Goodbye: Poems 1991–1997* (New York: Anchor Books/Random House, 1997), 27.

23. Orridge, interview by author.

24. Jordan, *Soldier*, 6.

25. Jordan, *Some of Us Did Not Die*, 141.

26. For a detailed and descriptive discussion of Jordan's childhood with Granville Ivanhoe Jordan and Mildred Maude Fisher, please see Jordan, *Soldier*.

27. June Jordan, interview by David Barsamian, "Childhood Memories: An Interview with June Jordan," March, 2000, http://www.zmag.org/Zmag/articles/mar01 barsamian.htm.

28. Orridge, interview by author.

29. Jordan, interview by David Barsamian, "Childhood Memories."

30. Orridge, interview by author.

31. Orridge, interview by author.

32. Jordan, *Some of Us Did Not Die*, 139.

33. United States Constitution, art. 18, sec. 1, http://www.house.gov/Constitution/Constitution.html.

34. Paul Laurence Dunbar, *Selected Works, Unabridged* (Mineola, NY: Dover Publications, 1997), 66.

35. William Shakespeare, *The Riverside Shakespeare* (Boston: Houghton Mifflin Company, 1974), 1751.

36. Jordan, *Soldier*, 19.

37. Ibid., 161.

38. Ibid.

39. Ibid., 176.

40. Orridge, interview by author.

41. Orridge, interview by author. Orridge tells me, "June admired my mother because . . . she was a principal. She [Lynne] had been a teacher, became an assistant principal, and then became a school principal."

42. Orridge, interview by author.

43. Jordan, *Soldier*, 134.

44. Orridge, interview by author.

45. Jordan, *Civil Wars*, 98.

46. June Jordan, *On Call: Political Essays* (Boston: South End Press, 1985), 51.

47. Alexis De Veaux, "Creating Soul Food: June Jordan," *Essence Magazine*, April 11, 1981, 82, 143.

48. Orridge, interview by author.

49. Ibid.

50. Ibid.

51. De Veaux, "Creating Soul Food," 145.

52. Jordan, *Civil Wars*, 16.

53. Jordan, *On Call: Political Essays*, 54.

54. Jordan, "Foreword," in *Civil Wars*, 1.

WHO LOOK AT ME

1. Jordan, "Foreword," in *Civil Wars*, 2.

2. Ibid.

3. Orridge, interview by author.

4. Ibid.

5. Around the time Jordan was writing her children's and young-adult novels, and shortly after her text, *Who Look at Me* (1969), was published, other important works by black women writers were being released: Toni Morrison's *The Bluest Eye* (1970), Alice Walker's *The Third Life of Grange Copeland* (1970), Maya Angelou's *I Know Why the Caged Bird Sings* (1969), Ntozake Shange's *for colored girls who have considered suicide/when the rainbow is enuf* (1975), and the reprinted edition of Zora Neale Hurston's *Mules and Men* (1970). These women, and many before them, used their writings to demonstrate that black women could exist as "revolutionary" artists and could offer a theory of black female creativity as connected to politics and identity.

6. Jordan, *Civil Wars*, xvii.

7. Jordan, *Things That I Do in the Dark*, 2. It should be noted that "Who Look at Me?" is a book-length poem published in 1968; the poem also appears as a part of a collection of other poems, as in the case of its inclusion in Jordan's *Things That I Do in the Dark* and *Naming Our Destiny: New and Selected Poems*.

8. In some of her writings, particularly in "One Way of Beginning This Book" (Jordan, *Civil Wars*, 1981), Jordan refers to her friend Huck: "My friend Huck, who had dropped out of Barnard a couple of years before I did, came by, all the way from the Bronx where she lived, about once a month. These visits were exhausting. Huck was a genius of sorts; incapable of superficial anything. Hence, any discussion or narrative had to be pursued into the early hours of the morning or it would represent shoddy exploration" (Jordan, *Civil Wars*, xxiii–xxiv).

9. Jordan, *Civil Wars*, xxvii.

10. Jordan, *Civil Wars*, xxvii. I cite Jordan's racial identification of Wiseman and Clarke because of the emphasis she places upon the political dynamics between the characters and the producer and director of the film: "the film 'starred' Black kids from the streets; it was the only feature film about what it means to be Black in a racist white country from 1954 to 1964 that I can recall"—and it was directed and produced by two white people who were not afraid to work with children of color in Harlem, New York.

11. Jordan, *Civil Wars*, 4.

12. Jordan has written briefly on her encounters with Malcolm X in New York City during the early-to-mid-1960s. In 1965, Malcolm X was murdered at the Audubon Ballroom on upper Broadway in Washington Heights, New York. The ballroom is now the site of the Malcolm X and Betty Shabazz Memorial and Educational Center.

13. The Congress of Racial Equality (CORE), founded as the Committee of Racial Equality, was formed by a racially diverse group of students from the University of Chicago. James Farmer, a black student, and George Houser, a white student, became the organization's primary leaders. CORE formed as an organized, nonviolent group in 1942 in many American cities, including New York, Baltimore, Los Angeles, and St. Louis. The history of CORE is often divided into three periods: (1) 1942–1961—nonviolent organizing with the ultimate goal being integration of public spaces and institutions; most members were Northern and white; (2) 1961–1964—nonviolence and coercive force combined as people protested and demonstrated against violence and inequality; black and white members addressed issues of housing and voter registration for Black Americans; and (3) 1964—the rise in Black Power groups and community organizing for poor and working-class black people with most of CORE's members being black. For more information on the history and work of CORE, see http://www.tcnj.edu/~doshi2/.

14. Jordan refers to her friend, Dorothy Moscou, in "Letter to Michael (1964)." In her letter, Jordan alludes to a moment when she turned her radio on and heard newscasters asking residents of Harlem to not resort to violent acts because of the murder of fifteen-year old Jimmy Powell by the police. Jordan writes that Moscou "came by, shared my dinner and accompanied me to the funeral establishment" to pay respects to Powell. Upon arriving in Harlem, Jordan and Moscou were met with scores of police officers and protestors in the streets. For more information, see Jordan, *Civil Wars*, 17–18.

15. Jordan, *Civil Wars*, 19.

16. Jordan, *Civil Wars*, xvii.

17. Adrienne Torf, interview by author, October 24, 2005.

18. Jordan was never specific about why she was not able to financially and completely take care of her son. In some of her writings, including "Letter to Buckminster Fuller (1964)," Jordan writes: "Michael was gone. I worked. I studied architecture. . . . I planned. I spent my life waiting. It was a gamble." She goes on to admit, "Those days I didn't eat. A few friends brought me cigarettes, Scotch, eggs, bread, and my mother gave me two or three dollars for gas. What I had left was my car: my tangible liberty was my car" (Jordan, *Civil Wars*, 23). This was a particularly difficult time for Jordan.

19. Jordan, *Civil Wars*, 24.

20. Ibid., 30.

21. Ibid., 38.

22. Before the Open Admissions Policy was passed at City College, the student population was predominately white. "Then, in 1969, riding the crest of the civil rights movement, a group of African American and Latino students shut down City College's South Campus. They demanded that the college reflect the racial and ethnic composition of Harlem. After numerous tense meetings, New York City's politicians agreed upon an open admissions policy that guaranteed every New York City high school graduate a place in CUNY." This proved monumental because the open admissions policy at City College did not restrict students of color to two-year institutions, but made way for them to receive undergraduate degrees from a four-year, or "senior," institution.

"The African American and Latino activists didn't want students of color to be restricted to two-year college degrees. So the activists sought and won an open admissions policy that permitted students who were in the top half of their high school class or who had a grade point average of eighty to enroll in the senior colleges." City College became an open admissions institution, and the student demographics quickly changed from that of a largely white population of students to one where "students of color," in 1969, "accounted for less than a fifth of all CUNY undergraduates." For more information, see "Open Admissions at the City University of New York" at http://www.aaup.org/publications/Academe/ 2003/03ja/03jacrai.htm. Accessed March 22, 2006.

23. Ibid., 46.

24. Ibid., 53.

25. Ibid., 55.

26. Adrienne Rich, *On Lies, Secrets, and Silence: Selected Prose, 1966–1978* (New York: Norton, 1979), 56.

27. Jordan, *Civil Wars,* 50, 55. In the essay titled, "Black Studies: Bringing Back the Person" (1969), Jordan argues various reasons for the existence of Black Studies programs on college campuses. Her participation, with colleagues and students at City College, for university approval of the Open Admissions policy instigated her insistence on diverse teaching methods and curricular practices, particularly in the education of nonwhite students.

28. David Vidal, "What Happens to a Dream? This One Lives," *New York Times*, original publication date unlisted. Archival date provided as March 24, 1977, NJ22. http://www.proquest.com or http://pqasb.pqarchiver.com/nytimes/results.html?st=advanced&QryTxt=&x=37&y=6&By=David+Vidal&Title=&datetype=6&frommonth=05&fromday=01&fromyear=1967&tomonth=03&today=31&toyear=1977&restrict=articles&sortby=REVERSE_CHRON.

29. This note is found in the prefatory pages to the actual text. Jordan acknowledged Milton Meltzer because he made the completion of the project possible; this highly acclaimed writer committed time and attention to providing Jordan with feedback and picture selection.

30. Cheryll Greene, "Women Talk: A Conversation with June Jordan and Angela Davis," *Essence Magazine*, May 1990, 63–68. http://www.findarticles.com/p/articles/mi_m1264/is_n1_v21/ai_9005541.

31. June Jordan, *Who Look at Me* (New York: Thomas Y. Crowell Company, 1969), 1.

32. Ibid., 90–91.

33. June Jordan, "Mississippi 'Black Home,'" *New York Times*, October 11, 1970, 65.

34. In a conversation with poet E. Ethelbert Miller, I was informed that Jordan's visits to Nicaragua and Lebanon had a large impact on her politics and art. In studying Jordan's poems and essays on both places and researching the political, economic, and social issues that were (and continue to be) pervasive during her "discoveries" of Nicaragua and Lebanon, I was able to draw connections between her concentration on space, identity, love, and resistance. See June Jordan, "Nicaragua: Why I Had to Go There," in *Some of Us Did Not Die*, as well as "Dance: Nicaragua" and "Apologies to All the People in Lebanon," in *Naming Our Destiny: New & Selected Poems* (New York: Thunder's Mouth Press, 1989) for an introduction to the poet's commitment to the two places.

35. Jordan, "Mississippi," 65.

36. Ibid., 81.

37. Ibid., 83.

38. Ibid.

39. Valerie Kinloch, "Black English as a Linguistic System: A Statement About Our Rights," in *Still Seeking*, 71.

40. June Jordan, *His Own Where* (New York: Crowell Company, 1971), 1.

41. Torf, interview by author.

42. Jordan, *Moving Towards Home: Political Essays* (London: Virago Press, 1989), 38.

43. Ibid.

44. Jordan, *Civil Wars*, 61.

45. Among other places, this essay can be found in the following text: George Orwell, *A Collection of Essays* (New York: Harcourt Publishers, 1970).

46. Interestingly, Jordan wrote the first known young-adult novel in Black English in America. Some thirty years later, the debate on the validity of Black English as a language surfaced in Oakland, California, and in 1996, the school board in Oakland decided that Ebonics was a language form that needed to be addressed in the education of its black students. June Jordan, however, hated the name Ebonics and insisted that the debate was not new. She always believed in the multiple forms of English and other languages that students bring with them to the classroom.

47. Jordan, *Civil Wars*, 78.

48. June Jordan, "May 27, 1971: No Poem," *Directed by Desire: The Collected Poems of June Jordan* (Port Townsend, WS: Cooper Canyon Press, 2005), 121–122. Originally published in *The Village Voice* (June 10, 1971), and originally accessed from the newspaper archives at Stanford University, November 2003.

49. June Jordan, *Fannie Lou Hamer* (New York: Crowell Company, 1972), 39.

50. Jordan has dedicated and written poems about her father, Granville. While the information that circulates around their relationship is not detailed, one can strongly speculate that their father-daughter relationship was not as strong as either of them would have wished. Granville wanted his daughter to be a doctor, not a poet; some of the decisions that June Jordan made did not coincide with the decisions that her father had hoped she would make.

51. Jordan, *Civil Wars*, 78.

52. Jordan wrote various works on her mother. For example, in her poem "Ghaflah," Jordan remarks, "I wish I had found her/that first woman/my mother/trying to rise up . . . /I wish I had given her/my arm" (Jordan, *Kissing God Goodbye*, 28). In the poem, "On the Spirit of Mildred Jordan," Jordan writes, "After sickness and a begging/from her bed/my mother dressed herself/grey-laced oxfords . . . /she took the street . . . /she wasn't foxy/*she was strong*" (Jordan, *Naming Our Destiny*, 13–14; author's emphasis).

53. Orridge, interview by author.

54. Orridge, interview by author.

55. Jordan, *Moving Towards Home*, 121

56. Ibid., 122.

57. Ibid.

58. Orridge, interview by author.

59. Orridge, interview by author.

60. Jordan, *Things That I Do in the Dark*, 37.

61. Ibid., 27.

62. Jordan, *Moving Towards Home*, 124–125.

63. Orridge, interview by author.

64. Jordan, *Affirmative Acts: Political Essays* (New York: Anchor Books/Doubleday, 1998), 134.

65. Jordan, *His Own Where*, 1.

NEW DAYS: POEMS OF EXILE AND RETURN

1. Jordan, *New Days: Poems of Exile and Return* (New York: Emerson Hall Publishers, 1970), 73.

2. Ibid., 73–74.

3. Even as Jordan sought to participate in public movements that highlighted the varied experiences of women, particularly black women, as evident by the inclusion of her writings in *Chrysalis*, her writing began to increase in its philosophical intensity; she read representative writings associated with Marxism, feminism, women's studies, ethnic studies, African and African American cultural scholarship, urbanism, and later, interdisciplinarity and world culture.

4. Alexis De Veaux, *Warrior Poet: A Biography of Audre Lorde* (New York: W. W. Norton & Company, 2004), 178. While Jordan was not close to Audre Lorde, she did value Lorde's literary contributions. It was Lorde who, upon her resignation from the National Education Association's policy committee for literature, suggested that the NEA consider filling her vacancy by appointing either June Jordan, Janice Mirikitami, or Alexis De Veaux.

5. For more information on June Jordan's arguments against the research of William Shockley, see Jordan, *Civil Wars*, 90.

6. Jordan, *New Days*, 6.

7. Ibid.

8. Ibid.

9. Jordan, *Moving Towards Home*, 70.

10. Ibid.

11. Walt Whitman, "Song of Myself," in *The Portable Walt Whitman*, ed. Mark Van Doren, 33 (New York: Viking Penguin Inc., 1973). Format is as it appears in *The Portable Walt Whitman*.

12. Bettina Knapp, *Walt Whitman* (New York: Continuum, 1993), 88, 91.

13. Jordan, *Moving Towards Home*, 70.

14. Ibid., 61.

15. Jordan, *Civil Wars*, 180.

16. Ibid.

17. Ibid., 181. Jordan offers her interpretation of this situation. In researching Piven and Jordan's relationship and differing opinions as concerns political involvement, gay rights, and civil rights, my attempts to contact Piven proved unsuccessful. My attempts to contact Jordan's son, Christopher David Meyer, were also unsuccessful. Jordan notes that it was her son who told her to read Piven and Cloward's book, *Poor Peoples' Movements: Why They Succeed, How They Fail.*

18. Jordan, *Civil Wars*, 181.

19. Around this time, Christopher David Meyer was a student at Harvard University; he was working on his AB in sociology and completing his thesis, "The Negro Dilemma: An Inquiry into the Political Programs of Frederick Douglass and W.E.B. Du Bois." He

completed this degree in June 1981 and graduated cum laude. For more information, visit the libraries and archives at Harvard University.

20. Jordan, *Civil Wars,* 85.

21. Walker first came across the writer Zora Neale Hurston in a footnote when she was doing research, and from that discovery, Walker sought to expose the literary genius that was Hurston. She shared Hurston's novel, *Their Eyes Were Watching God,* with Jordan.

22. Jordan, *Civil Wars,* 86.

23. Ibid., 84.

24. At City College, Jordan worked to prepare students to move out of remedial, "basic writing," courses and into the general education curriculum by teaching writing and grammar. Her work at City College came after her divorce from Michael Meyer and her mother's death. Around the same time, Jordan was "caring" for her son and gaining popularity with initiatives throughout Harlem, New York's political movements.

25. Jordan, *Naming Our Destiny,* 71.

26. Ibid.

27. According to online information, Yaddo was "founded in 1900 by the financier Spencer Trask and his wife Katrina, herself a poet." It is "an artists' community located on a 400-acre estate in Saratoga Springs, New York. Its mission is to nurture the creative process by providing an opportunity for artists to work without interruption in a supportive environment." Residencies are provided to "professional creative artists from all nations and backgrounds working in one or more of the following media: choreography, film, literature, musical composition, painting, performance art, photography, printmaking, sculpture, and video." For more information, see http://www.yaddo.org/Yaddo/index6.shtml. Accessed March 22, 2006.

28. Jordan, *Moving Towards Home,* 90.

29. According to the organization's online materials, "The MacDowell Colony was founded in Peterborough, New Hampshire, in 1907. The Colony's mission today, as it was then, is to nurture the arts by offering creative individuals of the highest talent an inspiring environment in which to produce enduring works of the imagination. More than 250 writers, composers, visual artists, photographers, printmakers, filmmakers, architects, interdisciplinary artists, and those collaborating on creative works come to the Colony each year from all parts of the United States and abroad." For more information, see http://www.macdowellcolony.org/history.html. Accessed on March 22, 2006.

30. The other Reid Lecturer was writer Alice Walker.

31. Jordan, *Some of Us Did Not Die,* 3, 4. The author's original indentations and format are provided in this citation.

32. Valerie Orridge, interview by author, December 14 and 18, 2005. Orridge tells me that sometime after the death of Mildred, Granville sold his Brooklyn brownstone and went back to Jamaica, where he eventually died. Before his return to Jamaica, Granville asked to be buried with his wife, Mildred, in New Jersey. Upon his death, Jordan went to Jamaica and for undisclosed reasons, buried her father there.

33. June Jordan to Joanne Braxton, January 1970.

34. Karla Hammond, "An Interview with June Jordan," *Kalliope* 4, no.1 (Fall 1981): 39.

35. June Jordan, ed., *Soulscript: A Collection of African American Poetry* (New York: Harlem Moon/Broadway Books, 2004), xvii.

36. Ibid.
37. June Jordan, ed., *Soulscript: Afro-American Poetry* (New York: Zenith Books, 1970), xviii–xix. Throughout the discussion of *Soulscript*, I refer to the first edition of the collection, which was published in 1970, unless otherwise noted in the text.
38. Ibid., xvi.
39. Ibid., xvii.
40. Ibid., xvi.
41. Ibid., xvii.
42. Ibid., 2.
43. Ibid., 6.
44. Ibid., 7. Original spelling of the lowercase "I" belongs to the author, Linda Curry.
45. Ibid., 18.
46. Ibid., 134.
47. Ibid., 135.
48. June Jordan, *Some Changes* (New York: E. P. Dutton & Company, 1971), ix.
49. Ibid., 9.
50. Ibid..
51. Jordan was in fact very close to her son, and provided for him in ways that Michael Meyer did not.
52. Jordan, *Some Changes*, 3.
53. Ibid.
54. Ibid.
55. Ibid., 47.
56. Ibid.
57. Ibid., 3.
58. Ibid., 9.
59. Interestingly, Jordan's father resembled a white man and Jordan, herself, married a white man. Her son, Christopher, looks like a white man. The construction and presence of images of whiteness, then, in June Jordan's family structure and in her associations with personal friends and colleagues make for startling commentary on how she interrogated race, racial dynamics, and the "privilege" of whiteness in her family and in literature, politics, and activism.
60. Jordan, *Some Changes*, 55.
61. Ibid., 56.
62. Jordan, *Things That I Do in the Dark*, 37–38.
63. Ibid., 38–39.
64. June Jordan, Jan Heller Levi, and Sara Miles, eds., *Directed by Desire: The Collected Poems of June Jordan* (Port Townsend, WA: Cooper Canyon Press, 2005), xxi.
65. Ibid., xxii.
66. Jordan, *Things That I Do in the Dark*, 64.
67. Ibid.
68. Ibid.
69. During a few email exchanges, E. Ethelbert Miller informed me that Jordan's poem, "For Ethelbert," was indeed a response to his poem, "FOR JUNE." Sincere appreciation is due to Miller for providing me with invaluable information and for helping me to make particular connections.
70. E. Ethelbert Miller, "For June," in *Whispers, Secrets, and Promises*, 115 (Baltimore: Black Classic Press, 1998).

71. Jordan, *Naming Our Destiny*, 29.

72. Jordan, *Things That I Do in the Dark*, 64.

73. Jordan, *Some Changes*, 9.

74. Hammond, "An Interview with June Jordan," 41.

75. June Jordan, *Passion: New Poems* (Boston: Beacon Press, 1980), 79.

76. Ibid.

77. Ibid., 80.

78. Ibid., 86.

79. Ibid. Poet's original structure, including line breaks and the use of the solidus, or front slash, in the last two lines of the cited excerpt from the poem.

80. Jordan, *Naming Our Destiny*, p.103. Many of Jordan's poems are reprinted in her various poetry collections. For this particular excerpt of "Poem about My Rights," I refer to the *Naming Our Destiny* version.

81. Ibid., 104. This particular excerpt of "Poem about My Rights" appears in *Naming Our Destiny*. Italics belong to the author, June Jordan.

82. Jordan, *Passion*, 86.

83. Ibid., 87.

84. E. Ethelbert Miller, "My Language, My Imagination: The Politics of Poetry," May 4, 1998, http://www.eethelbertmiller.com/essay.html. Accessed October 2005.

85. Jordan, *Naming Our Destiny*, 158.

86. Ibid., 159.

87. Ibid., 159–160.

88. June Jordan, *Living Room: New Poems* (New York: Thunder's Mouth Press, 1985), 25.

89. Jordan, *Things That I Do in the Dark*, 158–159.

90. Marilyn Hacker, "Provoking Engagement," *The Nation* 250, no. 0004 (January 29, 1990): 135.

91. Jordan, *Naming Our Destiny*, 24.

92. Amiri Baraka, "SOS," in *The Leroi Jones/Amiri Baraka Reader*, 2nd ed., 218 (New York: Thunder's Mouth Press, 1999).

93. Gil Scott-Heron, "The Revolution Will Not Be Televised," performed by Gil Scott-Heron on *Our Souls Have Grown Deep Like the Rivers* (New York:Rhino/Wea Records, 2000), compact disc.

94. Jordan, *Civil Wars*, xx.

95. Jordan, *Affirmative Acts*, 39.

MOVING TOWARDS HOME: POLITICAL ESSAYS

1. Writer-activist Kalamu ya Salaam pinpoints the Black Arts Movement's beginning at 1965 and its eventual ending, not death, at 1976. For information on BAM, see www.black-collegian.com/african/bam1_200.shtml.

2. Woodie King, Jr., *The Forerunners: Black Poets in America* (Washington, DC: Howard University Press, 1975), xxiii.

3. Ibid., xxiii–xxiv.

4. Ibid., xxvii.

5. Jordan, *Some of Us Did Not Die*, 44.

6. Ibid.

7. Ibid., 45.

8. In 1963, King was again arrested, this time for participating in demonstrations and a civil rights campaign in Birmingham, Alabama. In jail, he wrote his famous "Letter from Birmingham Jail," which, in part, reads, "Moreover, I am cognizant of the interrelatedness of all communities and states. I cannot sit idly by in Atlanta and not be concerned about what happens in Birmingham. Injustice anywhere is a threat to justice everywhere. We are caught in an inescapable network of mutuality, tied in a single garment of destiny. Whatever affects one directly affects all indirectly. Never again can we afford to live with the narrow, provincial 'outside agitator' idea. Anyone who lives in the United States can never be considered an outsider anywhere in this country." For more information, see the following: Martin Luther King, *I Have a Dream: Writings and Speeches that Changed the World*, ed. James M. Washington, 85 (San Francisco: HarperSanFrancisco, 1986/1992).

9. King showed support for the Civil Rights Act and delivered his famous speech, "I Have a Dream," to hundreds of thousands of demonstrators, including members of SCLC, SNCC, NAACP, and of Asa Phillip Randolph's labor group, gathered at the Lincoln Memorial in Washington, DC. In part, the speech reads, "Let us not seek to satisfy our thirst for freedom by drinking from the cup of bitterness and hatred. We must forever conduct our struggles on the high plane of dignity and discipline. We must not allow our creative protest to degenerate into physical violence. Again and again we must rise to the majestic heights of meeting physical force with soul force." For more information, see the following: King, *I Have a Dream*, 103. Other events by King that Jordan took note of include King's leadership of the March 1964 march, with civil rights activists and supporters from Selma to Montgomery, Alabama. (This comes after "Bloody Sunday," during which protestors were attacked by Alabama officers and supremacist groups, and after the violent "hate" murder of James Reeb, a northern minister.) The march culminated at the Alabama capital. In August of the same year, Congress approved the Voting Rights Act, proposed under the Johnson administration.

10. Jordan, *Moving Towards Home*, 194.

11. Ibid., 195.

12. Ibid.

13. Ibid.

14. Ibid., 196.

15. Paul A. Winters, ed., *The Civil Rights Movement* (San Diego: Greenhaven Press, 2000), 69. The version included in Winters' edited book is excerpted from James H. Cone, "Malcolm X: The Impact of a Cultural Revolutionary," in *The Christian Century Journal*, Vol. 109 (1992 December 23–30): 1189–1191, 1193, 1195.

16. The following are just a few significant political events for Malcolm X: In June 1954, just two years after Malcolm was released from prison, Elijah Muhammad appointed him head minister of Harlem's Temple Number 7. In the early 1960s, Malcolm X began to directly attack the nonviolent teachings of Martin Luther King and the Civil Rights Movement, believing that integration and nonviolent tactics were fundamentally wrong—his attacks were delivered in speeches, news broadcasts, and private and public meetings. In 1959, Malcolm increased his travels, visiting such places as Sudan, Nigeria, Ghana, the Middle East, and the United Arab Republic. With Mike Wallace and Louis Lomax, Malcolm was featured in the weeklong televised program, *The Hate That Hate Produced*, discussing the workings of, and his role in, the Nation of Islam. His appearance on the program solidified his popularity as a political leader of black people. March 1964 was met with Malcolm's permanent departure from the Nation. In the

same year of his departure, Malcolm opened the Muslim Mosque, Inc. in New York City and traveled to Mecca, Saudi Arabia where he was convinced that it was important to join hands and fight for rights with all people regardless of race. His growing desire for an international freedom movement began to take shape.

17. Julie Quiroz, "'Poetry is a Political Act:' An Interview with June Jordan," *Colorlines* 1, no. 3 (Winter 1999), unlisted page numbers. http://www.arc.org/C_Lines/CLArchive/story1_3_05.html.

18. Quiroz, "'Poetry is a Political Act,'" unlisted page numbers.

19. Jordan, *Affirmative Acts*, 170–171.

20. Ibid., 171–172.

21. Ibid., 172.

22. Ibid.

23. Ibid., 173.

24. Torf, interview by author.

25. Jordan, *Civil Wars*, 118.

26. Ibid.

27. Jordan, *Things That I Do in the Dark*, 40.

28. Ibid., 41.

29. Ibid.

30. Ibid., 40.

31. Ibid., 41.

32. Jordan, *Some of Us Did Not Die*, 263.

33. Ibid.

34. Ibid., 266.

35. Ibid., 263.

36. Jordan, *Technical Difficulties: African-American Notes on the State of the Union* (New York: Pantheon Books, 1992), 136.

37. Jordan, *Some of Us Did Not Die*, 263.

38. Jordan, *Technical Difficulties*, 137.

39. Jordan, *Civil Wars*, 75.

40. Ibid., 79.

41. Ibid., 80.

42. Ibid., 79.

43. Ibid., 80.

44. For more information on this conference, see Jordan, *Affirmative Acts*, 260.

45. Jordan, *Civil Wars*, 143.

46. Jordan, *Living Room*, 66.

47. Ibid., 66.

48. Ibid., 66–67.

49. Ibid., 103. Original quotation marks and format.

50. Jordan, *Technical Difficulties*, 37.

51. Ibid.

52. Ibid., 39.

53. Jordan, *Kissing God Goodbye*, 86.

54. Ibid., 87.

55. Jordan, *Technical Difficulties*, 23.

56. Ibid., 93.

57. Jane Creighton. "Writing War, Writing Memory" in *Still Seeking an Attitude,* eds. Valerie Kinloch and Margret Grebowicz, 250.

58. Jordan, *Naming Our Destiny*, 143.

59. Ibid.

60. Sally Ann Brunot, Lori M. Evans, Daniela Kocoska, Megan Quinn, and Carla Silva, Website Researchers. "June Jordan, 1936–2002," *Voices from the Gaps: Women Writers and Writers of Color, an International Website*, May 12, 1998. Unlisted page numbers. http://voices.cla.umn.edu/vg/Bios/entries/jordan_june.html.

61. Jordan, *Some of Us Did Not Die*, 229.

62. Torf, interview by author.

63. Hammond, "An Interview with June Jordan," 43.

THE VOICE OF THE CHILDREN

1. Jordan, *Some of Us Did Not Die*, 277.

2. June Jordan and Terri Bush, eds. *The Voice of the Children* (New York: Holt, Rinehart and Winston, Inc., 1970), 53. This poem was written by then fourteen-year-old Juanita Bryant.

3. Jordan and Bush, *The Voice*, ix.

4. Ibid.

5. Ibid., from the "Foreword."

6. Ibid., ix.

7. Ibid., 97.

8. On the group, "The Voice of the Children," editorial writer Eve Merriam, in a *New York Times* article, writes that the group "is the name of a group of twenty-odd black and Puerto Rican youngsters who have been meeting in a Brooklyn Community Center every Saturday for the past two years to "rap, dance, snack, browse among the books lying around, and write their stories, poems, editorials, and jokes." For more information, see Eve Merriam, "For Young Readers," *New York Times*, listed date is January 24, 1971, http://www.proquest.com or http://pqasb.pqarchiver.com/nytimes/91264361 .html?did=91264361&FMT=ABS&FMTS=AI&date=Jan+24%2C+1971&author=EVE+ MERRIAM&pub=New+York+Times++(1857-Current+file)&desc=For+Young+Readers, BR24.

9. Jordan and Bush, *The Voice*, 98.

10. Martin Gansberg, "Voice of the Children is Stilled," *New York Times*, listed date is November 7, 1971, http://www.proquest.com or http://pqasb.pqarchiver.com/ nytimes/91312247.html?did=91312247&FMT=ABS&FMTS=AI&date=Nov+7%2C+19 71&author=By+MARTIN+GANSBERG&pub=New+York+Times++(1857- Current file)&desc=Voice+of+the+Children+Is+Stilled, A18.

11. Jordan, *Some of Us Did Not Die*, 275.

12. Ibid., 277.

13. Ibid., 279.

14. Ibid., 282.

15. Torf, interview by author.

16. E. Ethelbert Miller, e-mail message to author, November 1, 2005.

17. In *Solider: A Poet's Childhood*, Jordan informs readers of her first "true" love, sixteen-year-old Herbie Wilson, Jr.

18. June Jordan, *Fannie Lou Hamer*, 4.

19. Ibid., 24.

20. Ibid., 12.

21. Ibid., 15.

22. Ibid., 17–18.

23. Alexis De Veaux, "Creating Soul Food," 82, 138–150.

24. Alice Malsenior Walker and June Millicent Jordan were friends. Walker won the Pulitzer Prize in 1983 for her epistolary novel, *The Color Purple*. It tells the survival story of central character and Southern black woman, Celie, who writes letters to God about her life, particularly her various "women" responsibilities as mother, wife, and daughter. Walker includes in the novel a community of other black women: Celie's sister, Nettie; Blues singer, Shug Avery (Celie's husband is, consequently, in love with Shug Avery); the reflective Squeak; and the daughter-in-law, Sofia.

25. Alice Walker, "Fannie Lou Hamer: Can't hate anybody and see God's face," *New York Times*, listed date is April 29, 1973, http://www.proquest.com or http://pqasb. pqarchiver.com/nytimes/97135122.html?did=97135122&FMT=ABS&FMTS=AI&date =Apr+29%2C+1973&author=By+ALICE+WALKER&pub=New+York+Times++(1857-Current+file)&desc=Fannie+Lou+Hamer, 8.

26. June Jordan, "Mrs. Fannie Lou Hamer: In Memoriam," *New York Times*, June 3, 1977, http://www.proquest.com or http://pqasb.pqarchiver.com/nytimes/75081647 .html?did=75081647&FMT=CITE&FMTS=AI&date=Jun+3%2C+1977&author=&pu b=New+York+Times++(1857-Current+file)&desc=Mrs.+Fannie+Lou+Hamer%3A +In+Memoriam, 16. This poem is also published as "1977: Poem for Mrs. Fannie Lou Hamer" in Jordan, *Passion*, 40–41.

27. June Jordan, *Dry Victories* (New York: Avon Books, 1972).

28. Jordan, *Dry Victories*, 104.

29. Janet Harris, "Review of *Dry Victories*," *New York Times*, date listed as February 11, 1973, http://www.proquest.com or http://pqasb.pqarchiver.com/nytimes/90916358. html?did=90916358&FMT=ABS&FMTS=AI&date=Feb+11%2C+1973&author=By+JA NET+HARRIS&pub=New+York+Times++(1857-Current+file)&desc=Dry+Victories, 360.

30. June Jordan, *New Life: New Room* (New York: Crowell Company, 1975), 1.

31. Ibid., 12.

32. Ibid., 33.

33. June Jordan, *Kimako's Story* (Boston: Houghton Mifflin Company, 1981), inside cover.

34. Ibid., 1.

35. Ibid., 32.

36. Ibid., 37.

37. Ibid., 40–41.

38. Torf, interview by author.

39. In the newspaper story, "Newark Pride Gets Allies," journalist Mick Meenan writes about local slain females in Newark, New Jersey: fifteen-year-old Sakia Gunn who "was stabbed to death on the morning of May 12 on the corner of Broad and Market Streets in Newark as she waited with a group of other young women for a bus," and thirty-one-year-old Shani Baraka and her partner, thirty-year-old Rayshon Holmes, who "were shot multiple times in the head and body as they stood in the Piscataway home of Ms. Baraka's sister, Wanda Pasha" (*Gay City News*, 2, no. 36, September 2003).

Shani Baraka was the daughter of poet and political activist Amiri Baraka, whose only sister, Kimako Baraka, was killed some years before. Meenan writes, "In a follow up interview, he [Amiri Baraka] told how his sister, Kimako Baraka, herself an out lesbian, was brutally slain in 1984 during an attempted rape in Manhattan Plaza, a well-known residence for artists and entertainers. Kimako was a Broadway dancer and actress." For more information, see Mick Meenan, "Newark Pride Gets Allies," *Gay City News*, http://www.gaycitynews.com/ gcn236/newarkpride.html.

40. Jordan, *Living Room*, 99.

41. Jordan, *Some of Us Did Not Die*, 224.

42. Ibid., 225.

43. Ibid.

44. Julius Lester, letter to author, October 2005.

45. Ibid.

46. Jordan, *Living Room*, 42–43.

47. Jordan was not the only person campaigning for the language rights of students. In 1974, the Executive Committee for the Conference on College Composition and Communication, for example, proposed a resolution that argued for the affirmation of students' right to use their language forms in educational settings so as to learn those skills deemed essential for the further acquirement of academic knowledge and discursive practices. Sociolinguistic scholars, including Geneva Smitherman, were actively involved in initiating this resolution, named *Students' Right to Their Own Language*.

48. Smitherman, Delpit, and Rickford, in individual studies, argue for the legitimization of Black English in classrooms and communities, believing that speakers of Black English Vernacular are well versed in specific structures, rules, and skills of accompanying speech acts. To diminish how such speakers communicate with members in their own communities and in communities where the "Language of Wider Communication" is used is to deny them access to multiple forms of engagement. These authors assert the need for educators to affirm the linguistic varieties of students as said students are taught/shown the codes of academic, or formal, English. See Geneva Smitherman, *Talkin and Testifyin: The Language of Black America* (Detroit: Wayne State University Press, 1977); Lisa Delpit, *Other People's Children: Cultural Conflict in the Classroom* (New York: New Press, 1996); and James Rickford, "The Creole Origins of African American Vernacular English: Evidence from Copula Absence," in S. S. Mufwene, et al., *African American English: Structure, History and Use* (London and New York: Routledge, 1998).

49. Latoya Hardman, interview by author, October 20, 2004.

50. June Jordan, "Mississippi," 65, 67–71, 80–83.

51. June Jordan, *His Own Where*, 1.

52. Jordan, *Civil Wars*, 128–129.

53. Violet J. Harris, "African American Children's Literature: The First One Hundred Years," *Journal of Negro Education* 50, no. 4 (1990): 540–555.

54. Jordan, *His Own Where*, 13.

55. Ibid., 9.

56. Torf, interview by author.

57. Jordan, *His Own Where*, 1.

58. Jordan's *Soulscript: Afro-American Poetry*, a collection of poetry that contains the works of June Jordan, Audre Lorde, Sonia Sanchez, Langston Hughes, James Weldon Johnson, Gwendolyn Brooks, Countee Cullen, Richard Wright, Claude McKay, Gayl

Jones, various young and emerging student poets, and countless other luminaries, was first published in 1970. Harlem Moon publishers released a revised and updated edition of the collection, named *Soulscript: A Collection of African American Poetry*, in November 2004.

59. Jordan, *Naming Our Destiny*, 102.
60. June Jordan, *On Call: Political Essays*, 123.
61. I discuss Jordan's essay and the educational implications of adopting her guidelines for Black English in my 2004 essay, "June Jordan and the Linguistic Register: A Statement About Our Rights." The essay can be found in Kinloch and Grebowicz, eds., *Still Seeking*, 71–86.
62. Jordan, *Naming Our Destiny*, 204.
63. Ibid., 205.
64. Ibid., 210.
65. Lauren Muller and the Poetry for the People Blueprint Collective, eds., *June Jordan's Poetry for the People: A Revolutionary Blueprint* (New York: Routledge, 1995), 7.
66. Ibid., 7.
67. Ibid., 200.
68. Ibid., 201.
69. Greene, "Women Talk," 63–68.
70. Jordan, *Naming Our Destiny*, 210.
71. Jordan, *Civil Wars*, 163.
72. Ibid.
73. Jordan, *Affirmative Acts*, 120.
74. Jordan, *Technical Difficulties*, 119.
75. Ibid., 121.
76. Jordan's discussion of censorship as pertains to Jackson's pursuit of the Democratic Presidential nomination is related to the role and significance of black leadership in this country, particularly after the 1960s Civil Rights Movement. For more information on this topic, see Robert Charles Smith, *We Have No Leaders: African Americans in the Post Civil Rights Era* (Albany: State University of New York Press, 1996). This book challenges conservative and liberal notions of U.S.-based political struggles for black Americans, institutional processes, and censorship in political discourse.
77. Jordan, *Technical Difficulties*, 121.
78. Ibid., 123.
79. Ibid., 132.
80. Jordan, *Civil Wars*, 3.
81. Jordan, *Affirmative Acts*, 120.
82. Jordan, *On Call: Political Essays*, 3.
83. Jordan, *Some of Us Did Not Die*, 41.
84. Ibid., 58.
85. Ibid., 28, 31.
86. Jordan, *On Call: Political Essays*, 115–116.
87. Jordan, *Naming Our Destiny*, 143.
88. Ruth Forman, "Travelin' Shoes (for June Jordan)," in Muller, *June Jordan's Poetry for the People*, 225, 227.

AFFIRMATIVE ACTS: POLITICAL ESSAYS

1. Forman, "Travelin' Shoes," 225, 227.

2. Ibid., 225.

3. In conversations with poet E. Ethelbert Miller, I was informed that Jordan was close to her students and appreciated the mutual support afforded by their collaborations and learning experiences.

4. Muller, *June Jordan's Poetry for the People*, 15.

5. Ibid.

6. In the brief course description of P4P included in the text, *June Jordan's Poetry for the People*, 15, is written the following: "We publish student poetry in suitably splendid form, and distribute these anthologies at the student readings and through the kind offices of Berkeley bookstores, such as Black Oaks Books and Cody's. This is an integral part of coursework."

7. On how the program began, Jordan writes: "I did not wake up one morning ablaze with a coherent vision of Poetry for the People! The natural intermingling of my ideas and my observations as an educator, a poet, and the African-American daughter of poorly documented immigrants did not lead me to any limiting ideological perspectives or resolve. Poetry for the People is the arduous and happy outcome of practical, day-by-day, classroom failure and success." It is important to note that Jordan collaborated with others at UC Berkeley and in the community to raise necessary funds and attract attention for the program—a program which, from its very first class, had an immediate student following. For more information, see Junichi P. Semitsu, "Course Profile: Poetry for the People," http://www.ocf.berkeley.edu/~micmag/issue1/poetryforthepeople.php. See also Muller, *June Jordan's Poetry for the People.*

8. Muller, *June Jordan's Poetry for the People*, 13.

9. Muller, *June Jordan's Poetry for the People*, 16. For additional information on June Jordan's P4P and the ground rules, see Junichi P. Semitsu, "Course Profile: Poetry for the People," http://www.ocf.berkeley.edu/~micmag/issue1/poetryforthepeople.php.

10. Junichi Semitsu, former director of Poetry for the People, who was appointed by June Jordan, writes the following in a 2005 online posting: "In the *Poetry for the People* ("P4P") program I direct at Berkeley, we include hip hop lyrics on our study of poetry. This year's reader includes Aceyalone's 'The Balance,' Talib Kweli's 'The Proud,' and 2Pac's 'Dear Mama,' which reflects the choices of numerous student teacher poets in the P4P program." See http://www.o-dub.com/weblog/2005_02_01_archive.html.

11. For more information, see Korina Joscon, "'Taking it to the Mic': Pedagogy of June Jordan's Poetry for the People and Partnership with an Urban High School," *English Education* 37, no. 2 (January 2005), 132–148; Kinloch and Grebowicz, *Still Seeking*; and The Poetry for the People Collective, *Poetry for the People, Speak on It! Smash the State: The Second Coming* (Berkeley: P4P, 2002).

12. For information on the Senior Seminar course, visit the online listing of courses at http://english.berkeley.edu/courses/upperf03ll.html. In the course description, the instructor writes, "in this class we will carefully and critically analyze Jordan's work, reading some of her writing (poetry, essays, plays, memoir and novel, and even course syllabi) very closely and placing it in a variety of contexts. Topics we'll follow Jordan in addressing include: autobiography, children's literature, and the politics of childhood."

13. Jordan, *Technical Difficulties*, 100.

14. Jordan, *On Call: Political Essays*, 5.

15. Ibid.

16. In her essay, "For the Sake of a People's Poetry: Walt Whitman and the Rest of Us," Jordan defines what she means by New World Poets. She writes, "New World does not mean New England. New World means non-European; it means new, it means big, it means heterogeneous, it means unknown, it means free, it means an end to feudalism, caste, privilege, and the violence of power." From this definition, Jordan provides lines from Walt Whitman's *Song of Myself* as an example. See June Jordan, *Passion*, xix.

17. Jordan, *On Call: Political Essays*, 14.

18. Ibid., 6.

19. Ibid., 14.

20. Van Doren, ed., *The Portable Walt Whitman*, xx-xxi.

21. Jordan, *On Call: Political Essays*, 15.

22. Ibid., 14.

23. Muller, *June Jordan's Poetry for the People*, 4.

24. Paulo Freire, *Pedagogy of the Oppressed* (New York: Continuum, 1970/1997).

25. Muller, *June Jordan's Poetry for the People*, 4.

26. Ibid., 5.

27. Ibid., 4.

28. Ibid., 5–6.

29. Ibid., 8.

30. Jordan, *Technical Difficulties*, 100.

31. Ibid., 99.

32. Lyndon B. Johnson, "To Fulfill These Rights," in *The Affirmative Action Debate*, ed. George E. Curry, 17–18 (Cambridge: Perseus Books, 1996).

33. Jordan, *Affirmative Acts*, 100.

34. Ibid. Placement of words and format are those of the author, June Jordan.

35. Ibid., 100–101.

36. Ibid., 101.

37. Ibid., 102.

38. Ibid., 102–103.

39. Ibid., 247.

40. Ibid., 101.

41. For a longer, critical discussion of these points, see essays included in the collection, Kinloch and Grebowicz, *Still Seeking*. In particular, see Christina Accomando, "Exposing the Lie of Neutrality: June Jordan's *Affirmative Acts*," 33–47, and Ramona Coleman, "Exploring the Space of Americanness and the Place of African American Women through the Works of June Jordan," 49–65.

42. In her discussions on affirmative action, Jordan cites the case of affirmative action in Houston, Texas, and how Houston residents voted in favor of affirmative action and against the use of the word "preference." Both affirmative action and bilingual education programs are important topics in a state such as Texas because of student demographics and the composition of that particular metropolitan city—the number of Spanish-speaking residents has rapidly increased over the last fifteen years and will continue to increase.

43. Jordan, *Affirmative Acts*, 115.

44. Ibid., 248.

45. For more information, see Nanette Asimov, "Big Victory for Measure to End Bilingual Education: Opponents Say They'll File Suit Today" in the *San Francisco*

Chronicle (June 3, 1998). See http://www.sfgate.com/cgi-bin/article.cgi?f=/c/a/ 1998/06/03/MN79691.DTL&hw=Proposition+227&sn =002&sc=701.

46. Ibid., 247.

47. Ibid., 249. Italics belong to the author.

48. Ibid., 252.

49. Ibid., 255.

50. Ibid.

51. Jordan, *Moving Towards Home*, 128.

52. California Poets in the Schools, or CPITS, is an important organization that offers support to teachers and students by placing culturally and ethnically diverse, established writers into classrooms to demonstrate the power of imaginative language and some of the many processes of writing. According to the organization's Web site, CPITS "became a statewide organization in the mid-1970s and there are now CPITS programs in 29 counties from Humboldt to San Diego. It is estimated that since 1964 a half million students have been introduced to creative writing by CPITS poets. Since 1987, CPITS has placed a yearly average of over 150 poets in more than 300 schools across the state to work with 25,000 students in grades Kindergarten through Twelfth." The significance of the program, as well as that of Teachers & Writers Collaborative (T&W), Writers-in-the-Schools (WITS), and Poetry for the People (P4P), is immeasurable. For more information, see http://www.cpits.org/.

53. See also Kinloch, "Poetry, Literacy, and Creativity: Fostering Effective Learning Strategies in an Urban Classroom," *English Education* 37, no.2 (January 2005): 96–114.

54. Jordan, *Affirmative Acts*, 255.

55. Muller, *June Jordan's Poetry for the People*, 3.

56. Ibid., 9.

57. Ibid., 225.

58. The June Jordan School for Equity is located at 325 La Grande Avenue in San Francisco, California.

59. Torf, interview by author.

60. For more information on the June Jordan School for Equity, see http://www.jjse.org.

61. For more information on this quote and/or *The Progressive*, see http://progressive.org/?q=node/11/print, accessed on August 7, 2005.

62. Jordan, *Some of Us Did Not Die*, 3.

63. Ibid., 8.

64. Ibid., .97.

65. Ibid., 98.

66. Jordan, *Technical Difficulties*, 219.

67. For more information, see Jordan, "Introduction," *Some of Us Did Not Die*, 3–15.

68. Jordan, *Technical Difficulties*, 14.

69. Ibid.

70. Jordan, *Some of Us Did Not Die*, 229.

71. Jordan, *Affirmative Acts*, 151.

72. Ibid.

73. Ibid., 147–148.

74. Ibid., 143.

75. Ibid., 155.

76. Ibid., 153.

77. Jordan, *Naming Our Destiny*, 99.
78. Ibid., 81.
79. Ibid., 142–143.
80. Ibid., 143.
81. A group of women joined together in 1988 to sponsor weekly, silent vigils for peace. The group continues to hold vigils in various Israeli cities as a way to "protest the illegal Israeli occupation of the West Bank, Gaza, and East Jerusalem." Their united presence has demonstrated "that Jewish Israelis and Palestinian Arabs can work together, and that while the men at the negotiating tables and in the halls of power seem intent on prolonging the conflict, women—always the greatest victims in war—are intent on making peace." It should be noted that the "Women in Black in Israel and Serbia were nominated" for the 2001 Nobel Peace Prize. For additional information, see http://www.wib-la.org/.
82. Jill Nelson, "A Conversation with June Jordan," *Quarterly Black Review of Books* Vol.1 (May 1994), 50–53. http://www.findarticles.com/p/articles/mi_hb3384/is_199405/ai_n8129832.
83. R. D.Laing, *Politics of Experience* (New York: Pantheon Books, 1983), 18–19.
84. Nelson, "A Conversation with June Jordan," 50–53. http://www.findarticles.com/p/articles/mi_hb3384/is_199405/ai_n8129832.
85. Jordan, *Technical Difficulties*, 189.
86. Jordan, *Affirmative Acts*, 176.
87. Jordan, *Technical Difficulties*, 188.
88. Ibid., 192.
89. Jordan, *Passion*, 13.
90. Ibid., 79.
91. Ibid., 78.
92. Ibid., 89.
93. June Jordan, *Haruko/Love Poems* (New York: High Risk Books, 1994), inside cover.
94. Ibid., ix.
95. Ibid., 7.
96. Ibid., 14.
97. Peter Erickson, "After Identity: A Conversation with June Jordan and Peter Erickson," in *Transition* 0, no. 63 (1994): 144.
98. Ibid.
99. Ibid., 147.

KISSING GOD GOODBYE

1. Jordan, Levi, and Miles, eds., *Directed by Desire*, 609.
2. E. Ethelbert Miller, interview by author, October 29, 2005.
3. For more information about this collection, see the library Web site, which provides full catalog details: http://special.lib.umn.edu/findaid/xml/scrbg004.xml. A special thank you is owed to poet E. Ethelbert Miller and reference librarian Karla Davis for making this collection available to the general public and for entertaining my queries.

4. Ibid.

5. Ibid.

6. Erickson, "After Identity," 147.

7. Jordan, *Affirmative Acts*, 217.

8. Ibid., 69.

9. Ibid., 70–71.

10. Orridge, interview by author.

11. Ibid. Memorial Sloan-Kettering Cancer Center is a widely known medical facility with locations throughout the greater New York area.

12. Ibid.

13. Jordan, *Affirmative Acts*, 159.

14. Ibid., 161.

15. Ibid., 74–75.

16. Ibid., 70.

17. Ibid., 161.

18. Ibid.

19. Ibid., 162

20. Ibid.

21. Ibid., 75.

22. Erickson, "After Identity," 148.

23. Orridge, interview by author.

24. Jordan, *Affirmative Acts*, 163.

25. Jordan, Levi, and Miles (Eds.), *Directed by Desire*, 629.

26. Ibid.

27. Ibid.

28. Jordan, *Kissing God Goodbye*, 69.

29. Miller, interview by author.

30. Miles, "Directed by Desire," 265.

31. Jordan, *Affirmative Acts*, 70.

32. Adrienne Torf, "For June's Memorial Celebration, 15 September 2002," in *The Women's Review of Books: A Feminist Guide to Good Reading*, 20, no.1 (October 2002): 15. http://www.wellesley.edu/womensreview/archive/2002/10/special.html#special.

33. Ibid.

34. Ibid.

35. Ibid.

36. Orridge, interview by author.

37. Jordan wanted to be cremated, and her friends fulfilled her wish. There were no funeral services for the poet; instead, close friends organized a memorial for the beginning of September in order for admiring students and colleagues from the University of California, Berkeley to attend. Orridge was pleased that there was not a funeral service: "I needed the two or so months between the time she died, June and September. But I needed some closure too, because I hadn't seen her, hadn't seen any dead body, hadn't attended a funeral. There was nothing in terms of reality to make me understand that she was gone" because Jordan was cremated even before Orridge was told of her death. Orridge exhibited sadness as she sat with me and recalled the occasion of discovering the death of her cousin: "When she died, a friend of mine, who was living up in Cape

Cod, phoned me and left this message on my machine because I was working . . . and he said, 'oh, I am so sorry to hear about June. I guess you're getting ready to go to California to the funeral.' And that's the first I'm hearing she died. I was just flabbergasted that nobody out there called me." Orridge, at the prompting of her son, eventually contacted Adrienne Torf, who informed her of Jordan's death.

38. For more information about this particular memorial service, see the official Press Release by Kathleen Maclay, "Memorial service to celebrate the life of poet June Jordan," http://www.berkeley.edu/news/media/releases/2002/06/17_jordan.html.

39. Thulani Davis, "June Jordan, 1936–2002," *Village Voice* (2 July 2002), www.villagevoice.com/print/issues/0226/davis.php.

40. Alexis De Veaux, "Freedom Fighter," *The Women's Review of Books: A Feminist Guide to Good Reading*, 20, no.1 (October 2002): 18, http://www.wellesley.edu/womensreview/archive/2002/10/special.html#special.

41. June Jordan, *I Was Looking at the Ceiling and Then I Saw the Sky* (New York: Scribner, 1995).

42. Jordan, *On Call: Political Essays*, 82.

43. Ibid., 83.

44. Jordan, *Kissing God Goodbye*, 13–14.

45. Adrienne Torf, *June Jordan and Adrienne Torf: COLLABORATION (Selected Works 1983–2000)* (San Francisco: ABT Music, 2003), compact disc liner notes.

46. Ibid.

47. June Jordan and Adrienne Torf, Track 1 on *June Jordan and Adrienne Torf: COLLABORATION*.

48. Jordan, *Things That I Do in The Dark*, 102.

49. Jordan, *Passion*, 52.

50. Torf, "For June's Memorial Celebration," 15.

51. Jordan, *Naming Our Destiny*, 37.

52. Ibid., 103.

53. June Jordan, and Adrienne Torf, "June Jordan and Adrienne B. Torf: On Collaboration," in *HOT WIRE: A Journal of Women's Music and Culture* 1, no.3 (July 1985): 28–30.

54. Jordan, *Technical Difficulties*, 42.

55. Torf, interview by author.

56. Jordan, *Technical Difficulties*, 46–47.

57. Torf, interview by author.

58. Pratibha Parmar, *A Place of Rage* (London, England: Women Make Movies, 1991), documentary film, http://www.wmm.com/filmcatalog/pages/c287.shtml.

59. Jordan, *Kissing God Goodbye*, 96.

60. Ibid.

61. Ibid.

62. Jordan, *Civil Wars*, 104.

63. Ibid., 108.

64. Ibid.

65. Jordan, *Some of Us Did Not Die*, 241.

66. Ibid., 275–276. One wonders if Jordan was actually writing about her cousin, Valerie, or whether she was referring to some fictional child.

67. I had the pleasure of meeting Mrs. Valerie Orridge on November 28, 2005 at a New York City bookstore during a second tribute to June Jordan on the publication of

the poet's collected poems. Mrs. Orridge is a phenomenal woman. We have kept in touch since.

68. Jordan, *Some of Us Did Not Die*, 7.
69. Ibid.
70. Jordan, *On Call: Political Essays*, 2.
71. Jordan, *Naming Our Destiny*, 122.
72. Jordan, *Some of Us Did Not Die*, 14.
73. Ibid., 14.
74. Jordan, *Things That I Do in The Dark*, ix.

Selected Bibliography

Allen, D., and W. Tallman, eds. *The Poetics of the New American Poetry*. New York: Grove Press, 1973.

Allen, F. "June Jordan, Poetry for the People: A Revolutionary Blueprint." *Library Journal* (December 1995): 115, 120.

Angelou, Maya. *The Complete Collected Poems of Maya Angelou*. New York: Random House, 1994.

Baker, David. *Heresy and the Ideal: On Contemporary Poetry*. Fayetteville: University of Arkansas Press, 2000.

Baldwin, James. *The Fire Next Time*. New York: Vintage International, 1993. First published 1962 by Dial Press.

Baraka, Amiri. *The Leroi Jones/Amiri Baraka Reader*. 2nd ed. New York: Thunder's Mouth Press, 1999.

Black, Les, and John Solomos. *Theories of Race and Racism*. London: Routledge, 2000.

Braxton, Joanne M. *Black Women Writing Autobiography: A Tradition Within a Tradition*. Philadelphia: Temple University Press, 1989.

Brogan, Jacqueline Vaught. "From Warrior to Womanist: The Development of June Jordan's Poetry." Pages 198–209. *Speaking the Other Self: American Women Writers*. Edited by Jeanne Campbell Reesman. Athens: University of Georgia Press, 1997.

———. "Planets on the Table: From Wallace Stevens and Elizabeth Bishop to Adrienne Rich and June Jordan." *The Wallace Stevens Journal* 19, no. 2 (1995): 255–78.

Brown, Wendy. *States of Injury: Power and Freedom in Late Modernity*. Princeton, NJ: Princeton University Press, 1995.

Butler, Judith. *Gender Trouble: Feminism and the Subversion of Identity*. London: Routledge, 1990.

Caroll, Rebecca, ed. *I Know What the Red Clay Looks Like: The Voice and Vision of Black Women Writers*. New York: Carol Southern Books, 1994.

Carpenter, Humphrey, and Mari Prichard. *Oxford Companion to Children's Literature*. New York: Oxford University Press, 1984.

Clifton, Lucille. *Good Woman: Poems and a Memoir 1969–1980*. Rochester, NY: BOA Editions, 1987.

Collins, Patricia Hill. *Fighting Words: Black Women and the Search for Justice*. Minneapolis: University of Minnesota Press, 1998.

————. *Black Feminist Thought: Knowledge, Consciousness, and the Politics of Empowerment*. New York: Routledge, 2000.

Crenshaw, Kimberlé. "Mapping the Margins: Intersectionality, Identity Politics, and Violence Against Women of Color." *Stanford Law Review* 43 (July 1991): 1241–1299.

Curry, George E., ed. *The Affirmative Action Debate*. Cambridge, MA: Perseus Books, 1996.

Davis, Angela. *Angela Davis: An Autobiography*. New York: International, 1989. First published 1974 by Random House.

————. *Blues Legacies and Black Feminism: Gertrude "Ma" Rainey, Bessie Smith, and Billie Holiday*. New York: Vintage Books, 1999.

————. *Women, Race, and Class*. New York: Vintage Books, 1983.

DeShazer, Mary K. *A Poetics of Resistance: Women Writing in South Africa, El Salvador, and the United States*. Ann Arbor: University of Michigan Press, 2000.

De Veaux, Alexis. "Creating Soul Food: June Jordan." *Essence* 11 (April 1981): 82, 138–50.

————. *Warrior Poet: A Biography of Audre Lorde*. New York: W. W. Norton and Company, 2004.

Dictionary of Literary Biography. *Afro-American Writers After 1955: Dramatists and Prose Writers*. Detroit: Gale Research, 1985.

Du Bois, W.E.B. *The Souls of Black Folk*. New York: Signet, 1995.

Dyson, Anne Hass. *The Brothers and Sisters Learn to Write*. New York: Teachers College Press, 2003.

Ellison, Ralph. *Invisible Man*. New York: Vintage Books, 1972.

Erickson, Peter. "After Identity: A Conversation with June Jordan and Peter Erickson." *Transition* 63 (1994): 132–49.

————. "State of the Union." *Transition* 59 (1993): 104–9.

————. "June Jordan 1936–." *Dictionary of Literary Biography*. Detroit: Gale, 1985. 146–62.

Espich, Whitney T. "Papers of Poet, Essayist, Critic and Activist June Jordan Acquired by Schlesinger Library at the Radcliffe Institute." *Radcliffe News and Publications* 3 (October 2003), http://www.radcliffe.edu/news/pr/031002_Jordan.html.

Fine, Michelle, Lois Weis, Linda C. Powell, and L. Mun Wong, eds. *Off White: Readings on Race, Power, and Society*. New York: Routledge, 1997.

Fisher, Maisha. "'The Song Is Unfinished': The New Literate and Literary." *Written Communication* 21, no.3 (2004): 290–312.

Forman, Ruth. We Are the Young Magicians. Boston: Beacon Press, 1993.

Frankenberg, Erica, and Chungmei Lee. "Race in American Public Schools: Rapidly Resegregating School Districts." The Civil Rights Project at Harvard University. http://www.civilrightsproject.harvard.edu/research/deseg/reseb_schools/ (accessed November 1, 2005).

Freire, Paulo. *Pedagogy of the Oppressed*. Translated by Myra Bergman Ramos. New York: Continuum, 2000.

Gaster, Adrian, ed. *The International Authors and Writers Who's Who*. 8th ed. Cambridge: International Biographical Centre, 1977.

Gates, Henry Louis, Jr., and Nellie Y. McKay. "From Phillis Wheatley to Toni Morrison: The Flowering of African-American Literature." *Journal of Blacks in Higher Education* 14 (1996/1997): 95–100.

Gayles, Gloria Wade. *Pushed Back to Strength: A Black Woman's Journey Home.* New York: Avon Books, 1993.

Gilbert, Derrick I. M., ed. *Catch the Fire!!! A Cross-Generational Anthology of Contemporary African-American Poetry.* New York: Riverhead, 1998.

Gilyard, Keith. *Let's Flip the Script: An African American Discourse on Language, Literature, and Learning.* Detroit: Wayne State University Press, 1996.

————. *Voices of the Self: A Study of Language Competence.* Detroit: Wayne State University Press, 1991.

Goodenough, Elizabeth, Mark A. Heberle, and Naomi Sokoloff, eds. *Infant Tongues: The Voice of the Child in Literature.* Detroit: Wayne State University Press, 1994.

Guy-Sheftall, Beverly, ed. *Words of Fire: An Anthology of African-American Feminist Thought.* New York: New Press, 1995.

Hacker, Marilyn. *Love, Death, and the Changing of the Seasons.* 1986. Reprint, New York: W. W. Norton and Company, 1995.

Hammond, Karla. "An Interview with June Jordan." *Kalliope* 4, no.1 (Fall 1981): 39.

Haney López, Ian F. *White by Law: The Legal Construction of Race.* New York: New York University Press, 1996.

Harper, Phillip Brian. "Nationalism and Social Division in Black Arts Poetry of the 1960s." *Critical Inquiry* 19 (1993): 235–55.

Harris, Violet J. "African American Children's Literature: The First One Hundred Years." *Journal of Negro Education* 59, no. 4 (1990): 540–55.

Henderson, Stephen. *Understanding the New Black Poetry: Black Speech and Black Music as Poetic References.* New York: William Morrow and Company, 1972.

Hill, Robert A., and Barbara Bair, eds. *Marcus Garvey: Life and Lessons.* Berkeley: University of California Press, 1987.

hooks, bell. *Teaching to Transgress: Education as the Practice of Freedom.* New York: Routledge, 1994.

————. *Wounds of Passion: A Writing Life.* New York: Henry Holt and Company, 1997.

————. *Yearning: Race, Gender, and Cultural Politics.* Boston: South End Press, 1990.

Hughes, Langston. "Books and the Negro Child." *Children's Library Yearbook* 4 (1932): 108–10.

————. *The Collected Poems of Langston Hughes.* Edited by Arnold Rampersad and David Rossel. New York: Alfred Knopf, 2000.

Hull, Gloria T., Patricia Bell Scott, and Barbara Smith, eds. *All the Women Are White, All the Blacks Are Men, but Some of Us Are Brave: Black Women's Studies.* Old Westbury, NY: Feminist Press, 1982.

Inge, M. Thomas, Maurice Duke, and Jackson R. Bryer, eds. *Black American Writers: Biographical Essays, Volume 2: Richard Wright, Ralph Ellison, James Baldwin, and Amiri Baraka.* New York: St. Martin's Press, 1978.

Irigaray, Luce. *Speculum of the Other Woman.* Ithaca, NY: Cornell University Press, 1985.

Jocson, Korina. "'Taking it to the Mic': Pedagogy of June Jordan's Poetry for the People and Partnership with an Urban High School." *English Education* 37 (2005): 132–48.

Johnson, Diane. *Telling Tales: The Pedagogy and Promise of African American Literature for Youth.* Westport, CT: Greenwood, 1990.

Johnson, James Weldon, Booker T. Washington, and W.E.B. Du Bois. *Three Negro Classics.* New York: Avon Books, 1965.

Johnson-Feelings, Dianne. "Children's and Young Adult Literature." Pages 133–40 in *The Oxford Companion to African American Literature*. Edited by William L. Andrews, Frances Smith Foster, and Trudier Harris. New York: Oxford University Press, 1997.

Jordan, June. *Affirmative Acts: Political Essays*. New York: Anchor Books/Doubleday, 1998.

———. "Bang Bang Uber Alles." Music by Adrienne Torf. Atlanta: Seven Stages Theatre, 1986.

———. "Black Women Haven't Got It All." *The Black Scholar* 10 (May–June 1979): 39–40.

———. *Bobo Goetz a Gun*. Willimantic, CT: Curbstone Press, 1985.

———. "The Break." New York: Staged Performance, 1984.

———. *Civil Wars: Observations from the Front Lines of America*. New York: Touchstone, 1981.

———. *Dry Victories*. New York: Rinehart and Winston, 1972.

———. "For the Arrow That Flies by Day." New York: Shakespeare Festival, 1981.

———. *His Own Where*. New York: Thomas Y. Crowell, 1971.

———. *Haruko/Love Poetry*. London: Virago, 1993.

———. "Hunters and the Hunted." *The Progressive* 63, no.10 (October 1999): 17.

———. "A Gathering Purpose." *The Progressive* 62, no. 1 (January 1998): 33+.

———. "I am Seeking an Attitude: Women's Rights' History." *The Progressive* 57, no. 5 (May 1993): 18+.

———. "In the Spirit of Sojourner Truth." New York: Public Theatre, 1979.

———. *I Was Looking at the Ceiling and Then I Saw the Sky*. New York: Scribner, 1995.

———. *Kimako's Story*. Boston: Houghton Mifflin, 1981.

———. *Kissing God Goodbye: Poems 1991–1997*. New York: Anchor Books, 1997.

———. *Living Room*. New York: Thunder's Mouth Press, 1985.

———. *Lyrical Campaigns: Selected Poems*. London: Virago, 1989.

———. *Mahfouz*. Berkeley: Poetry for the People Press, 1998.

———. "Mississippi Black Home." *New York Times*. October 11, 1970. ProQuest Historical Newspaper Archives: 65, 67–71, 80–83. http://www.il.proquest.com/.

———. *Moving Towards Home: Political Essays*. London: Virago, 1987.

———. *Naming Our Destiny: New and Selected Poems*. New York: Thunder's Mouth Press, 1989.

———. *New Days: Poems of Exile and Return*. New York: Emerson Hall, 1970.

———. "A New Politics of Sexuality." *The Progressive* 55, no. 7 (July 1991): 12+.

———. *On Call: Political Essays*. Boston: South End Press, 1985.

———. *Passion: New Poems, 1977–1980*. Boston: Beacon Press, 1980.

———. *Soldier: A Poet's Childhood*. New York: Basic/Civitas Books, 2000.

———. *Some Changes*. New York: E. P. Dutton, 1971.

———. *Some of Us Did Not Die: New and Selected Essays of June Jordan*. New York: Basic/Civitas Books, 2002.

———, ed. *Soulscript: Afro-American Poetry*. New York: Zenith/Doubleday, 1970.

———. *Technical Difficulties: African-American Notes on the State of the Union*. New York: Pantheon Books, 1992.

———. *Things That I Do in the Dark*. New York: Random House, 1977.

———. "Where is the Sisterhood: Gender Genocide Against Females." *The Progressive* 60, no. 6 (June 1996): 20+.

———. *Who Look at Me*. Toronto: Fitzhenry and Whiteside, 1969.

————. "Writing and Teaching." *Partisan Review* 36 (1969): 478–82.

Jordan, June, Jan Heller Levi, and Sara Miles, eds. *Directed by Desire: The Collected Poems of June Jordan*. Port Townsend, WA: Copper Canyon Press, 2005.

Jordan, June, and Adrienne Torf. *COLLABORATION: Selected Works, 1983–2000*. Compact Disc. San Francisco: ABT Music, 2003.

Jordan, June, and Terri Bush, eds. *The Voice of Children*. New York: Holt, Rinehart and Winston, 1970.

Joyce, Joyce A. "The Black Canon: Reconstructing Black American Literary Criticism." *New Literary History* 18, no. 2 (1997): 335–44.

King, Woodie, Jr. *The Forerunners: Black Poets in America*. Washington, DC: Howard University Press, 1975.

Kinloch, Valerie. "Poetry, Literacy, and Creativity: Fostering Effective Learning Strategies in an Urban Classroom." *English Education* 37 (January 2005): 96–114.

————. "Revisiting the Promise of Students' Right to Their Own Language: Pedagogical Strategies." *College Composition and Communication* 57, no.1 (September 2005): 83–113.

Kinloch, Valerie, and Margret Grebowicz, eds. *Still Seeking an Attitude: Critical Reflections on the Work of June Jordan*. Maryland: Lexington Books, 2004.

Knapp, Bettina. *Walt Whitman*. New York: Continuum, 1993.

Koch, Herbert. *Journal of an Experiment: Teachers and Writers Collaborative*. Washington, DC: Teachers and Writers, 1979.

Kozol, Jonathan. *Savage Inequalities: Children in America's Schools*. New York: Crown, 1991.

————. *Amazing Grace: The Lives of Children and the Conscience of a Nation*. New York: Harper Perennial, 1995.

Larrick, Nancy. "The All-White World of Children's Books." Pages 156–68 in *The Black American in Books for Children: Readings in Racism*. Edited by D. MacCann and G. Woodard. Metuchen, NJ: Scarecrow Press, 1972.

Livingston, Myra Cohn. *The Child as Poet: Myth or Reality?* Boston: Horn Book, 1984.

Lopate, Philip, ed. *Journal of a Living Experiment: A Documentary History of the First Ten Years of the Teachers and Writers Collaborative*. New York: Teachers and Writers, 1979.

Lorde, Audre. *Sister Outsider*. Freedom, CA: Crossing Press, 1984.

————. *The Collected Poems of Audre Lorde*. New York: W. W. Norton and Company, 1997.

————. *Zami, Sister Outsider, Undersong*. New York: Quality Paperback Book Club, 1982.

MacPhail, Scott. "June Jordan and the New Black Intellectuals." *African American Review* 33, no.1 (Spring 1999): 57–71.

Madison, D. S., ed. *The Woman That I Am: The Literature and Culture of Contemporary Women of Color*. New York: St. Martin's Press, 1994.

Miles, Sara. "Directed by Desire." *The Women's Review of Books* 20, no. 1 (October 2002): 17.

Morrison, Toni. *Lecture and Speech of Acceptance, Upon the Nobel Prize for Literature*. New York: Alfred Knopf, 1994.

Mostern, Kenneth. *Autobiography and Black Identity Politics: Racialization in Twentieth-Century America*. Cambridge: Cambridge University Press, 1999.

Mullaney, Janet Palmer. *Truthtellers of the Times: Interviews with Contemporary Women Poets*. Ann Arbor: University of Michigan Press, 1998.

Muller, Lauren, and The Poetry for the People Collective, eds. *June Jordan's Poetry for the People: A Revolutionary Blueprint*. New York: Routledge, 1995.

Orwell, George. *A Collection of Essays*. New York: Harcourt, 1970.

Pace, Patricia. "All Our Lost Children: Trauma and Testimony in the Performance of Childhood." *Text and Performance Quarterly* 18 (1998): 233–47.

Perry, Theresa, and Lisa Delpit, eds. *The Real Ebonics Debate: Power, Language, and the Education of African-American Children*. Boston: Beacon, 1998.

Pound, Ezra. *ABC of Reading*. New York: Laughlin, 1960.

Reed, Ishmael. *Mumbo Jumbo*. New York: Simon and Schuster, 1972.

Rich, Adrienne. *What Is Found There: Notebooks on Poetry and Politics*. New York: Norton, 1993.

Richardson, Judy. "Black Children's Books: An Overview." *Journal of Negro Education* 43 (1974): 380–400.

Rothschild, Matthew. "A Feast of Poetry." *The Progressive* 58 (May 1994): 48–50.

Rowe, Monica D. "Kissing God Goodbye: Poems 1991–1997." *American Visions* (February/March 1998): 13, 30–32.

Rush, Theresa Gunnels, et al. *Black American Writers Past and Present: A Biographical and Bibliographical Dictionary*. 2 vols. Metuchen: Scarecrow Press, 1975.

Scott-Heron, Gil. "The Revolution Will Not Be Televised." *Our Souls Have Grown Deep Like the Rivers*. Compact Disc. New York: Rhino/Wea Records, 2000.

Smitherman, Geneva. "Black Language and the Education of Black Children: One Mo Once." *The Black Scholar: Journal of Black Studies and Research* 27, no.1 (Spring 1997): 29–31.

———. *Talkin and Testifyin: The Language of Black America*. Boston: Houghton Mifflin, 1977.

———. *Talkin that Talk: Language, Culture and Education in African America*. London: Routledge, 2000.

Splawn, P. Jane. "New World Consciousness in the Poetry of Ntozake Shange and June Jordan: Two African-American Women's Response to Expansionism in the Third World." *College Language Association Journal* 39, no. 2 (June 1996): 417–32.

Sutton, Soraya Sablo, and Sheila Menezes. "In Remembrance of June Jordan, 1963–2002." *Social Justice* 29, no. 4 (2002): 205–6.

Tatum, Beverly. *Why Are All the Black Kids Sitting Together in the Cafeteria, and Other Conversations about Race*. New York: Basic Books, 1997.

Villanueva, Victor. *Bootstraps: From an American Academic of Color*. Urbana, IL: National Council of Teachers of English, 1993.

Walker, Alice. *In Search of Our Mothers' Gardens: Womanist Prose*. New York: Harvest Books, 1984.

———. *The Color Purple*. New York: Pocket Books, 1982.

Whitehead, Kim. *The Feminist Poetry Movement*. Jackson: University of Mississippi Press, 1996.

Williams, Patricia J. *The Alchemy of Race and Rights*. Cambridge, MA: Harvard University Press, 1991.

Williams, Robert L. *Ebonics: The True Language of Black Folks*. St. Louis: Institute of Black Studies, 1975.

Index

feminist, 86, 145, 163; political,
34–36, 51–52, 60–61, 70, 78, 110,
137; restoration, 54, 60, 81, 108;
service/outreach, 51, 54, 101, 108,
125–26, 133, 135, 163, 164, 165
CORE, 80

Datcher, Michael, 124
Davis, Angela, 52, 147, 160
Democracy, 10–11, 22, 40, 44, 48, 54,
59, 89, 90, 92, 116, 117, 119, 133,
137
DeVeaux, Alexis, 50, 52, 106
*Directed by Desire: The Collected Poems of
June Jordan*, 5, 115, 122, 149, 150
Diversity, 52, 111, 123, 132, 136, 140
Dry Victories, 5, 82, 95, 96, 101, 102,
105, 107, 108, 166
Du Bois, W.E.B., 157

Eady, Cornelius, 115
Ellison, Ralph, 11

Feminism, 50, 84, 87, 111, 113, 114,
140, 159, 162, 164
Fisher, Maisha, xi
Flanders, Laura, 52, 115
Foreman, Ruth, 106, 121, 122, 124
Freedom: academic, 37, 134; and democracy, 10, 44, 48, 51, 67, 80, 117; of
expression, 107, 137; fighters/fights,
2, 4, 8, 28, 40, 47, 48, 51, 65, 70, 73,
74, 80–81, 99, 115, 162, 163; human,
1–3, 5, 7, 32, 45, 59, 60, 62, 79, 91,
110, 116–18, 162; and love, 23, 28,
90, 107, 116, 164, 166; opportunity,
129–31; rides, 4, 5, 28, 32, 75, 78;
safety, 150, 156, 161, 162; sexual, 63,
83, 87, 140, 141, 142; struggles,
95–96, 112, 130, 153, 154
Freedom Now Suite, 103

Gaines, Ernest, 77
Garvey, Marcus, 9–10
"Getting Down to Get Over," 47, 56, 57

Hacker, Marilyn, 50, 65, 72, 106, 157–58
Haley, Alex, 77

Hamer, Fannie Lou: activist, 2, 32,
40–41, 44, 45, 46, 50, 55, 68, 71, 75,
77, 91, 101, 159; biography, 5, 45, 48,
82, 95, 96, 99, 100, 105, 107, 110,
112
Harjo, Joy, 115
Harlem Renaissance, 77
Harlem Riot of 1964, 7, 9, 32–35, 48, 77
Heller, Jan Levi, 115
Hemphill, Essex, 77
Heterosexism, 125, 127, 141, 160–61
Hill, Anita, 137
His Own Where, 1, 4, 5, 32, 41–43, 61,
96, 108–11, 132, 166
History: cultural/familial, 7, 14, 19, 29,
47, 66; discrimination/violence, 45,
48, 69–70, 161; exclusion, 21, 38;
human, 7–8, 38–39, 65, 101, 107,
145, 161; literary and linguistic,
54–55, 106, 116; sexuality, 28, 69,
158; United States, 101
Howard University, 87
Hughes, Langston, 2, 38, 48, 62, 65, 146,
155–57
Hurston, Zora Neale, 55–56

Identity: collective, 45, 76, 110, 116; cultural, 10, 23, 27, 50, 77, 97, 126, 158;
difference, 25, 39, 65, 70, 95; feminism, 18, 114, 140; gender, 48, 57,
69, 70, 126; individual, 2, 9, 22,
32–33, 45, 97, 158; national and
political, 8, 9, 27, 33, 36, 48, 57, 60,
63, 69, 96, 116, 129; power, 18, 33,
77, 88, 90, 96, 110, 138; race, 28
"In the Land of White Supremacy," 131
Israel, 90, 91, 92, 93, 107–8, 118, 140,
154, 164

Johnson, Angela, 96
Johnson, Lyndon B., 129
Jordan, Granville Ivanhoe, 1, 9–13,
15–26, 46–47, 59, 63, 65, 111, 142
Jordan, Mildred Maude Fisher, 1, 8, 9,
13–25, 27, 32, 35, 43, 46–47, 63,
65–66, 111, 162

About the Author

VALERIE KINLOCH is Assistant Professor of English Education at Teachers College, Columbia University. She is the editor of *Still Seeking An Attitude: Critical Reflections on the Work of June Jordan* and several journal articles.